Literature and Skepticism

SERIES EDITORS

David E. Johnson, *Comparative Literature, University at Buffalo*
Scott Michaelsen, *English, Michigan State University*

SERIES ADVISORY BOARD

Nahum D. Chandler, *African American Studies, University of California, Irvine*
Rebecca Comay, *Philosophy and Comparative Literature, University of Toronto*
Marc Crépon, *Philosophy, École Normale Supérieure, Paris*
Jonathan Culler, *Comparative Literature, Cornell University*
Johanna Drucker, *Design Media Arts and Information Studies, University of California, Los Angeles*
Christopher Fynsk, *Modern Thought, Aberdeen University*
Rodolphe Gasché, *Comparative Literature, University at Buffalo*
Martin Hägglund, *Comparative Literature, Yale University*
Carol Jacobs, *German and Comparative Literature, Yale University*
Peggy Kamuf, *French and Comparative Literature, University of Southern California*
David Marriott, *History of Consciousness, University of California, Santa Cruz*
Steven Miller, *English, University at Buffalo*
Alberto Moreiras, *Hispanic Studies, Texas A&M University*
Patrick O'Donnell, *English, Michigan State University*
Pablo Oyarzun, *Teoría del Arte, Universidad de Chile*
Scott Cutler Shershow, *English, University of California, Davis*
Henry Sussman, *German and Comparative Literature, Yale University*
Samuel Weber, *Comparative Literature, Northwestern University*
Ewa Ziarek, *Comparative Literature, University at Buffalo*

Literature and Skepticism

Pablo Oyarzun

Published by State University of New York Press, Albany

© 2022 State University of New York Press

All rights reserved

Printed in the United States of America

No part of this book may be used or reproduced in any manner whatsoever without written permission. No part of this book may be stored in a retrieval system or transmitted in any form or by any means including electronic, electrostatic, magnetic tape, mechanical, photocopying, recording, or otherwise without the prior permission in writing of the publisher.

For information, contact State University of New York Press, Albany, NY
www.sunypress.edu

Library of Congress Cataloging-in-Publication Data

Names: Oyarzun R., Pablo, 1950- author.
Title: Literature and skepticism / Pablo Oyarzun.
Description: Albany : State University of New York Press, [2022] | Series: Suny series, literature . . . in theory | Includes bibliographical references and index.
Identifiers: LCCN 2021014862 | ISBN 9781438486796 (hardcover) | ISBN 9781438486819 (ebook) | ISBN 9781438486802 (paperback)
Subjects: LCSH: Skepticism in literature. | Fiction--History and criticism. | LCGFT: Literary criticism.
Classification: LCC PN56.S576 O93 2022 | DDC 809/.93353--dc23
LC record available at https://lccn.loc.gov/2021014862

10 9 8 7 6 5 4 3 2 1

Contents

1 INTRODUCTION Literature and Skepticism

27 CHAPTER ONE Montaigne: Writing and Skepticism

49 CHAPTER TWO Superb Imposture: Satire, Common Sense, and Skepticism in Swift's *A Tale of a Tub*

85 CHAPTER THREE On the Insignificant: Figures of Lichtenberg

107 CHAPTER FOUR Kleist, the Puppets, and the Vanishing Point of Meaning

127 CHAPTER FIVE Kafka and Skepticism: A Note

153 CHAPTER SIX Borges: Essay and Fiction

179 A Few Words of Conclusion

189 Notes

211 Works Cited

217 Index

Introduction

Literature and Skepticism[1]

THE ARGUMENT

In his essay on "The Storyteller," Walter Benjamin proposes the idea of an *end of the art of storytelling* (see section 1 in this chapter) grounded in a radical crisis of the possibility of experience. What is formally at stake is a variation of the Hegelian thesis on the *end of art*. However, in view of the content of Benjamin's idea, one should say that it points to a radicalization of that thesis: if the latter maintains the insufficiency of art as a supreme mode in which Spirit takes charge of its actual—that is, *modern*—experience, Benjamin's formulation states that it is precisely the development of modernity as a world that brings about the crisis of the possibility of experience. If the beginning of the end indicated by Benjamin lies in the origin of the emergence of literature as a general form of the art of the word, which universally imposes itself from the Renaissance on (in Benjamin, the end of the art of storytelling gives place to the novel), then the modern condition of literature testifies precisely to this crisis. But this would mean that the end of the art of storytelling carries with itself *in nuce* the *end of literature as such*.

To this historical argument (see section 2), which refers the transformations of literature to the changes in the social modes and relations of production as a matrix for experience, it is perhaps possible to add a structural argument in order to make intelligible the inherence of both ends: storytelling, which seeks to give place to and inscribe the singularity of experience, is affected by a contradiction in terms, by a paradox, as it were—the impossibility of narrating (that is, repeating) the unrepeatable. In a certain way, then, the "end" is prescribed in this impossibility, and storytelling would prepare, laboriously, silently, and reluctantly, the crisis of experience. No doubt, it would be perfectly admissible to argue that the paradox is in itself speculative and that the history of storytelling in the broad sense—and all throughout what we call the "modern age"—is its practical overcoming: that storytelling belongs to the kind of "tasks" that, like translation, as Franz Rosenzweig says, are theoretically impossible but practically feasible. Moreover, one can maintain that the crux of this overcoming consists in the (impossible) repetition of experience becoming an (actual) experience of repetition, marked by the interest, participation, and enjoyment of narration itself.[2] But precisely for this reason one could assume that there is also a structural limit to this overcoming and that the limit is reached when such peculiar experience goes into crisis. Accordingly, the Benjaminian formulation could perhaps be modulated to say that modernity is the time in which this limit becomes the essential problem of literature, of its very possibility: the time in which literature as such becomes essentially uncertain.

And this could be the first sign of a relation between literature and skepticism (see section 3). Affected by the categorical evidence of the limit, faced with the inevitable urgency of the problem, literature acquires a peculiar lucidity: now it learns—now, in the context of modernity—that literature itself is no longer possible other than as the knowledge of that end, of that impossibility, of its primordial incertitude. It is left to ask if a knowledge of this kind was not lodged from the beginning in the bosom of literature, and if it is not precisely a certain lethargic state of that knowledge that determined its exercise and its articulation as a constructive principle of the space of fiction and as a basis for the legitimacy of repetition. If this is the case, this orphan knowledge, this paradoxical knowledge of incertitude, would determine in literature, in its own foundation, an essentially skeptical character.

But this is only one aspect of the problem we shall examine here.

We find a second remark in Benjamin's essay that can help us to round out the picture (see section 4). In characterizing the birth of the novel at the dawn of the modern age as the earliest sign of the process that will end up as the decline of the art of storytelling, Benjamin points to the break with the collectivity and with its shared ground of experiences (*Schriften* 2, pt. 2: 442–43/*Selected Writings* 2: 146–47).[3] The book is the essential destination of the novel; consequently, it resists oral transmission, which remains immersed in the existence of the community. The technical mediation of communication is connected to a fundamental distancing from experience, which the novelist is no longer capable of coining paradigmatically. He has lost that most peculiar certitude that is congenital to genuine experience. A certitude that does not tower over it, presuming to scan it from the pinnacle of universality—allegedly equipped with the sure organ of the concept—but a certitude that knows—with the knowledge, simultaneously fragile and firm, that suits the witness—that something has happened, that something has taken place, and that what has happened demands its memorable institution: in short, a certitude that knows about the event. Instead, the novelist, although he may have the feeling of what has happened, does not know exactly what or precisely where and, in order to find out, has to force his way through the thicket of language, searching the half-erased traces, extracting from the insufficient words at least the mere possibility. Radically uncertain, maintains Benjamin, the novel signs the perplexity of the subject—the isolated individual—in the middle of the euphoric existence.

This original position of the individual marks (see section 5) at once the source of a purely problematic narration *and* the principle of another literary form, which consists no longer in "the representation of human life [*Lebens*]" (Benjamin, *Schriften* 2, pt. 2: 443/*Writings* 2: 146, translation modified) but in the exposition of the primary perplexity that afflicts the living being, the self of that life. This form is the essay.

Unlike the art of storytelling, which has entered the dominion of literature and stands suspended in the space of fiction, the essay's intention is directed to truth. In principle, then, its movement is one of overcoming that elemental perplexity. Nevertheless, the truth that is at stake here can only be constructed by means of criticism, through the destruction of truths that have been handed down and transformed into prejudiced or scholastic heritage. It remains therefore always in suspension, menaced by the labor of trenching that gives place to it: its statute is, then, perennially provisional, and if the result of a particular essay may temporally overcome the perplexity that has motivated it, there is no guarantee that new material or a new point of view will not destroy the verisimilitude that was achieved. In consequence, the essay determines a perspectivist comprehension of truth and a disposition to appeal to the *vérité de faits* as the touchstone of every discursive truth. So, those who are judged the founders of the genre, Montaigne and Bacon, although they may be flagrantly opposed to each other in view of their respective projects and attitudes—the former's fortuitous, digressive, and personal, the latter's methodic, analytic, and detached—both have experience as a leveler of their "essay," as a medium of contrast and as a technique for the critical discernment of discourse's pretensions to truth. Whether as performance or as procedure, skepticism is notoriously the rule of the essay.

Lastly, we Latin Americans take a cue from the general consideration of the essayistic form, a sign toward the locality out of which we spell this "us." Montaigne as well as Bacon have at their backs the discovery of America. The uniquely experimental strategy of their works expresses the incalculable effect that this first de facto essay, which seems to verify the space of fiction, provoked in the European intelligence and imagination. With an unequivocally skeptic vein, Borges, one of "us," suggested that metaphysics could or should be esteemed as a branch of fantastic literature. Starting from the sketch attempted here, we may perhaps risk the assertion that it is possible to consider literature as a variant of skepticism.

If the preceding conjectures are somehow plausible, it would be advisable to follow the track of this skeptical connection, which would manifestly engage two fundamental forms of the literary. This is what I will do here, asking in general about the relationship between literature and skepticism. In view of this, it will be necessary to establish a rigorous concept of skepticism, one conceived under the guidance of its philosophic orchestration, ancient and modern, and to inquire into the character that adopts experience in such a context. Meanwhile, and referring to these two forms, I will say that both essay and narration, being different, even opposed, provide evidence that a certain non-knowing, and above all a certain relationship to non-knowing, open the possibility of writing.

THE DEVELOPMENT

1

Walter Benjamin's essay "The Storyteller" has as a subtitle, "Observations on the Works of Nikolai Leskov." Certainly, these remarks are not restricted to a commentary on Leskov, but they seek to make his work, as well as its narrative power, comprehensible from a historical perspective. Written in 1936, it is based on multiple notes that extend from 1928 to 1935 and aims, according to Benjamin's own declaration, at a "theory of the novel" or, more generally, at a "theory of epic forms."[4]

This perspective takes a peculiar turn. To present Leskov as a storyteller, says Benjamin, is not to bring him closer but rather to increase the distance that separates us from him. "This distance," he says, is

> prescribed for us by an experience which we may have almost every day. It teaches us that the art of storytelling [*die Kunst des Erzählens*] is coming to an end.... It is as if a capability that seemed inalienable to us, the securest among our possessions, has been taken from us: the ability to share experiences. (*Schriften* 2, pt. 2: 439/*Writings* 3: 143)

Continuing with his argument, Benjamin takes up a previous remark he made about the muteness of the soldiers who came back from the front during the Great War:

> Beginning with the World War, a process became apparent which continues to this day. Wasn't it noticeable at the end of the war that men who returned from the battlefield had grown silent—not richer but poorer in communicable experience [*an mitteilbarer Erfahrung*]? What poured out in the flood of war books ten years later was anything but experience that can be shared orally. And there was nothing remarkable about that. For never has experience been more thoroughly belied than strategic experience was belied by tactical warfare, economic experience by inflation, bodily experience by mechanical warfare, moral experience by those in power. A generation that had gone to school on a horse-drawn streetcars now stood under the open sky in a landscape where nothing remained unchanged but the clouds and, beneath those clouds, in a force field of destructive torrents and explosions, the tiny, fragile human body. (*Schriften* 2, pt. 2: 439/*Writings* 3: 143–44)

The point was already present, with little differences, in the essay "Experience and Poverty," probably written around 1933. The main difference was about the war as "one of the most monstrous [*ungeheuersten*] experiences of world history" (2, pt. 1: 214/2: 731). In a certain sense, the war that was destined to end all wars appeared to Benjamin as the experience that sealed the end of all experience. In the same text, with the intention of giving an account of the connection indicated in the title, he referred this unforeseen event to the dominion of technology and its devastating consequences for the individual and collective attempts to build and configure experience. "With this monstrous development of technology [*mit dieser ungeheuren Entfaltung der*

Technik]," Benjamin stresses, "a completely new poverty has descended on mankind," a poverty that brings about the eroding of culture. "For what is the value of all our culture if it is divorced from experience?" This new poverty is, then, a poverty of experience, one that "is not merely poverty on the personal level, but poverty of human experience in general. Hence, a new kind of barbarism" (2, pt. 1: 214–15/2: 732, translation modified). In this continuation of the earlier essay, Benjamin advocates for a positive concept of barbarism, consisting in the need to begin anew and to get by with few resources. By contrast, "The Storyteller" focuses on the crisis that affects the very possibility of sharing experiences by relating them.

There are many things, I guess, that are worth underlining in Benjamin's argument. I am especially interested in one of them; notwithstanding the fact that it cannot be literally read in the text, I think it is possible to infer it without risking overinterpretation. Of course, Benjamin does not only restrict himself to recording a transformation of the ways in which human experience takes place, due to historical changes and profound social upheavals; nor does he remark, properly speaking, on a merely factual disturbance of the truth content of common and communitarian experience.[5] No, the historical *factum* to which Benjamin refers brings along with it a transcendental effect: it is the very *possibility* of experience that is radically questioned, inasmuch as those transformations take away the very conditions of truth, sharing in common, appurtenance, and identity that determine it as such.[6] Precisely in these terms may be understood the assertion that in the soldiers' silence there begins to appear a thorough "denial" of the experiences that give subjects place and orientation in the world: if "the experiences" are the way in which human beings relate to the truths of existence, their "denial" involves a structural crisis. Consequently, the war is not conceived here as an event inserted in a chain of events, no matter the magnitude attributable to it; it isn't an event in a series of meanings (under the name of history), but the subversion of the meaning of history itself. A symptom of this perspective is the use of the term *ungeheuer* ("monstrous, violent, terrible, utterly unusual") to describe both war and technology, and the former precisely because of its being an essentially technical war; this designation indicates that war itself is conceived as the radically unusual event—that is, as the advent of the technical dominion.

It is precisely this nucleus of Benjamin's argument that allows us to confront sharply his assertion with the judgment that Hegel pronounced more than a century before and with which it has a close link, although this link is not remarked upon. The idea of an "end of art" became meaningful for Hegel inasmuch as it could be maintained that the advance toward a new form of historical experience of Spirit demanded a different kind of configuration and appropriation of experience, whose truth could not be satisfied anymore by fantasy as the essential source of art.

What is this experience—the experience that determines the present from which the "end of art" is decreed? As Hegel formulates it in the *Introductory Lectures on Aesthetics*, it may be said that the crucial index of the "present" is the *complexity* of relations that constitute the modern world, a complexity that imposes everywhere the work of mediation (*Vorlesungen über die Ästhetik* 24–25/*Introductory Lectures on Aesthetics* 12–13). Nevertheless, it is not complexity as a given fact but as the result of the world as such being progressively construed by diligent and patient human agency. The world as a human work removes the work of art as the reflection of the world: this would be the meaning that modernity has for Hegel at the aesthetic level. Thence, also, the only condition by which it is possible to take charge of such a complexity, leading to the concrete fulfillment of that world as a historical space of accomplished freedom, is the same condition that is at the base of its progressive construction—that is, the full development of *reflection*. The latter, in a general sense, could be described as the mode of production of the modern world as such, whose chief experience will have to be, from now on, reflexive, not reflected.

What distances Benjamin from Hegel on a *theoretical* level is the materialistic reinterpretation of mediation by Marx, for whom it can only be (figuratively) spoken of as the work of mediation on the condition of understanding that it is actually the mediation of work, which acquires in the modern context the character of a universal system of production. This entails consequences for the conception of art, as becomes manifest in the sketches that Marx left about the issue (cf. *Ökonomische Manuskripte* 43–45/ *Foundations* 109–11). In developing these sketches, Benjamin conceived that it was possible, indeed necessary, to approach the development of art starting from the transformations of the modes and means of production inasmuch as these condition and affect the changes in artistic creation: he proposed, then, to establish a historical and systematic relationship between the transformations of both technology and art in order to make the latter intelligible from a materialistic point of view, emancipated from ideological burdens.

But it was precisely this unrestricted technical disposition and realization of mediation (to which Benjamin refers, in his celebrated essay on the work of art, as "technical reproducibility"—that is to say, as a mode of production based on reproduction) that resulted in an essential transformation affecting the experience of Spirit, so that this experience can no longer be thought of as a space or reappropriation of Spirit through the process of reflection, can no longer be elaborated and purified as an identitary capital of the metaphysical subject. Spirit's experience could only now be described as the experience of a loss, one that is not merely the loss of an attribute or property but the loss of Spirit itself, and therefore the experience of the mourning for this loss, which is formulated in Benjaminian terms as the evanescence of the aura.

It is this evanescence that marks the critical historical situation to which Benjamin refers under the title of the "end of the art of storytelling," meaning by that the termination of an atavistic mode of transmission of experience based on craftwork or artisanal production.

This is, then, what allows us to think that the Benjaminian assertion of the end of the art of storytelling involves a radicalization of Hegel's thesis.

2

I have pointed to the intimate connection between these aforementioned "ends": the end of the "art of storytelling" and the end of literature in general. My argument has, as a trait associated with its thetic character, an interpretive nuance concerning the Benjaminian approach, as I presume is by now obvious. This is the thread linking a conceptual point of view with the "end of the art of storytelling"; in other words, the collapse of the "epic form" with the end of "literature" as a whole is the common reference to *experience*. This reference, which is consubstantial to what Benjamin says, presupposes a certain characteristic of experience itself, to which I am alluding here in a summary way under the notions of the singular and the unrepeatable: in a word, under the theme of the *event*. And it is precisely this question, the acuteness of the event, that could allow us to confront the problem or, better, the paradox, of narrativity in the way I'm trying to sketch here, as the repetition of the unrepeatable. By this I refer to the idea—or, if you prefer, the *desideratum*—of narration, which would tell the event so that it would be possible for narration to satisfy both requirements: to render the event disposable for its remembering while indicating at the same time its absolute singularity—that is, the whole said at once, to institute the event as such.

No doubt, you may recall immediately in this context the paradox of iterability as proposed by Jacques Derrida with reference to the date in Paul Celan's poetry: "How can one date what does not repeat if dating also calls for some form of return? But how can one date anything other than that which never repeats itself?" (*Schibboleth* 13/*Sovereignties* 2). In a similar way to what, according to Derrida, constitutes the possibility of this repetition of the unrepeatable—of "an event without witness, without other witness" (37/15)—that is to say, similar to the erasure of the date by the very act of its inscription, similar to the announcement of a reappearance (*revenance*), to a spectral return of what cannot return by virtue of the same erasure that assures the legibility of the date: in this way, narration repeats the event that it narrates to the extent that it denies its status as the impossible repetition of the event, doing so precisely in and through the event that now comprises the narration itself, and insofar as it disposes itself as the place of a spectral (i.e., fictitious)[7] return of the event itself. Beneath the story of the event narration tells, it whispers at the same time its own end as the condition of possibility of such a story.

Put differently, a narration is never a *simple* repetition, if it is even possible to think that there is such a thing. Consequently, it is necessary to take into account that narration is determined by the structure of a *repetition of the repetition*. The paradox of the iterability of the event can only be solved by iterability itself. This structure not only allows for a relation to the narrated event that repeats the event in another time—the time of writing, of hearing, of reading—but also administers all the possible repetitions of this relation (from hearing and understanding to commentary, explanation, interpretation, etc.). In a certain sense, one could say that the repetitive structure of narration not only makes possible the repetition of the event in its singularity and the encounter of the hearer's or reader's singularity with the former—as well as, if you prefer, the encounter of the hearer's or reader's idiom with the idiom of the repetition—but also governs the reiterative repetition of the impossibility and therefore of the end. As I have tried to suggest, each narration not only repeats the event it narrates but also repeats (also in the mode of anticipation) its own end, in order to make the inscription of the event possible. Every narration contains its own denial with respect to the truth of the narrated event, but, in doing so, it incorporates this truth into the space that opens this auto-critical operation: the space of fiction.[8]

It is from this point of view that I maintain that narration's character could be associated with what Franz Rosenzweig, at the beginning of his essay

"Scripture and Luther" (1926), defines as the task of translation, which is a paradoxical task too. I think it won't be pointless to transcribe the two initial paragraphs. Let us begin with the first:

> Translating means serving two masters. It follows that no one can do it. But it follows also that it is, like everything that no one can do in theory, everyone's task in practice. Everyone must translate, and everyone does. When we speak, we translate from our intention into the understanding we expect in the other—not, moreover, some absent and general other, but *this particular* other whom we see before us, and whose eyes, as we translate, either open or shut. When we hear, we translate words that sound in our ears into our understanding—or, more concretely, into the language of our mouth. We all have our own individual speech. Or rather: we all would have our own individual speech, if there were in truth such a thing as monologic speaking (as logicians, those would-be-monologists, characteristically postulate) and all speaking were not already dialogic speaking and thus—translation. ("Schrift" 749/"Scripture" 47)

The (theoretical) impossibility of translation, if conceived as the repetition of the same in a medium essentially different than the one in which the same has been coined, is its (practical) necessity. This necessity is evinced by the fact that all speaking is translating. Therefore, the true significance of the theoretical impossibility of translating, "in the succession of 'impossible' and necessary compromises we ordinarily call life," consists in giving us "the courage of modesty, which asks of itself not what is recognized as impossible but what is given [*aufgegebenen*] as necessary" (749/47). This is Rosenzweig's "task of the translator," which, as a task (*Aufgabe*), has the fundamental ethical meaning of recognition of and openness to the other:

> In speaking and hearing, what is asked is not that the other possess our ears or our mouth—in that case translation would be of course unnecessary, as indeed would be speaking and hearing as well. And in speaking and hearing between peoples it is not asked that the translation be either the old original—in which case the hearing people would be superfluous—or a new original—in which case the speaking people would be annihilated. Only a mad egoism could desire either of these, mad enough to imagine itself satisfied with its own personal or national being, and to long for empty desert all around it. But the world was not made an empty

desert, but rich in distinctions and kinds; and there is no room in it for such an attitude. (749–50/47–48)

In Rosenzweig's account, the whole of language, from common talk, intimate or public, to the most complex literary creations, and even to the divine word shaped in text, is susceptible to being conceived and experienced under the model of translation. Such a model has not only a descriptive value but a prescriptive dimension as well. The peculiarity of Rosenzweig's proposal consists in offering, under the concept of translation, an ethics of communication that has its core in its dialogical articulation. Obviously, not every communication is *in fact* a dialogue in the sense of a relationship between free subjects mutually irreducible; but every communication *ought* to be a dialogue, with a duty of opening to free otherness. To steal oneself from this duty, to enter into a unidirectional communication that would not expect from the other the revelation of an unforeseen meaning, brings with it the risk not only of turning the world into a desert but also of abolishing it.

If we link this postulate with what we have previously seen of the Benjaminian approach (with whose general premises finds such affinity in Rosenzweig), we can assume that what Benjamin calls "war" in its transcendental efficacy denies precisely the possibility of the "mad egoism" to which Rosenzweig refers.

A hint of the suppression of dialogue that Rosenzweig warns against and that Benjamin underlines with his idea of the "communicability of experience" (there seems to be some justification for approaching both notions together) is given by the attention that the latter dedicates to the emergence of a new form of communication in mature capitalism, which has its proper medium in the press: this new form, which bears the principal responsibility for the crisis of narration, no matter the degree of affinity that could be found between both, is *information*, which encompasses "almost everything" that happens (Benjamin, *Schriften* 2, pt. 2: 444–45/*Writings* 3: 147–48). This hint may help us to complement what we have said about the crisis of experience. Benjamin quotes a declaration of Hyppolite de Villemessant, the founder of *Le Figaro*, in which he claims to recognize "the essence [*Wesen*] of information": "To my readers ... an attic fire in the Latin Quarter is more important than a revolution in Madrid." To which Benjamin replies, "This makes strikingly clear that what gets the readiest hearing is no longer intelligence coming from afar, but the information which supplies a handle for what is nearest" (2, pt. 2: 444/3: 147). I set aside the meaningful addenda to this commentary (the verifiability and verisimilitude of information as confronted with the authority and the wonder of narration) in order to focus on the change to which Benjamin points: the dissolution of the experiential opening proper to narration in the exactness of the explanation that gives access to what has happened. If one would wish to update Villemessant's statement with respect to the renewed conditions of information brought by late capitalism, it would probably be suitable to say, "For my readers any event, no matter if near or distant, is equivalent, to the extent that it is already formatted by the technology of information." This, which by now is a moderate way to announce those conditions, should also show not only how the Benjaminian "art of storytelling" sinks into the night of the archaic under the weight of the informational totalization of communication, but also how "literature" in general is thrown by this totalization into a critical situation. A consideration of the relations in course between literature and globalization may help to clarify the point.

The mere mention of this issue awakens contrariety: what we call "literature" and are accustomed to subsuming under the general principle of possibility—in that peculiar variant that is fiction—gets on badly with the idea of a saturation of contexts involved in the regime of globalization, whether it be understood from the point of view of the thorough integration of markets or conceived from the perspective of the planetary expansion of communication. Immediately seen, it gets on badly with that integration, for the dictatorship of the "sellable" obstructs the freedom of the play of signs and meanings (otherwise, if it does not obstruct it, it becomes predictable) and fixes and puts in order—in a sort of preestablished menu—the viscous matter of desire, which the so-called literature thickens and helps in its slow fluidity. And it gets on badly, too, with the communicative expansion, because the linguistic homogeneity that this promotes with no respite cheapens the nuances and slippages and paves the narrow passes of translation. But more decisively, in one way or another in globalization—and of course between both there is a bond as strict as it is indiscernible—the saturation to which I refer suppresses the diversity of experiences, the difference of places. In speaking of both—places and experiences—I mean to refer to one and the same complex: that which may happen, the eventful, that which "takes place" or is in course of taking place. Whether this "place" is envisaged in terms of geographical locations or as knots in a web of relations, in terms of situations and circumstances, of happenings, of subjects, each bears the signature of an experience, as encounter or discovery, as warning or wonder, as routine or incident—a diversity of experiences, a diversity of places, then, as one and the same constellation, which the regime of information suppresses. And it happens that the so-called literature is—or is supposed to be—the production and inscription of that difference, of such diversity.

Almost with a nostalgic aftertaste, one could say that this was formerly the case: "literature" worked as the drilling (or even the blowing up) of the granite of indurate experiences, which brought back the vertiginous instant of the irruption of the unexpected in experience itself: for the same reason, the instant of the susceptible to remembrance, the worthy of being narrated. For this exercise of the "literary," the context of experience was always—one could say by definition—a porous block, and the "place" was, in turn, the proper dimension of that experience, as the gap through which it opened to otherness. But now the subtle fabric of the webs proper to globalization serves to unnerve that altering force. In the multiple intersections of the reticular system, the "things," the facts and events, the "lived" itself are no more than fugacious flickerings and titillations. All that was known under the name of "experiences," which hinged on the possibility of its exchange on precisely its reciprocal irreducibility, on its "usage value," is now subsumed under a general faculty of format whose application is as unlimited as it is indifferent. Nor is experimentation still an option: it has lost its point, which consisted in producing the experience not yet lived, and even the impossible experience. The "possible" as much as the "impossible"—and the very difference between the two—turn out to be atmospheric variations in the space of the virtual. The context of globalization brings along with it the virtualization of experience, wherein the latter tends emphatically to its extinction.[9]

3

Obviously, this is the critical point of my argument. What consistent relation could be established between literature and skepticism? Does this imply that we must refer literature to knowledge, conceiving it, for instance, as a form of knowledge of the world in order to show it immediately, and paradoxically, as a form that teaches the impossibility of such knowledge? And am I not taking the notion of "skepticism" in a looser way?

Of course, I cannot offer here an exhaustive determination of this putative relation. Moreover, I'm afraid that there cannot be a conclusive demonstration that could make the hypothesis of such a relation fully persuasive. This *problem* is established as the horizon of the essays that follow in this book, and this also means that the legitimacy of the approach to this sort of problem can only be decided by means of a work that tries to prove it by dwelling upon certain instances that may have some force of suggestion. Anyway, it is necessary to secure at least a principle of verisimilitude for that relation, which, although suggestive, is not patently obvious.

To begin with, it is useful for us to try an explanation of the concept of literature with which I'm working here. This concept has already been insinuated in my first paragraph, although in a surreptitious and therefore ambiguous manner. This I have done by suggesting that what Benjamin conceives as the end of the "art of storytelling" coincides with the emergence of literature "in the proper sense" (not only with the novel), and this "propriety" has to do with the meaning of what in the long term has been understood as "belles lettres": I'm referring to literature as a *system* whose primary criterion of validity rests in aesthetic experience. The Benjaminian concept of an "art of storytelling" points already to this sense, inasmuch as it supposes an artistic intentionality of form and effect, which, although not entirely alien to everyday narration, is in no way a thematic or preexisting aspect of it. By the way, one could ask if it is possible to give a thorough account of this art by taking as a measure of the narrative act its artistically elaborate forms as such, much in the way the notion of the "art of storytelling" refers the universe of narration to the archetypes of the sedentary peasant and the merchant seaman as "past masters of storytelling" (Benjamin, *Schriften* 2, pt. 2: 440/*Writings* 3: 144). Would it not be beneficial to look at the incipient and spontaneous forms and usages of everyday storytelling, from the gossip to the confession and the testimony? Certainly, for the argument Benjamin is interested in developing this consideration could be relatively superfluous, but for our present aim it may have some relevance. This relevance comes into greater focus when we pay attention to what in the Benjaminian approach constitutes the essential difference between the "art of storytelling" and the "novel" as successive, historical articulations of the epic form. As we have already seen, the difference rests in the continuity of a substantial ground of common and communicable experiences (common as communicable and communicable as common) at the heart of that "art": a ground that one naturally also has to presuppose with respect to the spontaneous everyday storytelling but that would no longer be in force in the "novel."

Following this track, we could say that literature "in the proper sense" arises with its eradication from experiences, not at all with the loss of the ability to communicate experiences proper to the radical crisis of the "art of storytelling" in Benjamin's conception, but rather in a process that tends to diminish the value of actual experiences—a process, then, in which these experiences gradually prove to be somewhat superfluous to the configuration of individual and collective life. Put differently, it may be possible to maintain that literature arises as *vicarious experiences* become more and more important. From a historical point of view, this is the moment that Aristotle marks for the first time when he defends poetry's aptitude for universal truth in contrast with history (*Poetics* 1451a39–b11). This distinction is crucial if we are to recognize the turning point in narration itself, by virtue of which it becomes an "art": the point at which, starting from a common ground where history, myth, and invention remain more or less confounded (as is indicated by the double meaning of the word *(hi)story* in Western languages), these discursive forms begin to separate from each other. As is well known, Aristotle distinguishes history and poetry by the fact that the former tells things that happened while the latter tells things that should happen (*hoia an genoito*). With poetry's reference to the domain of the possible (*to dynaton*), a space is opened where the discourse of non-actual experience can prove its relevance and efficacy.[10]

Starting from this characterization, it is perhaps possible to lend an appearance of verisimilitude to the relation I am outlining. To this end, it will be necessary to turn now to philosophical skepticism, providing a minimal review of its fundamental traits. Obviously, this will have an allusive and provisional value and is no substitute for the indispensable precisions and distinctions on the basis of which one can trace the full picture of this school.

Skepticism maintains that, because our information about the world is grounded merely in our experiences, it is impossible for us to forge a secure or certain knowledge of the world. The beliefs we have, the opinions we pronounce about the world, its elements and conditions, cannot be grounded so that we could defend an opinion—concerning a determinate issue or set of issues—as true and incontrovertible without it being possible to put forward reasons of equal weight supporting the opposite opinion. To the extent that the doubt concerning the truth or falsity of opinions provokes mental unease in the doubtful subject, skepticism commends as a general strategy the suspension of judgment—that is to say, leaving undecided the matter with which those opinions deal. Such suspension provides the abstinent with the cure for the obsessive search for truth, opens him to the plain presence of the phenomenon, and gives him the consequent tranquility of mind.

Granting for the sake of hypothesis the concept of literature previously advanced, and admitting this brief sketch of skepticism, it would be entirely natural to ask whether the relation between skepticism and literature is not immediately suppressed by the confrontation of both. While the former seems to insist on rescuing phenomena from the attempts of colonization and reduction undertaken by the philosophical *logos*, the latter seems to be occupied in providing the discourse with new modes of interpretation of experience, new modes of relation to it (I was alluding to this in speaking of experiences that are no longer actual), by virtue of which those phenomena usually appear in a light as different and unsuspected as any metaphysical explanation. In both cases the phenomenon—as an irreducible remnant of the suspension of judgment—would tend to be obliterated under the weight of a powerful, discursive articulation. However, there is something that literature manifestly does not share with the reductive *logos* of metaphysics: its *dogmatism*—that is, the marks of universality, necessity, and exclusiveness that this *logos* claims for itself. The pluralism of the experiences that are no longer actual, its particularity (its specification in a determined universe of meaning), its suspension in the dimension of possibility (the hypothetical projection of this universe), indicates another configuration of *logos*.

To the extent that literature exposes us to non-actual experiences, it contributes to the sense that it is not possible in the end to establish the truth or falsity of the judgments we form about every experience. In fact, implied in the literary exercise is a primary suspension of judgment, which lends fiction (as the domain of possibilities) its peculiar efficacy. Without this suspension of judgment, the structure of the repetition of repetition, which solves the paradox of iterability, would be impossible. If, as we have seen before, every narration more or less implies its own denial with reference to the truth of the narrated event, literature "in the proper sense" actualizes this denial in the very configuration of the non-actual experience.[11]

It is this suspension that emerges as such through the exercise of literature in modernity, rendering evident literature's inveterate skeptical affinity.

In any event, it is necessary to say that I'm not simply defining literature as a form of skepticism. Rather, I would suggest that there is a skeptical matrix in the literary phenomenon, and I am suggesting, too, that the discernment of this matrix should help us to better understand the structural traits of the literary phenomenon, as much from the point of view of forms as of realizations.

4

The second remark appears in the fifth chapter of Benjamin's essay. It is worth quoting the whole passage:

> The earliest indication of a process whose end is the decline of storytelling is the rise of the novel at the beginning of modern times. What distinguishes the novel from the story (and from the epic in the narrow sense) is its essential dependence on the book. The dissemination of the novel became possible only with the invention of printing. What can be handed on orally, the wealth of the epic, is different in kind from what constitutes the stock in trade [*Bestand*] of the novel. What distinguishes the novel from all other forms of prose literature—the fairy tale, the legend, even the novella—is that it neither comes from oral tradition nor enters into it. This distinguishes it from storytelling in particular. The storyteller takes what he tells from experience—his own or that reported by others. And he in turn makes it the experience of those who are listening to his tale. The novelist has isolated himself. The birthplace of the novel is the individual in his isolation, the individual who can no longer speak of his concerns in exemplary fashion, who himself lacks counsel and can give none. To write a novel is to take to the extreme that which is incommensurable in the representation of human life [*Leben*]. In the midst of life's fullness, and through the representation of this fullness, the novel gives evidence of the profound perplexity of the living. Even the first great book of the genre, *Don Quixote*, teaches how the spiritual greatness, the boldness, the helpfulness of one of the noblest of men, Don Quixote, are completely devoid of counsel and contain not a scintilla of wisdom. If now and then, in the course of the centuries, efforts have been made—most effectively, perhaps, in *Wilhelm Meisters Wanderjahre*—to implant instruction in the novel, these attempts have always amounted to a modification of the novel form. The bildungsroman, on the other hand, does not deviate in any way from the basic structure of the novel. By integrating the social process with the development of a person, it bestows the most brittle justification on the order determining that process. The legitimizing of this order stands in direct opposition [*steht windschief*] to its reality. The unattainable is event—precisely in the bildungsroman. (Benjamin, *Schriften* 2, pt. 2: 442–43/*Writings* 3: 146–47, translation modified)

In Benjamin's explanation, the reference to technology plays a central role. We have already seen that what he himself calls the "monstrous development of technology," which finds in the Great War the laboratory in which its crucial experiment is carried out, is what stipulates the transcendental crisis of experience. The paragraph just quoted indicates another milestone of this tension between technology and experience, an inaugural milestone in the process that reaches its pinnacle with the war. The technique of printing introduces a crisis in communication, in the mutual sharing of experiences within a community, which is equivalent to the crisis or the auratic experience of the work of art brought about by the intermittent expansion of the techniques of reproduction.[12] This critical condition, if it does not suppress the possibility of sharing experiences, eradicates them from the communitarian context of meaning and tends to expose them to the nude facticity that remained latent in them and that narrative communication—indeed, in an imperceptible way—has kept in line. The "subject" of experience, who is not yet a subject in the proper sense within its communitarian configuration, becomes in this way an individual.[13]

The two novelistic paradigms Benjamin mentions account for the duality of fates that are reserved for this "individual" throughout the development of the modern novel. If *Don Quixote* may be described as a novel that precisely shows the individual exercising with importunate and comical heroism the derangement into which his primary perplexity throws him, if it may be said that the work is something like a story of the deformation of the subject, a story of its de-constitution *in statu nascendi*, the bildungsroman wants to show the itinerary through which, no matter how labyrinthine the path, one comes to be such an individual. But, despite the difference and even the flagrant opposition between both fates, at their bases lies the same premise of existence and (not) knowing. In the passage quoted above, two terms set the standard for understanding the way in which Benjamin conceives this premise: the incommensurable (*das Inkommensurable*) and the unattainable (*das Unzulängliche*). These concepts attempt to characterize the essential statute of what we call the "individual." Stressing the loss of a substantive *measure* of the organic relations between human being and the world, a measure that the narration was in charge of coining, recreating, and transmitting time and again, both indicate the radical change of experience that forces its way from now on. The notion of "event" lies at the center of this mutation, but in a very specific way, for there is also event in the universe of narration. The inherent measure of the art of storytelling is the event of a continual refoundation of the community through the continual reference to the event that establishes it. Instead, what is thought under the heading of this notion in modern times is precisely the event of the incommensurable, of the insufficient, which refers the individual time and again to the loss that constitutes him.

Maybe this can give us occasion to insist on the intersection between the historical and the structural hypothesis about which I spoke at the beginning, in order to justify the idea of an implication of the "end of literature" in the "end of the art of storytelling." For I think that from this characterization of the event there follows an essential modification of the relations between event and language with respect to the structure they assume within the narrative communication. Paying close attention to the statement with which Benjamin concludes his brief account of the bildungsroman—which presumably also sets the tone of his comprehension of the rise of the novel— we could say that the eventfulness of what Benjamin calls "insufficient," and by virtue of which the advent of the individual is marked, makes manifest, for the individual, the insufficiency of the event. And if from the point of view of the individual's being it is likely that this insufficiency may be the main stimulus of its becoming a subject, the same insufficiency raises, from the point of view of the appropriation of the event in language, the necessity of compensating for it by means of discourse. Discourse is now the institution of the event in an entirely different way than it could have been before and must involve—this is a question to which one should give the form of a hypothesis—an essential alteration of what I have formerly named the structure of repetition. Whereas in oral narration the event has an original certification (an original truth) due to its being the very condition that makes it possible to produce and receive its story, and the story has only the task of augmenting this certification (also in the sense of invention) without ever impairing it (without refusing the event, in the last instance, its primary right to truth). In the technically mediated narration, then, the discourse provides the event with the certitude of which the latter on principle lacks; that is to say, discourse does not share the event but mediates it. It is precisely this determination that contains as an essential possibility, starting from the mass communication that printing and print media permit, the new form that Benjamin characterizes as information, which does not offer anything of "what happens" without the addition of an explanation for the sake of the plausibility of information itself.

5

The essay, a literary form proper to the modern era, is undoubtedly the one that most immediately satisfies the relation of literature with skepticism. This relation also comprises the affinity that the essay has with the epistemological worries that drive the theoretical inquiries in the same epoch. Indeed, the weight that has skepticism as a problem and a strategy for the project of the foundation of knowledge—a gravitation that remains throughout the entire development of modern thinking in Descartes, Hume, Kant, and Hegel—finds one of its primary means of staging and exploration in the essayistic form, shaped as it is by the authors who may be considered its initiators: Michel de Montaigne (1533–92) and Francis Bacon (1561–1626). It is precisely in this sense that I am associating with the question of the essay what Benjamin says about the perplexity of the individual, linking the existential character that he attributes to it with the demand for knowledge—or a kind of knowledge—that may permit this individual at least to confront that perplexity, if not to administer or overcome it.

Resorting to the same terms with which Benjamin establishes his thesis about the novel, I would say that in the essay the question concerns an *exposition*, not of life in its fullness, as with the novel, which presents the human being entangled in the dense web of reality, forcing his way through it or succumbing to its incidents, but an exposition of the primary perplexity that affects him because of this web, a perplexity that touches even the true meaning that may be attributed to the word *reality*, for the emphatic characteristics that may be attributed to it have been suffocated by the experience of incertitude.

In the warning *Au lecteur* of the grounding document of the essayistic genre, Michel de Montaigne's *Essais*, the idea of the *exposition* I'm talking about as origin of this form is appropriately expressed. This exposition is an intention and a passion of *truth*, but of a truth whose only content is Montaigne's "I myself"—whole, plain, and unadorned. "Good faith [*bonne foy*]," maintains the first statement of this warning (which is at the same time an exoneration and a dissuasive gesture), is the matrix and the mood of the book (*Essais* 27/*Essays* lix, translation modified). "Good faith," then, on behalf of which the author wants only to be seen "in [his] simple, natural, and everyday fashion, without striving or artifice" (27/lix), with no desire to hide one's faults and frailties: the truth of the self—the faithful picture of the self—is opposed to concealment, cosmetics, and makeup, in a word, to fiction. Wholeness and nakedness are, in the last instance, the *desideratum* that governs the work:

> And therefore, Reader, I myself am the subject of my book: it is not reasonable that you should employ your leisure on a topic so frivolous and so vain. (27/lix)

Whatever you may think of it, the question of truth is the matrix of the essay. In Montaigne's exemplary case, it is about the truth of the self in its minute commerce with the world as the eclipse or abolition of every Truth, in capital letters, particularly that of the opinions that feign an allegedly assured knowledge. Unlike the way in which, sixty years later,[14] Descartes will articulate this condition, a kind of doubt without method defines here a sort of tabula rasa, which is only frailly counterbalanced by the memory of the readings of classical authors, who provide the array of quotations—with various functions: illustrative, prudential, or decorative—that fills up the book's pages.[15] It is a paradoxical and singular truth, then, to the extent that it supposes the suppression of *the* truth on behalf of what characterizes the becoming of the self that is now its sole content, as well as its form and principle—that is, the *experience*, the essential synonym of *essai*. But you should not think that this mode of conceiving truth is condemned to sink into solipsism. On the contrary, the reference to the individual, personal, and idiosyncratic releases the punctual and peculiar little truths of things from the mold of a great exclusive and excluding truth. As La Rochefoucauld puts it,

> Truth, wherever it is found, cannot be overshadowed by comparison with any other truth; and whatever differences there may be between two entities, what is true in one can never overshadow what is true in the other. They may be more or less extensive and more or less conspicuous, but they are always equal in truth—which is no truer in the greater entity than in the lesser. (*Collected Maxims* 193–94)

Montaigne's essay defines, in the inauguration of the form, a first fundamental source of it. The other is established in the work of Bacon.[16] Here, it is also about experience as the fundamental context in which the individual maintains his relations with reality. Here, the essay also breaks with the necessity of orientation and counsel, the demand for an accurate judgment of things. But Bacon's work exhibits a sharp difference with Montaigne's. The latter, seized by doubts about every matter—since in each case there are contrary and plausible opinions that contend for primacy—refrains from every decision that, from a theoretical standpoint, would be unjustifiable and instead favors one of those opinions only if the situation becomes pressing. Perplexity is the epistemological dimension that the individual inevitably inhabits; it is his everlasting condition of knowing. For Bacon, as well as for Descartes later, the task will be to settle matters with the primordial perplexity, to overcome its defective state, not only to the extent that this has consequences for the theoretical situation of man, but above all because there will follow decisive effects for his practical life. The purpose of a knowledge that is certain arises, then, as an essential project, although its breeding ground is incertitude and confusion, the same as it is for Montaigne's practical occasionalism.

There follows from here a different notion of experience, or, if you prefer, an internal difference in what for Montaigne appears as a plural and indistinct mass. In the first place, Bacon conceives of a kind of automatic experience, one that is permanently assailed by reality and its unpredictable vicissitudes. One cannot expect from such *vague* experience any reliable guide for conducting cognitive enterprises or for life itself, although it is precisely this experience to which all former thinkers have had recourse for one end or another. To this vague experience is opposed the *ordered* experience, which can systematically gather these past attempts, mend them, and take a secure road. With this distinction, Bacon grounds the act of *experiment*. The experiment has the particular feature of being, just as Bacon says, an experience that is sought after (*experientia quaesita*), not one that "simply" restricts itself to recording in a passive way (that is, without purpose) what "happens," what "comes up" by chance (*occursus rerum*). What distinguishes the *experimentum* from vague or simple experience is the intentional search, the *quaesitio* or *quaestio*—that is, the intention to know formulated in a question, not raised, of course, by the mere apparition of things but born from intellectual spontaneity—which leads to the insertion of experiences in a general plan of research fashioned out of reason. So, ordered experience must replace vague experience so as to assure the progress of science toward its proper goal, according to a structure and a strategy of investigation that coordinates different experiments, experiments with axioms, and axioms, again (progressively), with experiments.[17]

But beyond the differences that may exist between one source and the other and between the diverse intermediate modalities, the essential affinity of the form of the essay with skepticism is justified in the first place because the essay is the literary formalization of an opinion, a point of view concerning the world, concerning an element or a set of elements in it, or a certain state of it. This formalization is unavoidably affected by doubt inasmuch as it has as its only support the standpoint of the individual who expresses his opinion, and this, in turn, can only be based on the individual's experiences. However positive an essay could be, its enunciation is in advance played down by the position of the individual, and it carries out, in the proper sense, a suspension of judgment rather than a positive and decisive judgment; anyway, the latter is only possible starting from such a suspension. But it is not only about this formalization. What is at stake in the essay is the exposition of a particular way in which a self looks for orientation in the world and, therefore, these two things: that wherever it is possible to assert a truth (if this is at all feasible), the latter demands and presupposes the witnessing of a self who betrays its position in its assertion (for which reason there is no categorical character one could assign to that truth); and that the world itself, which the essayist has always at the forefront of his intention but which only presents itself to him in experience, through the concreteness and the detail of phenomena, can only be comprehended (and this is, for certain, an exiguous comprehension) according to the key of *complexity*.

You may consider Montaigne and Bacon two fundamental pillars of the modern epoch, what over the course of time we still call modernity and—with yet another turn—what could be legitimately termed "the age of complexity." But they are two essentially different origins of the "modern project." One is cast in insurmountable doubt, stimulating an indefatigable process of reflection, which goes hand in hand with a discursive performance that is true to the vicissitudes and varying fortunes of this process: the only truth that can be attained in this case. Starting from the other origin, all effort focuses upon contriving a wonderful ruse to anticipate every vicissitude and eventuality—"method" will be the formal name of this ruse—in order to stay true to the call for truth, even if this truth might be continuously and always amendable.

Here, I intend to follow the path opened by the first of these two origins. Certainly, it does not conform to a univocal line of progression, not even what may be called, in a more or less loose way, a tradition; rather, it is a firmament of scattered and eccentric shining points, each one for its own sake, although I'm inclined to think that there is a certain kinship between them, a kind of skeptical fraternity. Needless to say, a complete map of such points is a sheer impossibility. Accordingly, I make my own selection of cases that might lend my overarching hypothesis, as I said before, a minimum of plausibility: companions to Montaigne will be Swift, Lichtenberg, Kleist, and Kafka. And I should add just one more, whom I will mention in the following and last section.

6

I alluded to complexity. This hint points to a "region" in which the relation of literature and skepticism, in the double form of narration and essay and above all in the mixture of both forms, reaches a critical point of its efficacy. If complexity is the condition under which literature—but also thinking, by extension, all its forms—evolves in the modern era, the emergence of this "region" not only as a province within the already known orb, as a new domain in which to continue searching for familiar realities, but also as a "new world" would be the most flagrant data of such complexity.

In an essay presented at the Sorbonne on the occasion of an awards ceremony for Latin American essayists, the Colombian historian, diplomat, journalist, and politician Germán Arciniegas announced right from the title the conviction that motivated his lesson: "America is an essay." Arciniegas poses a question about the predilection that people have in Latin America for the essayistic form, the documentation of which, he argues, is so long-standing that its first products precede by years the instauration of the genre by Montaigne. He ascribes this predilection to a fundamental historical motive:

> The reason for this singularity is obvious. America appears in the world, with its geography and its men, as a problem. It is an unsuspected novelty that breaks with traditional ideas. America is already, in itself, a problem, an essay of a new world, something that tempts, that provokes, that challenges intelligence. [La razón de esta singularidad es obvia. América surge en el mundo, con su geografía y sus hombres, como un problema. Es una novedad insospechada que rompe con las ideas tradicionales. América es ya, en sí, un problema, un ensayo de nuevo mundo, algo que tienta, provoca, desafía a la inteligencia.] (331)

I will not insist on the arguments with which Arciniegas seeks to lend support to his hypothesis, which in a very marked way touch the topic of racial mixing, *mestizaje*. I'm just trying to draw the reader's attention to a "region," as I said—a geographical "region," indeed, but first and foremost a historical and cultural one that bears the original stamp of assay and incertitude, of a new beginning that ceaselessly begins time and again. No wonder the exercise of the essay—and of fiction—is a privileged mode of guessing (which is a feeble but not negligible mode of knowing) our own traits. And this merits some study.

A guide for this reflection could be drawn from the phlegmatic creed of the Argentinian writer Jorge Luis Borges, in which that essayistic, Latin American coinage finds one of its inescapable paradigms. His assertion, according to which it is worthier to take metaphysics (or theology) as a branch of fantastic literature, sums up in a manner as absolutely economic as it is humorous the skeptical refusal of every emphatic pretension of truth, of last or definitive truths. Through the same assertion, Borges alludes to a fictitious totalization of the universe of discourse, not only in that all its products and items are susceptible to being aesthetically consumed, but also according to a comprehension of this experience (the aesthetic one) that distinguishes it fundamentally from any positive yield of truth: you should remember that Borges maintains that the aesthetic fact is perhaps the imminence of a revelation that in the end does not happen. The indication of this imminence may be, in turn, a sign of that deferral, of that temporality of deferral that I deem to recognize at the origin of what we call "fiction" and that would relate literature, at least problematically, to the suspending strategy of skepticism. It is precisely in this sense that I think it is possible to respond to Borges's assertion, assuming that this preserves some affinity with its tenor, by saying that literature, in its entirety, could be considered as a branch or a variant of skepticism.

Chapter One

Montaigne

WRITING AND SKEPTICISM

INTRODUCTION

In philosophical terms, skepticism can be considered in at least three ways: as a school, as an attitude, as a strategy. It can become stronger alternately in the methodical demolition of dogmatic pretensions, in the administration of life in the middle of a world constantly changing, or in the tenacious criticism of the prejudiced restrictions of knowledge in order to secure the improvement of knowledge. In a certain case, skepticism will be a frame of mind, in another a principle, in a third, perhaps, cunning. In any case, there is something one cannot deny: skepticism is an original and inseparable moment in the philosophical enterprise, to the point that the mark of the search for truth characteristic of philosophy (or so it proudly claims) is precisely the primary dispute it furthers against the putative knowledge that dominates the scene of human conversation. The virtue of ancient skepticism, and above all the legendary figure of Pyrrho, consists in conferring autonomy to that moment, identifying it with philosophy in general.

In the introduction to this volume, I suggested that something analogous could be thought about literature, that there could also lie in it (albeit in a tacit or surreptitious way) a skeptical moment, original and inseparable, hypothetically present in every literary exercise, and possibly emancipated and converted into the epitome of literature in general. The first instance in which a conjecture like this could be put to the test—in both its variants—is the work of Michel de Montaigne (1533–1592).

My approach in this chapter is relatively simple. I'm going to suppose that the skepticism professed in fact by Montaigne is the matrix of a relation between self and experience—this is of course a medullary issue of his work—that has its proper dimension in writing. Consequently, I'm inclined to think that writing could be described as the skeptical operation par excellence to the extent that it exercises the constant "assay" of that relation. This assay finds its form in the essay, and it will be necessary to give an account of this coinage. My first point will be to discuss the nature of Montaigne's skepticism; I'll then try to sketch the connection between essay and experience, ending with some considerations concerning the questions of the self and of writing. Although I might also refer to other pieces in Montaigne's oeuvre, for each of these three sections I have in view, respectively, an essay that I have chosen for its exemplarity: "An Apology for Raymond de Sebond," "On Experience," and "On Practice."

MONTAIGNE'S SKEPTICISM

Montaigne counts as one of the great names in the tradition of skepticism. Nevertheless, his affiliation and militancy are not confirmed by the rigorous application of established titles. Montaigne is not what we properly and ordinarily call a philosopher; he is, rather, as he himself declares, a "new character: a chance philosopher, not a premeditated one!" (*Essais* 578/*Essays* 614).[1] His office is none other than writing and, of course, an entirely peculiar practice of writing in which the writer uses exposition as an instrument to spy on himself. Despite everything, the contribution Montaigne made to the renaissance of the skeptical stance at the dawn of modern times is a powerful one. Thanks to him, and especially his propagation of skepticism's epistemological critique in "An Apology for Raymond de Sebond," Sextus Empiricus—his source for that critique—attains a philosophical notoriety that has not decreased since. Surely, Montaigne's skeptical signature is perceptible everywhere in his *Essays*. But if one wants to document more clearly his connection with that philosophical stance, one has to turn to the "Apology."

This piece, the largest in the *Essays*, has a religious and moral grounding. From the beginning, the author's intentions appear quite plainly. Admitting—more or less ironically—that science may have its utility, he denies that it is "the Mother of virtue and that all vice is born of Ignorance" (458/489). In view of the human relationship with God, the essay's declared purpose is to discuss the rights of supposed mystical illumination and of knowledge by way of reason. Concerning the former (I shall speak of the latter below), if we actually had access to divine truth through supernatural favor, its distinctive mark would be virtue, "the most worthy thing that Truth produces" (462/493), and the spectacle of the world plainly proves that men use religion in the most vicious and arbitrary ways, fitting its principles and precepts to the particularity of their characters, interests, and circumstances. As a corollary to the rejection of any direct link to God, it appears that obedience is humanity's sole noble quality. A particularly sharp expression of this assertion reads,

> Only humility and submissiveness can produce a good man. We must not let everyone work out for himself what his duties are. Duty must be laid down for him, not chosen by him from his own reasoning; otherwise, out of the weakness and infinite variety of our reasons and opinions, we will—as Epicurus said—end up forging duties for ourselves which will have us eating each other. (513/543)

Nevertheless, it doesn't seem that this allegation constitutes the nucleus of the *Apology*, above all if one thinks that the conformity and conservatism established in religion could steal an individual's autonomous capacity, since one cannot but attribute to Montaigne the assertion of that freedom. But we will treat this in more detail later.

Anyway, the critical approach adopted by Montaigne from the very beginning betrays the irony of the apology for Sebond: the *Theologia naturalis*, which was established on the scholastic conviction of a consummated unity of reason and revelation, is defended here in a very oblique manner, one that soon shows the signs of a refutation. In the end, this rebuttal entails a question of principle. If the human being does not receive the prescription for which Montaigne advocates—the one allowing the preservation of the possibility of virtue—by immediate divine inspiration, and if it cannot be appropriated by humans with the aid of means as weak as those at their disposal, then the simplicity and candor of nature might afford the rule for a good life. Consequently, Montaigne eradicates the traditional foundation of religiousness (whether it be mysticism or rationalism) and entrusts it to nature instead, but precisely to a nature that cannot be made to fit into the mold in which our knowledge wishes to place it. In asserting the thorough inadequacy of "divine science" with respect to human measure, and in suggesting that nature avoids the subject's cognitive intentions, Montaigne challenges all the titles of human science, referring as much to its epistemological reach as to its moral influence. The means of which he makes use for this purpose are drawn from Sextus's array, and the target is philosophy's conflictive tradition.

I do not pretend to offer a registry of the use—and frequently the repetition—of Sextus's arguments, which are here organized in a more or less loose manner according to a scheme of ten tropes. I'm interested in two things: briefly discussing Montaigne's concept of knowledge and, as I've already said, discerning his peculiar way of professing skepticism.

Concerning my first interest, Montaigne's judgment is unequivocal. All our knowledge—and, of course, its epitome, philosophy—is essentially and irremediably human: "Man cannot be other than he is; he cannot have thoughts beyond his reach" (549/581–82), reads a phrase whose invocation in this polemic is by now de rigueur. The search for truth is not governed by truth itself—such that, as Aristotle (and later on Hegel, for certain) formerly wished, even error is a moment of truth—but, rather, stems from embarrassment and remains forever affected by human weakness; original perplexity is unredeemable, and the effort to overcome it produces only new perplexities, which the forms of knowledge can only deceptively cover and decorate: "Certainly, philosophy is poetry adulterated by Sophists" (567/602). The well-known panorama of the acute controversies of philosophers is the richest source from which Montaigne extracts the proofs by which he demonstrates "the vacillations of the human mind over any subject whatever" (538/569). Once our supposed and presumptuous knowledge is stripped of all its sophisticated garments—and this is a proverbial practice in Montaigne's critique—what lies at its foundation becomes manifest: not an absolute imperative but the sting of appetite. The desire to know is, finally, only a desire that, at least in its form, has no more worth than any other desire thriving in man. Accordingly, its only motive is pleasure: "We ought not to find it strange that people who despair of the kill should not renounce the pleasure of the hunt: study is, in itself, a delightful occupation, so delightful that, among the forbidden pleasures which need to be held on a tight rein, the Stoics include pleasure arising from exercising the mind. They find intemperance in knowing too much" (538/569).

Nevertheless, in view of its content, it is a special desire, because of which the obsessive ends up risking his own integrity, whether mental or physical. As Paul de Man suggests, at the basis of Montaigne's argumentation lies the conviction that "the object of knowledge is contradictory in essence—in contradiction with the existence of its own intentional structure. In every act of knowledge there is a profound flaw that leads to an insoluble dilemma: its object can be known only at the price of the existence of the knowing agent.... Without this sacrifice, there can be no really objective knowledge" (*Critical Writings* 6).

The imperative to give up this obfuscating desire consolidates the skeptical attitude in Montaigne, precisely at the point where he asserts the irreducible character of the self, which is captive in the cognitive enterprise and left only with the odious alternative of either succumbing in the process of achievement or sinking into the despair of not achieving. It is, then, the self, Montaigne's *moi-même*, that enounces itself as the vortex of the impossibility of knowledge but also as the instance that discovers, in the interval of its enunciation, the possibility of accounting for itself as this vortex, which is— let us put it in these terms—the very issue of Montaigne's *Essays*. There lies in this a nuance that distinguishes him from his predecessors.

The review of the skeptical philosophers offered by Montaigne (529–33/559–63) is based on a faithful rendition of Sextus's exposition. But there is perhaps an issue in his subsequent commentaries (there are numerous places in which he returns to the various aspects of their stance) that are germane to my present aim. A passage in which Montaigne argues that the weaknesses and flaws of language—"most of the world's squabbles are occasioned by grammar"—points to the difficulty of formulating the constitutive ideology of Pyrrhonism:

> Pyrrhonist philosophers, I see, cannot express their general concepts in any known kind of speech; they would need a new language: ours is made up of affirmative propositions totally inimical to them—so much so that when they say "I doubt," you can jump down their throats and make them admit that they at least know one thing for certain, namely that they doubt. To save themselves they are constrained to draw an analogy from medicine: without it their sceptical humour would never get purged! When they say *I know not* or *I doubt* that affirmation purges itself (they maintain) along with all the others, exactly like a dose of rhubarb, which evacuates all our evil humours, itself included.[2] (556–57/590)

In the indecisiveness of the interrogation (accompanied by a shrugging of one's shoulders, which in turn represents a balancing of the scales)—which is to say, in an indecisiveness that leaves precisely knowledge and its emphatic assertions in the air—a breech opens in which we might witness the dehiscence of the self.

Where could we recognize the main difference that makes Montaigne a peculiar skeptic? Maybe the most succinct way to express this difference is to call attention to the apparent distance that separates the skeptical canon, comprised as it is of the suspension of judgment, from the constant judgment that Montaigne exercises in his *Essays*, which gives many of his enunciations a characteristically sententious tone. However, such an activity lacks any external criteria: it is an individual and personal judgment, without axioms or a priori rules, whose pertinence is located in the opportunity, the situation, and the conjuncture in which the subject finds himself. One of the most illustrative descriptions of the situation of judgment can be read in the *Apology*: "I go backwards and forwards: my judgment does not always march straight ahead, but floats and bobs about" (600/638). Despite everything, it is a free and singular force, on which the individual self bases all the authority and sovereignty feasible for it:

> Within me judgement holds the rector's chair, or at least it anxiously strives to do so. It permits my inclinations to go their own way, including hatred and love (even self-love) without itself being worsened or corrupted. Though it cannot reform those other qualities so as to bring them into harmony with itself, at least it does not let itself be deformed by them: it plays its role apart. (1121–22/1219)

This vacillating and at the same time independent judgment is, first of all, a version that is in no way alien to what Montaigne himself calls the "humor" of the skeptical position. And perhaps this could tell us something about Montaigne's modulation of skepticism, allowing time, in the suspension of the *epoche*, for a labor of self-inscription that relies on its own experience.

ESSAY AND EXPERIENCE

The stance that I'm inclined to call Montaigne's "incidental skepticism" raises immediate difficulties for the reader familiar with philosophical texts fashioned from the zeal of coherence and rigorous reasoning, a zeal that in metaphysics appears as the will to know the condition of all knowledge. Montaigne displays a reluctance in the face of all systematic cogency and every programmatic emphasis, and he constantly claims his right to contradict himself and to change his opinion. It is true that, if we take this reluctance to its extreme, we shall arrive at the unlimited scrutiny of "Montaigne's thought," which would entail even that domestic right and its circumstantial occupation, undermining the possibility of risking judgment about anything. Yet instead of the catastrophe of thinking and its stunned reclusion within an isolated and blind self, we find in his work the most intense and ductile dynamism, one that draws its very possibility from the imminence of this catastrophe.[3]

In Montaigne's assay (in his *essai*) lies, therefore, an active, paradoxical nucleus. The question of experience is not foreign to this nucleus, and a symptom thereof appears in the fact that the word *essai* also means "experience" and that Montaigne employs it repeatedly in this sense. In fact, *essai* (from *exagio*, "to ponder," with the same etymological root as the word *examination*) meant "attempt," "proof," and "experience" long before it acquired the meaning of "didactic work of a light and provisional character." Montaigne peruses and permanently combines these meanings in his work to the point that the limits between them become diffuse. The general effect of this semantic fluidity could perhaps be described as an inevitable contamination, diligently exercised, of the realms of writing and experience. This contamination determines the efficacy of what I call the paradoxical nucleus of the essay. If we recall that paradox goes against common opinion (as far as it follows, with respect to the latter, an aberrant and marginal course) and that *doxa* has been conceived as the essential creature of experience, as its proper wisdom, then we may assume that the aforementioned nucleus implies a peculiar kind of relation to experience. What becomes manifest in this relation would be the paradoxical efficacy of experience itself, its particular reticence toward all foresight and every program.

How should this experience of the paradox of experience, which forms the basis of the *Essays*, be conceived? I exclude on principle the possibility of conceiving it in the style of an aporia in its classic shape, which frees thinking from doxical atavisms and opens in this way the space of its epistemic claim. It is precisely this claim that Montaigne wishes to discourage, such that what here could be termed "aporia" refers not to a trans-empirical dimension of knowing (the dimension of the non-manifest, the first cause, or the ultimate ground, the essential, etc.) but to a return to experience itself as the sole context of validation and display of knowledge. However, the form of knowledge is not here, properly speaking, that of *doxa*, ingratiated with its verisimilitude. The paradoxical efficacy of experience demands a power of discernment, capable of taking into account the fact that the truly regular is precisely that difference. Such power—I have already anticipated it—is judgment, on the condition that one understands it, if I may put it this way, as the *life of thinking*.

Judgment, in this case what I have called Montaigne's "vacillating judgment," has a peculiar rigor, one that is alien to systematic coherence and compatible with empirical versatility. This rigor has nothing to do with the disposition of a method whose rules could be established in advance and in the absence of themes, matters, and objects. Montaigne insists that the infinity of differences and nuances in everything invalidates the aspiration to an organic closure of knowledge; he provides the proof of experience (use, practice) with its unlimited variety in order to undermine any scholastic project. The "knowledge" he proposes overtly shows its characteristics: lack of firmly established rules, nondeductive generality, mere attempt, rhapsodic, sequential, and fragmentary; these are the very tokens of the "essay." But certainly the essay does not consist in chance encounters and an incidental mode to cope with them. One should pay attention to the term with which Montaigne continually describes his own occupation, which is inseparable from the notion and practice of the essay: *study* (*étude*, *studium*, related to *spoudeo*, *speudo*), the scrupulous application of one's attention to anything in order to pronounce a verdict about it and to determine oneself exclusively with this ability to judge acquired by constant exercise. The essay's studiousness indicates the singular rigor I mentioned above; its matrix—if it can be put this way—would be a *logic of occurrence*, a *logic of invention*, which articulates the incidental occurrence of the case with the timely judgment upon it.

Therefore, the "essay" is not the result of an inquiry but of its very movement, and never even the present process of searching, if you understand by the latter an attempt that organizes itself around the possibility of reaching secure knowledge by its mediation. Let us see what Montaigne hints at in the long essay that closes his entire oeuvre, which has the title "On Experience":

> The learned do arrange their ideas into species and name them in detail. I, who can see no further than practice informs me, have no such rule, presenting my ideas in no categories and feeling my way—as I am doing here now; I pronounce my sentences in disconnected clauses, as something which cannot be said at once all in one piece. Harmony and consistency are not to be found in ordinary base souls such as ours. Wisdom is an

edifice solid and entire, each piece of which has its place and bears its hallmark: "*Sola sapientia in se tota conversa est*" [Wisdom alone is entirely self-contained]. (*Essais* 1123–24/*Essays* 1222)

Experience and study would form the essay's essential structure, at least according to what this final essay teaches. Now we have to see in what cardinal context these notions find themselves inscribed and what relations are governed by this context.

At the beginning of the essay, one notices an argumentative move that is directed precisely toward fixing the premises from which it is possible to reach the aforementioned conclusion about knowledge, whose skeptical turn is unmistakable. This move tends to establish the bases of a circumscription of the desire to know that results in its extenuation. To start with, it concerns finding out what those bases are; afterwards, it will be necessary to determine what kind of outcome Montaigne expects to attain from such undermining labor. Anyway, if I talk about circumscription, I'm not implying the mere refusal of every possibility of knowledge. It is not, in other words, the abolishing of every ground and every prospect of knowing or the tracing of knowledge's narrow limits in view of human precariousness and of the variegation of phenomena, but rather the essential transformation of knowledge's very statute, making its subject its exclusive theme.

The text begins—one should note Montaigne's ironic slant—by establishing what we could generally call the *philosophical principle*: "No desire is more natural than the desire for knowledge" (1111/1207). In order to bring satisfaction to this desire, we try every means. Montaigne refers to two resources that are fundamental: reason and experience. The latter "is a weaker and less dignified means" (1111/1207), but we cannot despise it if truth is at stake. With respect to *truth*, "so great a matter" (1111/1207), reason and experience are the means; the difference between them is one of *certainty* and of *rank*. But the text immediately questions the first of these two differences. The certainty of reason in view of the possession of truth fades away as soon as one pays attention to the multiplicity of its forms, wherein it does not differ from experience; such multiplicity weakens the possibility of observing what reason commends to us: "Reason has so many forms that we do not know which to resort to: experience has no fewer" (1111/1207). As we will see, this first attempt to erase the difference tends to preserve rank, hierarchy, as the only actual difference, and this is mainly a formal difference.

From the first steps of this essay forward, we witness a serious alteration of the relations between reason (as the capacity for well-founded and certain possession of truth) and experience.

A first meaning of the notion of experience plays a capital role in this alteration, well accredited by the traditional determination of this concept: "The induction which we wish to draw from the likeness between events is unsure since they all show unlikenesses. When collating objects no quality is so universal as diversity and variety" (1111/1207). This is a deeply rooted conviction of Montaigne's thought. However, it is not to be treated as an exclusive point of view. Later, in the course of the discussion of interpretations, Montaigne will complete this idea with another, which counterbalances it:

> Just as no event and no form completely resembles another, neither does any completely differ. What an ingenious medley is Nature's: if our faces were not alike we could not tell man from beast: if they were not unalike we could not tell man from man. All things are connected by some similarity; yet every example limps and any correspondence which we draw from experience is always feeble and imperfect; we can nevertheless find some corner or other by which to link our comparisons. (1116/1213)

We have, then, a double condition: the endless diversity of events and forms and *also* the existence of particular similarities among things, the fact that there is no thing identical with another in all respects and *also* that there is no thing absolutely different from another in any respect. Undoubtedly, Montaigne attributes both conditions to the essential and original disposition of nature: "Nature has bound herself to make nothing 'other' which is not unlike" (1111/1208). But it doesn't make any sense to change these assertions into enunciations of metaphysical principles. It is, rather, the contrary that seems to fit in this case. The denial that the absolute principles of identity and difference have validity and applicability when confronting the universe of events excludes the possibility of circumscribing "nature" in categorical terms, and nature, let's say, is conceived here as the disjunctive unity of things and events. So the denial discourages every claim of reason to embrace that universe exhaustively. The function of these premises is, then, eminently critical, negative, and there is no room to assign them a wider reach than that of the polemical argument to which they belong.

In order to understand what is here at stake, I will restrict myself to discussing what constitutes a first part of the text, which examines the problem of laws and their interpretations (1111–19/1207–17). This is the field in which reason preeminently is in force, such that it implicitly appears under the guise of a faculty of law, as well as a faculty of interpretation. For interpretation is not a merely extrinsic addition to law but represents a moment that inevitably belongs to law; it is the moment of application—that is to say, of the necessity of coping with the hiatus that separates the generality of the law and the minute singularity of events.

Montaigne's argument advances through paradoxical junctions. First, it is erroneous to limit the judge's freedom in the interpretation of laws by establishing new laws that frame the preceding ones. Each new law is a new stimulus for interpretation, and, therefore, it can only aggravate the evil that one tries to remedy with such an expedient, and there is no law that could, by its own force, put a stop to the hermeneutical process, because it will itself be an issue of opposite exegeses, even in the case of "the express words of the Bible" (1112/1208). Second, the futility of the multiplication of laws comes from the impossibility of achieving precisely that in which its validity would consist—namely, shortening the distance that separates the law from the case. Therefore, this is not a simple difference of degree but an ontological difference. Its marks are the absolute disproportion of number (the contrast between generality and singularity) and the rigidity and firmness of the law as opposed to the inconstancy of deeds and facts (1112/1208). Third, this same variation suggests that the only valid laws would be those that nature gives to us, "always ... happier laws than those we give ourselves" (1112/1208–09). This is a point of great consequence: it concerns the second inscription of the concept of nature in Montaigne's text, conceived now as the primordial source of legality, to which, from the side of human creations, would correspond those laws that are the "most desirable," the "fewest, simplest, and most general" (1112/1208), like the laws of the Golden Age imagined by poets or as insinuated by the prescriptions of King Ferdinand of Castile, who did not want to send jurisconsults to the colonies in the Indies. The idea governing this assertion is an idea of nature's wisdom: if nature is the fabric of diversity (cf. 1112/1208), then the legislation of this diversity should be entrusted to nature. This amounts to assuming that nature does not produce without a rule, although this rule is not humanly knowable. Fourth and finally, the incertitude of law (the unavoidable fact that it is exposed to a proliferation of interpretations) is deepened not only by the impossibility to cope with the hiatus between law and particular cases, but also by the fact of being made out of words, each of which is susceptible of exegesis: "Why is it that our tongue, so simple for other purposes, becomes obscure and unintelligible in wills and contracts?" (1113/1209). Here we can observe that the spring of this linguistic incertitude is interest, which seems to be suggested by the example of contracts and testaments. At any rate, it would certainly be impossible to separate the question of interest from the question of law, for every law has to rule our interests.

A first outcome of this line of argumentation is a specifically epistemological one: it concerns the effacement of truth, that which is "so great a matter" that it awakens all our efforts. In connection with this, there occurs in the text a second inscription of the concept of experience, one that discretely makes of it a criterion: "All I can say is that you can feel from experience that so many interpretations dissipate the truth and break it up [*Je ne sçay qu'en dire: mais il se sent par experience, que tant d'interpretations dissipent la verité, et la rompent*]" (1113/1210). At work in this epistemological collapse are the multiplication and relativity of opinions, which blur the comprehension of any assertion carrying with it an emphatic aspiration to truth: "Never did two men ever judge identically about anything, and it is impossible to find two opinions which are exactly alike, not only in different men but in the same men at different times" (1114/1210). Here we observe an amplification of the proliferating effect that this entire argument exploits to controversial ends. The unlimited multiplicity of events is answered by the unlimited multiplicity of opinions, such that the law remains captive between both sides, emptied by both of its force of truth. The knowledge that lies in it is undone and condemned to ignorance by the unrestrained possibility of glossing.

This possibility is not merely theoretical: it is a human impulse whose consequences cannot be more frustrating:

> do we ever find an end to our need to interpret? Can we see any progress or advance towards serenity? Do we need fewer lawyers and judges than when that lump of legality was in its babyhood?
>
> On the contrary we obscure and bury the meaning: we can no longer discern it except by courtesy of those many closures and palisades. Men fail to recognize the natural sickness of their mind which does nothing but range and ferret about, ceaselessly twisting and contriving and, like our silkworms, becoming entangled in its own works ... (1114/1210–11)

In the recognition of this impulse we find again the diatribe that Montaigne addresses against the ambition of knowing in the *Apology*;[4] it is now infinite interpretation that embodies that peculiar appetite: "It is only our individual weakness which makes us satisfied with what has been discovered by others or by ourselves in this hunt for knowledge: an abler man will not be satisfied with it.... There is no end to our inquiries: our end is in the next world" (1114–15/1211). A human being is a "hermeneutical animal" who finds himself driven to interpret without end, not only because of the spur to interest in the narrow sense (the concern for what is his own) but also because of interest in the wider sense (the curiosity for what concerns the other). This unlimited interpretation ("it is more of a business to interpret the interpretations than to interpret the texts" [1115/1212]) now offers a new fundamental fact—namely, that of the virtually self-generating movement of glosses. Nature, as the fabric of diversity, is perversely reflected by the distorting mirror of the fabric of meaning. The difference between them lies in the creative richness of the former and the sterility of the latter.

Unlike the first result of Montaigne's argument, a second general outcome of the critique of law is moral: it concerns now its essential disconnection with regard to justice, which it is supposed to express and serve. In the same way that the proliferation of commentaries and interpretations blurs the truth, rendering the meaning of the law and its pertinence to the case completely uncertain, the similitude of cases—at least in one point—destroys or distorts justice in the application of the law—that is, again, in its interpretation:

> Since the moral laws which apply to the private duties of all individuals are so difficult to establish (as we see that they are), not surprisingly those laws which govern collections of all those individuals are even more so. Consider the form of justice which has ruled over us: it is a true witness to the imbecility of Man, so full it is of contradiction and error. Wherever we find favouritism or undue severity in our justice—and we can find so much that I doubt whether the Mean between them is to be found as frequently—they constitute diseased organs and corrupt members of the very body and essence of Justice. (1116–17/1214)

Of course, Montaigne does not have to make any great effort to accumulate examples. Men's congenital obfuscation proliferates in all jurisprudence, such that there is no way to make justice in detail and justice in the big picture accord: the invariable result is general damage. So the foundations are laid to round off the critique of law in a radical sense, which anticipates certain defamations from Nietzsche, unmasking what is in its origin and its destiny nothing other than the fateful combination of the stupidity and narrow interest of men:

> Now laws remain respected not because they are just but because they are laws. That is the mystical basis of their authority [*C'est le fondement mystique de leur authorité*]. They have no other. It serves them well, too. Laws are often made by fools, and even more often by men who fail in equity because they hate equality: but always by men, vain authorities who can resolve nothing. (1119/1216)

One could say that this is the epitome of Montaigne's thought about the law, in which most of his skeptical approach is contained. The duality of reason and mysticism we recognized in the *Apology* now shows its entire fundamental unity: in the end there is not a real discord between both but, rather, a close solidarity. It is the very human longing for knowledge that, exasperated, seeks refuge, if not in the fraudulent appearance of discourses, at least in the supposed autarchy of its privileged faculty. Dogmatism is the perverse synthesis in which both presumptions find satisfaction, canceling the independent use of everyone's capacities. The main damage provoked by laws and their functionaries concerns that which most concretely defines the individual and that which is his most precious good: his liberty. "I so hunger after freedom that if anyone were to forbid me access to some corner of the Indies I would to some extent live less at ease" (1119/1216). Montaigne's attitude toward the law is certainly non-Socratic. The private individual must do his most not to fall under its jurisdiction, to keep himself as far away as possible, in order not to be exposed to the corrupted sentence of the magistrates. Individual liberty, which is postulated here not as a principle or as an idea but as freedom to move from one place to another—"my freedom to come and go," says Montaigne (1119/1216)—is settled above every eminence of the law, particularly if what comes into question is the chaotic heap of French law.

THE WRITTEN SELF

Experience and study, as I've said, form the essential plot of the essay. Its knot, though, is the self, the individual self of Michel de Montaigne. If in the essay "On Experience" there is a long stretch devoted to playing down, on all sides, the relation between reason and experience and to defrauding men's confidence in their dubious resources, the remnant that this leaves in view of the inquisitive tasks of knowledge, a remnant that, starting from its declared insignificance, extends itself endlessly, is the consideration of oneself. So, at the end of the discussion to which I referred in the last section, Montaigne says, "I study myself more than any other subject. This is my metaphysics, that is my physics" (1119/1217). This rubric of the self defines the decisive modification that Montaigne brings to the statute of knowledge, starting from the imbrications of its subject in experience, and it is also the condition under which experience can be deemed the quintessence of wisdom, as long as it is "enough to instruct us in what we need" and affords us the necessary knowledge for life: "Were I a good pupil there is enough, I find, in my own experience to make wise" (1120/1217–18). The consistency of experience is due to the fact that the original commerce between the self and the world (nature) takes place in it, that is to say, that there is not one event that does not presuppose the self, a witness, an individual, or living instance that forms an inseparable part of the definition of the event itself.

The fundamental rule of this knowledge is minimal and at the same time difficult: it concerns observing the "world's general law" (1120/1217), the rules of nature. This concern and this intimate wisdom were precisely what were becoming apparent in one of the paradoxical junctures of the critique of human laws. Montaigne says in "On Experience," "I, unconcerned and ignorant within this universe, allow myself to be governed by this world's general law.... The more simply we entrust ourself to Nature the more wisely we do so" (1120/1217–18). And experience is the space to which the "laws of nature" refer, the space in which these laws exert their efficacy across the minuteness of events. For this very reason nature is not conceived here as an actual or virtual totality of such rules, inasmuch as it is not a predictable order of events. The essential factor that seems to operate in all this is time. Nature ("the world") is given to us temporally, from one moment to another, as we come gradually to acquaint ourselves with it. This implies two things: first, that the relation between self and nature is a relation governed by necessity (nature offers me what is necessary for conducting my life in every circumstance, on the condition that I am a good apprentice), but a necessity that is always local, punctual, inscribed in the contingency of the relation itself; and, second, that nature never offers itself in its totality, neither extensive nor intensive nor, needless to say, absolute (which contradicts its essential parsimony), but always circumstantial and through its "ingenious medley" of similitude and dissimilitude.[5]

But the self that is the principle of this knowledge is not invoked as a pre-constituted entity to which the events of experience would be referred as accidents of a substance, or as an entity that is gradually formed through the vicissitudes of its life until it manages to offer a consummate profile, or, in the end, as an entity that, from the vantage point of an accomplished moment of its existence, gives an account of and shares its opinions about the facts of which it has been the protagonist or witness. Thence its "essay" does not constitute an autobiography, a kind of memoir, or a bildungsroman, even if certain passages of its work could evoke in one way or another the first two genres, maybe above all the second. So, the main literary form of the essays is not narration, though there are periods that are articulated as narratives. Such periods always subordinate themselves to the swaying of the author's ponderings or, otherwise, give illustrative support to his sententious pronouncements. Yet, although the calling of the *Essays* is essentially reflexive, the self who speaks in them neither constitutes, in Cartesian fashion, the synthetic instance of an invariant relationship between thinking and existence nor presents its written reflex.

If we look at the shape of Montaigne's work from the point of view of the accidents that befall the subject, one should have to say that everything (or almost everything, if we don't consider the power of discernment, which neither has a stable nature nor is the faculty of a substance) is accident; all (or almost all) stuff of which the self is made is incidental. The self is formed in and through experience. This formation is not cumulative: a sequence of facts does not produce an ontological density of the self as a solid sediment that could last in the long term; the reminiscent integration of the whole experience of a life is not possible, for memory is fragile and fallible.[6]

One should say that the accident takes on its full scope inasmuch as it becomes emancipated from its metaphysical framing. In experience, as the ultimate referent of every discourse, passion, and opinion, the accident appears very different compared with the aspect it shows as a mere acolyte of consistent things. It is the element and rhythm of things, and, for the same reason, it is the most acute provocation to which the self can be subject. Its proper mark is the mark of death. And surely there is no other place in Montaigne's work where this quality is more unequivocally manifest than the sixth essay of book 2, entitled "On Practice" (*De l'exercitation*). A brief review may be suitable.

Reason and instruction, argues Montaigne, are insufficient when it comes to orienting our actions: exercise is needed, the acquisition of experience. The most illustrious philosophers have made laborious efforts in order to deliberately expose themselves to the rigors of fortune. But exercise is impotent in front of death. Of course, it is possible to strengthen oneself against pains and other evils, "but as for dying, we can only assay that once; we are all apprentices when it comes to that" (389/416). Nevertheless, there is a way of experiencing it—namely, when one has suffered a violent misadventure, which makes the victim lose all her or his bodily and spiritual faculties. Montaigne then recounts the serious accident that he suffered when he fell off his horse on the way back home. In great detail, with an astounding prolixity, he describes the entire process of his agony and of his gradual recovery, always oscillating on the threshold of death. In this description, the idea that the passions and thoughts that one has in such a critical situation are not one's own plays a fundamental role: the soul, with no force to recognize itself, is driven by fancies and superficial impressions. And as "any pain which our foot or our hand feels while we are asleep does not belong to us," so the thoughts of the injured person are

> empty acts of apparent thinking provoked by sensations in my eyes and ears: they did not arise from within me. . . . My reactions were trivial ones, produced by my senses themselves, doubtless from habit. Any contribution from my soul, which was only very lightly involved and as though licked by the dew of some light impression of the senses. (395/422)

The record of this peculiar state of alienation and of the tardy regaining of consciousness counts theoretically as an inverse *cogito*, inasmuch as it evidences the insurmountable contamination of subjectivity by what happens, its originally vulnerable condition, and the radical impurity of its thought. It is precisely the accident and the impossibility of appropriating it at the moment of its happening that constitute and determine subjectivity. Montaigne's admirable annotations on the embarrassment of his memory illuminate the point:

> I must not overlook the following: the last thing I could recover was my memory of the accident itself; before I could grasp it, I got them to repeat several times where I was going to, where I was coming from, what time it happened. . . . But some time later the following day when my memory happened to open up and recall to me the circumstances which I found myself in on that instant when I was aware of that horse coming at me (for I had seen it at my heels and already thought I was dead, but that perception had been so sudden that fear had no time to be engendered by it),

it appeared to me that lightning had struck my soul with a jolt and that I was coming back from the other world. (396/223)

After this meticulous report (and it is not a minor thing to observe how essay and narrative are interlaced, here as in other places in the work), Montaigne justifies his exclusive occupation with himself in the face of the censure that is frequently addressed against any egocentric discourse. It concerns not only the lesson that he has drawn for himself from this mishap, and from his proximity to death, but also the general purpose of examining oneself, of spying at every moment on one's own thought. This thinking and scrutinizing oneself in the act of thinking are Montaigne's permanent itch, one that he can only mitigate by the constant scratching of the quill. And writing betrays precisely the impossibility of any categorical and clear coincidence of the self with itself:

> It is a thorny undertaking—more than it looks—to follow so roaming a course as that of our mind's, to penetrate its dark depths and its inner recesses, to pick out and pin down the innumerable characteristics of its emotions.... For many years now the target of my thoughts has been myself alone; I examine nothing, I study nothing, but me; and if I do study anything else, it is so as to apply it at once to myself, or more correctly, within myself.... I am chiefly portraying my ways of thinking, a shapeless subject which simply does not become manifest in deeds.... It is not what I do that I write of, but of me, of what I *am*. (396–98/424–26)

But, certainly, statements like these, although so abundant in the *Essays* and tempting to take for general assertions of the work's plan, cannot be divorced from their context, because it is precisely in this context that they attain their real weight. I have already tried to suggest it: the accident, as the form of the event in experience, bears the stamp of death. And this stamp also seals the act of writing. The tension between the lethal situation caused by the fall, characterized by giving oneself up, and the obsessive occupation with oneself, marks a task of writing as a repetitive act of capturing the self during the brief and risky interval during which its being is extreme vulnerability.[7]

However hard this labor may be—"no description is more difficult than the describing of oneself; and none, certainly, is more useful" (397/424)—and although the self could never be restored through such labor to what would presumably be its bare integrity (and you know already that it is not, that it cannot be), there is something entirely decisive resulting from this for the construction and installation of the self. To write the self in every moment on the edge of death is to inscribe oneself at every moment as an irreducible trace in the world. The essay "To Philosophize Is to Learn How to Die," the twentieth in the first volume, which strings together reflections by Cicero, Seneca, Horace, and Lucretius with the author's own ponderings, insists that the fatal denouement is unforeseeable and refuses the vulgar escape that consists in not thinking about it. If one wants to be free of the oppressive power that death exerts on us, it is necessary to confront it, to grow accustomed to it by means of thoughtful habituation. It is in this way that Montaigne favors the idea that "to practise death is to practise freedom" (88/96). And yet in the very middle of his learned reflections, the person of Montaigne bursts onto the scene, obstinately occupied with "thoughts about death," which chase him even in his vigorous youth: "Every moment it seems to me that I am running away from myself.... I am untying all the knots. I have already half-said my adieus to everyone but myself. No man has ever prepared to leave the world more simply nor more fully than I have. No one has more completely let go of everything than I try to do. The deadest deaths are the healthiest" (89–90/97–98).[8] One should ask what the self gains from this gloomy intimacy. Well, as the essay suggests, as "Of Exercise" teaches, it gains the peremptoriness of its present.

In this sense, the self is the point of an acute temporalization: it is uttered in the "now" and is inseparable from it. The beginning of the essay "On Repenting," the second in the third volume, is perhaps one of the most salient places in which this condition is formulated, accompanied as it is by a lucid indication of the urge to fix the fugacity of the time in which the self comes into itself. Under the motto "The world is but a perennial see-saw [*branloire*]," Montaigne declares,

> I am unable to stabilize my subject: it staggers confusedly along with a natural drunkenness. I grasp it as it is now, at this moment when I am lingering over it. I am not portraying being but becoming: not the passage from age to another (or, as the folk put it, from one seven-year period to the next) but from day to day, from minute to minute. I must adapt this account of myself to the passing hour [*à l'heure*]. I shall perhaps change soon, not accidentally but intentionally. This is a register of varied and changing occurrences, of ideas which are unresolved and, when needs be, contradictory, either because I myself have become different or because I grasp hold of different attributes or aspects of my subjects. So I

may happen to contradict myself but, as Demades said, I never contradict truth. If my soul could only find a footing I would not be assaying myself [*je ne m'essaierois pas*] but resolving myself. But my soul is ever in its apprenticeship and being tested. (845/907–08)

The truth of which Montaigne is speaking here is entirely different from the one that science seeks to identify: universal, stable, objective. The constant trembling that is the world—an open constellation of events—neatly suppresses the possibility of an invariable truth. Therefore, temporality affects truth itself: "for truth itself is not privileged to be used all the time and in all circumstances: noble though its employment is, it has its limits and boundaries" (1125/1223). But for the same reason, neither is it the fixation of the fact—that is, of the historical form of truth. Strictly speaking, there are no facts in Montaigne's universe, or rather, everything that may be considered as fact—in the sense of an undeniable and accomplished instance of experience on which experience could firmly stand—is essentially uncertain, inasmuch as the fact depends not on its own weight but on the conjuncture in which the self relates to it, and indeed, the supposed "fact" is nothing other than this conjuncture. As de Man says of Montaigne,

> His tense is exclusively the present.... But ... this present tense is not the present of Montaigne living through this or that experience; it is the present of Montaigne writing. No separation of the written phenomenon from the moment when he writes, but a formal separation between the action really performed and his observation by means of discourse. (*Critical Writings* 11)

This suggestion, added to what I indicated earlier, could offer a clue for the explanation of the *Essays*, on the condition that we foreground the act of writing. If the care of one's own life is the sum of all knowledge,[9] one should ask: Why, if the "art of living" is such a sum, is it necessary to open the gap of writing? Nevertheless, writing the book and building the self are one and the same thing. As Montaigne puts it, "Here, my book and I go harmoniously forward at the same pace" (*Essais* 846/*Essays* 909). Writing, then, is the inscription of a self in the present, a present that remains, so to speak, dated once and for all but that in turn has no privilege over the rest of present times in which that inscription takes place. The essentially restless, incidental, and problematic character of the act of writing is what gives the self its present each time; it is what gives rise to the self in each present. Writing is the truthful body of the self, and this is a self that is nothing outside this body.

On the one hand, from the point of view of knowing, the inscribed self possesses a negative universality as a power and passion of inscription. It does not rest on the reliability of an identity but always relapses into the vacuity of ignorance. Just as the temporalization that I mentioned affects truth itself, which remains restricted to the "limits and boundaries" of opportunity, so, too, experience deepens here its relation to error, being therefore deprived of its potential capacity for truth by the establishment of laws and constant rules: we learn from our errors, yes, but what we learn from them is no more than that about which we used to be mistaken.

On the other hand, this universality has a positive side. The knowledge that I have of myself (characterized, paradoxically, by the vacuity I was discussing) is also valid for all other people, and so amounts to the universal "human being." Insisting on the point that differentiates Montaigne's purpose from preceding attempts at anthropological knowledge that were all obsessed with the zeal of instruction ("I am not teaching, I am relating" [846/909]), "On Repenting" stipulates this very clearly: "Every man bears the whole Form of the human condition" (846/908). In the acute awareness that Montaigne brings to the essential novelty of his enterprise, which consists in the omission of every authorial credential, the idea of a "universal being" of the individual is stated for the first time: "Authors communicate themselves to the public by some peculiar mark foreign to themselves; I—the first ever to do so—by my universal being, not as a grammarian, poet or jurisconsult but as Michel de Montaigne" (845/908).

Experience is the medium of this (double) universality, and writing its organ, or, as I was saying, its body.

Why in the end could or should there be a deep connivance between skepticism and writing?

Earlier I observed the signification that the individual self acquires in skepticism, as well as its precise location in the "now," in the present of its passion, in the actuality of its experience. The skeptical self lacks any substantive unity and remains attentive to the diversity and dispersion of phenomena, with which, setting aside all the abusive attributions and abstruse explanations of the philosophical *logos*, it enters into contact through the instant's ephemeral passage. I was supposing that it could perhaps be possible to think that this narrow passage that discursive reason can neither exploit nor administrate, because reason needs time to carry out its mission, might be enhanced, dilated, and give rise to other forms and uses of discourse: in this way, a certain idea of literature could be insinuated. I think it plausible to maintain that Montaigne's work gives an account of such a possibility. In this work occurs that rare thing that consists not in chasing knowledge but in chasing oneself, not in stalking reality but in spying on the individual himself, not in searching for oneself but in finding it by chance: "This, too, happens in my case: where I seek myself I cannot find myself: I discover myself more by accident than by inquiring into my judgement" (73/40). The fragmentary quality—intermittent, digressive, almost absentminded—of Montaigne's essay outlines the splintered and fortuitous constitution of the self, and writing is not the thread that gathers the pieces and moments but the operation in which these fragments reverberate in various ways, marking the feeble consistence of the self in each present. Writing occupies—now—the place that knowledge left vacant.

Chapter Two

Superb Imposture

SATIRE, COMMON SENSE, AND SKEPTICISM IN SWIFT'S *A TALE OF A TUB*

IT SEEMS THAT AROUND 1697 Jonathan Swift (1667–1745) concluded his first major work, *A Tale of a Tub*, which was published anonymously in 1704 together with *A Full and True Account of the BATTEL Fought Last FRIDAY, Between the* Ancient *and the* Modern *BOOKS in St. JAMES's LIBRARY* and *A DISCOURSE Concerning the Mechanical Operation of the SPIRIT. IN A LETTER To a FRIEND*.[1] The *Tale*, having a rapid and powerful (and ambiguous) impact, has been considered since its early days one of the fundamental pieces of the universal satirical tradition. Dr. Johnson, the great eighteenth-century arbiter of English literature, famously pronounced this Swift's masterpiece and claimed that it was not surpassed by any of his other works, including *Gulliver's Travels*.

The satire betrays an invective tone, which is, so to speak, the first civil form of the genre. It attacks vehemently what the author deems intolerable offenses against the morals, principles, and the beliefs that should keep the world and human beings in order. At the same time, it sets a trap for the reader, who has to clearly discern the game in which he or she is involved, with the risk of remaining on the side of the one who is castigated if his discernment fails.

The *Tale* takes aim at a double target: on the one hand, the institution of religion; on the other, the forms and institutions of learning, along with—by way of association or consequence, depending on the particular case—political institutions. The sections of what would conventionally be called the central body of the work are alternately devoted to these two main targets, carrying out a demolishing critique of what the author deems to be their respective perversions, whose effects reverberate in the forms of government.[2] The critique has its premises in the opposition between the ancient and the modern, the latter being the unlimited breeding ground of the perversions in question. As usually happens with satire, the accuser does not assail his victim frontally but in an oblique manner: he establishes a fake complicity with the accused, feigning a persona that allows him to present himself as the author of the text, though he remains, like the real author, anonymous. The perversions have their history, which is a history of decadence, of a progressive loss of the relationship with the original sources of faith and learning, and of increasing corruption of the principles of civil government. The extreme of this decay is the modern, which does not cease to deepen and boundlessly propagate evil. What is represented as progress in the ideology of the modern is nothing other than a creeping deterioration.

But the modern is not an abstract monolith. In its multiple facets, which the *Tale* exposes, the names of its champions are inscribed: Paracelsus, John Calvin, Francis Bacon, Thomas Hobbes, John Milton, James Harrington, Isaac Newton, John Locke, John Toland, Bernard Le Bovier de Fontenelle, Lord Shaftesbury, and others.[3] From these names and their respective stances, notoriously dissimilar in most cases but amalgamated by Swift into a great intellectual front, one can infer the penetrating comprehension that the future dean of St. Patrick's in Dublin had concerning the complexity and implications, near and remote, of what he himself conceived as the gist of the modern: the organization of the fabric of the world and of life according to systems of interpretation and explanation that mythologically project the unchallenged dominion of a self-sufficient reason and its subject, the *animal rationale*.[4]

In this chapter, I will discuss the Swiftian attack on these schemes, assuming that it can be conceived as a skeptical critique destined to disarticulate and root out the pretensions of the modern program.

THE BOOK

The *Tale of a Tub* announces from the very start the game in which the reader will be invited to partake. It is not an innocuous game, as shall be seen promptly (and as I already warned), and it is a game that obliges the reader to ask about his or her statute no less than the statute of what we understand by the notion of an author and the nature of what we call a book.

A book, yes. Not only the book as a vehicle of meanings, truths, opinions, fantasies, errors, but a book as an apparatus, as a device, a machine. The page layout matters here: the silence of its printed being; the diverse forms in which its material is ordered and turned into conventions that are taken entirely for granted; the material and graphic signs by means of which the genre under which its content is accredited announces itself; and, of course, the mode in which all that the book contains becomes accessible to the reader by way of a quick glance.

The feigned perpetrator of Swift's text speaks in a certain passage about the importance of tables of contents, of their use and how they represent, in short, the key to the modern method for the acquisition of wisdom:

> The whole Course of Things being thus entirely changed between *Us* and the *Antients*; and the *Moderns* wisely sensible of it, we of this Age have discovered a shorter and more prudent Method to become *Scholars* and *Wits*, without the Fatigue of *Reading* or of *Thinking*. The most accomplished Way of using Books at present is twofold: Either first, to serve them as some Men do *Lords*, learn their *Titles* exactly, and then brag of their Acquaintance. Or Secondly, which is indeed the choicer, the profounder, and politer Method, to get a thorough Insight into the *Index*, by which the whole Book is governed and turned, like *Fishes* by the *Tail*. For, to enter the Palace of Learning at the *great Gate* requires an Expence of Time and Forms; therefore Men of much Haste and little Ceremony are content to get in by the *Back-Door*. For the Arts are all in a *flying* March, and therefore more easily subdued by attacking them in the *Rear*. Thus Physicians discover the State of the whole Body by consulting only what comes from *Behind*. Thus Men catch Knowledge by throwing their *Wit* on the *Posteriors* of a Book, as Boys do Sparrows with flinging *Salt* upon their *Tails*. Thus Human Life is best understood by the wise man's Rule, of *Regarding the End*. Thus are the Sciences found like *Hercules's* Oxen, by *tracing them Backwards*. Thus are *old Sciences* unravelled like *old Stockings*, by beginning at the *Foot*. (*Tale* 96)

Apart from providing a first sample of Swift's unbeatable satiric power in this work, the passage also displays one of its major rhetorical devices. Beginnings and ends (appendices, to be more precise), heads and tails, tips and stumps, entries and exits, all form one of the master oppositions with which the scabrous architecture of the *Tale* is built: you can see very clearly the odd rigor of a consistent delirium, the paranoid logic of a discourse that develops a fervor for analogy at the service of bastardized premises and conclusions, a discourse that does not hesitate to venture comparisons that undermine its own composition. As to the theme of the moment, the epistemic function of tables of contents is matched here with a question of power: the management of books, conceived as depositories of knowledge and apparatuses of instruction, depends on the exhaustive inspection of the tables of contents. They gather, as summary tables, all the knowledge that is inventoried in the book and offer in this manner the best, most expeditious, and most economic method of possessing knowledge. They are digital devices, if I can say so. They fulfill the rare desideratum of "an Iliad in a *Nut-shell*," about which the narrator says, at the beginning of section 7, he has *heard*, instead of the more usual case of finding a "*Nut-shell* in an Iliad" (95).

> A glance into the table of contents of this book is immediately lost in a fog of confusion:
>
> Treatises wrote by the same Author ...
>
> *An Apology for the* [*Tale of a Tub*]
>
> To the Right Honourable John Lord Somers
>
> *The BOOKSELLER to the READER*
>
> *The Epistle Dedicatory*
>
> *The Preface*
>
> SECT. I. *The Introduction.*
>
> SECT. II. [*A Tale of a Tub.*]
>
> SECT. III. *A Digression Concerning* Critics.
>
> SECT. IV. *A Tale of a Tub.*
>
> SECT. V. *A Digression in the Modern Kind.*
>
> SECT. VI. *A Tale of a Tub.*
>
> SECT. VII. *A Digression in Praise of Digressions.*
>
> SECT. VIII. *A Tale of a Tub.*
>
> SECT. IX. *A Digression concerning the Original, the Use, and Improvement of Madness in a Commonwealth.*
>
> SECT. X. [*A Farther Digression.*]
>
> SECT. XI. *A Tale of a Tub.*

Setting aside the *Apology*, which Swift added to the fifth edition (1710) in order to confront the multiple interpretations and gossip to which the book had given rise, the preliminary pieces add up to five, not counting the first section, despite its introductory character, since it occupies an ambiguous place due to that same character. Then you have ten sections in which the narrative parts and the digressions alternate. The last of these sections, which bears the title of the story under consideration here, is in fact a final digression.

This quick glance suggests that we are dealing with a book that explicitly poses the question at which I hinted above: What is a book? The question must have been latent and, in its latency, insistent in the epoch in which Swift writes the *Tale*, considering the growing proliferation of books, the inceptive installation of the publishing industry, and the ever-wider circulation of such products under the guise of treatises, essays, manuals, breviaries, compendiums, pamphlets, and other works meant for general entertainment. But, in the configuration that Swift gives to *his* book, what seems to be at stake above all is not the very materiality of the object (although that is very important), and certainly not the contents that can be incorporated by it in terms of the conditions of its production—say, as a set of preconceived meanings of which this object is the depository and the platform for their transmission—but rather, as I was beginning to say, the book as apparatus, as machine, device, which inseparably connects the *thing* that is the book with the production of meaning that has been entrusted to its pages and with the meaning that its reading motivates. The multiplication of preambles, which seems to highlight the essential difficulty of the beginning (how and where to commence the chain of meaning) and at the same time serves as a line of defensive trenches, is the index of what I'm trying to suggest; the alternating sequence of narrative sections and essayistic sections, each of the latter under the title of digressions, has the same function, as if the text were always in a centrifugal relation to itself. Lastly, there are the footnotes that Swift himself adds to the edition of 1710, interweaving them with other notes extracted from the glosses of William Wotton, one of the addressees of the assault against the moderns.[5]

Seen from the point of view of content, the ironical and parodic complexity of this structure is redoubled—I say *parodic*, because Swift is using the various resources that were already giving the institution and industry of the book its properly modern form. The sections that correspond to the *Tale*, beginning with the well-known "once upon a time," develop the allegorical story of three brothers who receive from their father as inheritance three identical coats (which are supposed to represent the Christian religion), giving them precise and rigorous instructions for their wear and care, at the risk of severe penalties that should affect the future destinies of the heirs: instructions that command them not to make any addition to the garments. After the father's death and the departure of the sons from the home and into the wider world, it isn't long before transgressions occur, together with the dominion of one of the brothers over the other two—namely, Peter (representative of the Catholic Church), who soon turns despotic, causing the brothers' separation. Another brother, Jack (who is alternatively identified with John Calvin or John of Leyden and is the representative of the dissident Protestant sects in Great Britain: Presbyterians, Methodists, Anabaptists, and Quakers), founds an eccentric cult that has at its core the doctrine of the wind as origin of all things, a frank mockery, of course, of spiritualistic pretensions (I will return to this later). The last brother, Martin (who is occasionally related to Martin Luther but is mainly the representative of the Anglican Church, the English religious establishment of which Swift himself was a member), the most sober of all three, decides to get rid of as many of his coat's fashionable additions as possible without destroying it. Nevertheless, Martin's role as a counterpoint to the authoritarian ambition of Peter and the spiritualistic delirium of Jack is rather ambiguous.[6]

By contrast, the digressions are marked by their diversity, but they all converge on the same goal, the ridicule of modern transformations, either through the repetitive harangues of the narrator seeking to accredit himself as an author (abounding in motifs that are already present in the prefatory texts), or through the derisively erudite disquisitions on certain issues that the tale touches, or, finally, through the characterization of modernity as an era of madness, as occurs in the dazzling ninth section. None of these parts could be considered indifferent to the formal structuring of the book, or vice versa; the book's overall structure actively cooperates with these parts in the satirical aggression against the work's central target.

Therefore, a fundamental point in all of this, a spur to the question I posed, concerns, in the relation between the material thing that is the book and the order of meaning (the ideality of discourse), the extreme tension that takes place between the book as a depository of meaning and writing as a process by which meaning is produced. The instability of discourse, of which its putative author and its reader become the victims (I will return to this), has to do with the continual surpassing of the container (the book) by a form of writing that should supply and reinforce the content but, thrown as it is into semiotic ruin, means that the book could never coincide with itself anywhere and irretrievably undermines the ideality of enunciation—that is, the conformation of a stable meaning and of a controllable communication.

Accordingly, it makes sense to say that the *Tale of a Tub* is a general device of equivocation. As such, it incites its readers to take charge of what they are doing: to become critically conscious of their activity and of the position they occupy when reading the book, which is to say the position in which the peculiar device that is this book locates them. The conventional a priori status of the act of reading is in this way called into question and exposed to analysis, and several questions follow from this scrutiny: What is a book? What is an author? What is his or her intention? What is the context of his or her performance? What is a reader, and, to cut the chase, what is the very institution of the literary, of writing? Many long-established assumptions are shaken by this book. If, to put it most succinctly, the key to satirical discourse is the exploitation of the relation between figurative and literal meanings, the critique of the figurative *by* the literal, then *this* book is satirical not only because of its content but also because of its very fabric, form, and organization: it makes entirely explicit all of its structural conditions of possibility.

The *Tale of a Tub* is a general device of equivocation, as I said. Herein, too, one can observe its satirical strategy, its parodic exercise. But the most general implications of Swift's critique are nonetheless inseparable from that exercise. If we pay attention to the premises of this critique, we might maintain that equivocation is the constitutive defectiveness of the *animal rationale*, a condition under which all vices prosper precisely because it disguises them or lends them expeditious alibis. According to the homeopathic medication that satire regularly administers, then, it is precisely the exacerbation of equivocation that has to alert us to its tremendous and insidious efficacy, confronting us with the uncomfortable predicament of being either absolutely lucid about this equivocation or complicit victims, and this is a predicament that in the case of Swift could be declared a priori irresoluble.

THE NAME

In the "Metaphysical First Principles of the Doctrine of Right," the first part of the *Metaphysics of Morals*, Kant has a chapter entitled "What Is a Book?," the explicit aim of which is stipulating that the reproduction of a book that has not been authorized by the author "*is forbidden as a matter of right*" (sec. 31, AB 128/72).[7] "A book," says Kant, is a writing ... which represents a discourse that someone delivers to the public by visible linguistic signs. One who *speaks* [*spricht*] to the public in his own name is called the *author* [*autor*]. One who, through a writing, discourses [*redet*] publicly in another's (the author's) name is a *publisher*. When a publisher does this with the author's permission, he is the legitimate publisher; but if he does it without the author's permission, he is an illegitimate publisher, that is, an unauthorized publisher [*Nachdrucker*]. (sec. 31, AB 128/71)

In a certain way, Kant's question is not one among others; rather, it touches the very lawful condition of the place in which it is formulated, the book of the *Metaphysics of Morals*, whose discourse Kant addresses to the public and to Friedrich Nicolovius of Königsberg, published in two editions (1797 and 1798) under the mandate of the author himself. In connection with this, Kant's question also touches on the determination of a compatibility between book and truth that is anterior to the question of the veracity of what is said in the book: a compatibility that concerns the authenticity that supports this saying. And the answer turns upon the speaking (the writing) and the name: the legal link, legally valid, between he who speaks (writes) on his own behalf and he who speaks on behalf of the former, under express contractual condition. The publisher who prints the book outside this condition, who for the same reason lacks the author's permission, acts illegally. This is what is known today under the opprobrious name of *piracy*.

There are plenty of things that could be missed in this Kantian explanation. For the same reason, one could think that there are many things that are taken for granted without discussion. In a certain way, they could all be charged to the account of authenticity, whose presupposition is not confronted here with what printed mediation means for the discourse, its production, and its reception. The use of the verbs *sprechen* and *reden*, primarily associated with orality (the "speaking"), is already a symptom thereof; this condition of printed mediation is not incorporated into the explanation. What is more—and this particularly interests me now—Kant's definitions do not take into account the case of anonymity.[8] Neither the name's omission nor its masking (the alias) receive any determination here; they remain, therefore, in a juridical limbo, so to speak. Anonymity or masking seriously disrupts the economy of property on which rests the right that secures the entity of the book, but they are not liable to the sanctions that the Kantian doctrine establishes. One might say that Swift took advantage of this sort of impunity a hundred years earlier. As Robert Phiddian notes, "in *A Tale*, more than anywhere else in Swift's writing or eighteenth-century writing at large (except, perhaps, *Tristram Shandy*), the author renounces property rights over meaning and the filiation of meaning through prior texts" (115).

If there is a "name" for the putative "author" of the *Tale*—which is a collective name, covering like an umbrella a host of narrative voices—the one that seems pertinent, as has been suggested many times, is *hack* (Phiddian 121), although it does not appear in the *Tale*. The term *hack* designates a writer of poor quality who offers his services like a mercenary. This is a good possibility, then. Various others have been suggested and argued, all of them, in one way or another, marked by a collective covering; besides the name *modern* (which obviously points to what is considered the fundamental target of the *Tale* and corresponds well to the affinities that the supposed author declares), there are others that are innocuous, such as *the Tale-teller*, and others that are instead abbreviations of the problem, such as *persona* (in the sense of the character that is Swift's mask). It has been suggested that, in the history of commentaries and exegeses of the *Tale*, and after Edward Said's essay "Swift's Tory Anarchy,"[9] the focus on this narrative voice and its relation to the author has turned toward "the *Tale's* self-conscious textuality and its purportedly consequent radical indeterminacy" (Connery 159). The turn is consistent with an analytic view that conceives the authorship of a text not as an already given condition—related to the idea of the subject as the source of meaning—but as an effect of its writing, a view, consequently, that understands that the work of analysis is first of all determined by the autonomy of the text.

The point that seems clear in this respect is that the de-affiliation, the dismantling of intellectual property, is not brought about merely by the omission of the name of the veridical author on the frontispiece and the title pages of the book or by other masking or concealing maneuvers. Instead, it is the product of a consistent writing exercise that systematically dismisses the tutelage of meaning and provokes, therefore, a general state of uncertainty regarding intentions and references, which can reach the radical instability of semiosis.

To this extent, it is appropriate to ask about the statute of the self that claims for itself the authorship of the discourse, a question that naturally cannot be dissociated from the question of the autonomy of the text, because it is in this autonomy that the former has to be decided.

In this respect, a picture comes rapidly to the fore, either by the explicit protests of that self or by the multiple reflections that one notices in the crevices of the discourse, of a voice in permanent stress, tension, at times exasperated, worried by the control of what it proffers, which at every moment threatens to escape from its control and at times does indeed escape, generating contradictions and short circuits that, of course, contribute much to the ironical effects of the text. If you think that this voice and its vicissitudes are sufficient to build a character endowed with some traits of identity, you should talk about someone who is obsessed with something I call the "anxiety of authorship." A first sign is the list of "Treatises written by the same Author," inscribed in the *Tale*'s advertisement, and other signs certainly abound in the text: recommendations and apologies misspent everywhere, the comparing of the author's own manner of proceeding with others judged erroneous or incongruous (in which the author also engages), flatteries and emulations, literary or scholarly professions of faith, the enunciation of infallible principles—none of them, of course, exempt from misprints and slips that undermine the harangue. The anxiety itself has a *momentum* of exacerbation in the following declaration of primacy: "But I here think fit to lay hold on that great and honourable Privilege, of being the *Last Writer*. I claim an absolute Authority in Right, as the *freshest Modern*, which gives me a Despotick Power over all Authors before me" (85).

There are few things in the *Tale* that can illustrate the anxiety in question better than this proclamation that ruins itself—the title to literary preponderance is no more than the pathetic insecurity of being the last in writing—and that shows the sharp edge of Swift's attack against the "moderns." Anyway, this very intense anxiety, which is very perceptible at every moment of development, has mischievous implications not only, I would argue, for what might be said about the narrative self of this piece—which in the end could be a mask worn by the real author, through which it could be feasible to have a glimpse of the true (and univocal) intentions that have guided him—but also for what might be said in general, on the basis of this same exercise, about the statute of what we call an "author." After all, the minute one lacks control, the noncoincidence between the author and what he says, the readings and exegeses to which his marginal emissions are susceptible beyond and at times against what he himself has *meant*, is not merely an accident of this *Tale*, which expands the moment to the time of the whole text, but truly a trait of every writing practice. Only in *that* writing (scripture) that pretends to be one and the same with "the Book" would the absolute (or, if you prefer, transcendental) author that is the model of all finite authors, relating to them asymptotically, be conceivable. *That* author remains safe and outside of the drift of all the voices it assumes and, from that reserve, continues to be the source and criterion of the unity of meaning that sustains those voices. Only for such an author is there no difference between saying and meaning, not an *intention* of saying but a pure saying. Wherever the intention of saying prevails as authorial endeavor, the aforementioned anxiety and the misfortune stemming from the lack of control also prevail. The misfortune or the luck: for the former becomes the latter where the lack of control reverts by and in writing into a renunciation of the *intention* of saying. In some way, this is what happens here, where this reversion has been driven to its most acute expression, such that the self betrays itself as a castaway subject to the violent ups and downs that set the book's unity in tension with the dispersion of its text. This tension traces a *field*—a field of writing—in which the narrator is dispersed into a multiplicity of discourses that amount to so many instances of the parodic efficacy of the writing(s) of that "author" whom we call "Swift." If we have recourse to the usual metaphor, there is not *one* voice that lets itself be heard in the *Tale*—not even under the supposition of masking—but *many*, and these "voices" are, epistemologically considered, the hypothesis of the author and at the same time his or her refusal (for they are asymptotically referred to that transcendental place as its very denial); this suggests in the end that every author is nothing other than that hypothesis.[10]

THE TUB

The expression "*Tale of a Tub*," which gives the work its title, designates in the epoch's contemporary usage (and it was already old by that time) a discourse that has an intention to swindle or defraud. This relation between the words *tub* and *discourse* might appear strained, but it comes from associations that were progressively forged starting from the initial meaning. Already in Chaucer, a *tub* is a wooden receptacle, open at one end, made with staves and hoops. Following the similarities between shape and appearance, in the sixteenth century the meanings of the words *bathtub* and *vessel* emerge, and playfully, in the following century, they come to designate the pulpit, which has the shape of a barrel: compound words such as *tub-preacher* and *tub-thumping* (to harangue) are forged to name religious and political talkativeness. In this way, burlesque talking for talking's sake is related to the petulance of preaching as well as to cheating and deception. We thus get a glimpse of the significance that the cheat and the fraud have for the constitution of Swift's satirical writing—writing *as* cheating—so intimately determinant for the organization of the *Tale* and taken up again in *Gulliver's Travels*.

The hypothetical author does not make this pejorative signification explicit (although he allows it a furtive peep from within the text); rather, he assumes his task with studied gravity, ready to affirm instead with "a great Ease to [his] Conscience that [he has] written so elaborate and useful a Discourse without one grain of Satyr intermixt; which is the sole point," he continues to say, "wherein [he has] taken leave to dissent from the famous Originals of our Age and Country" (*Tale* 29). However, the joke of the title appears from another angle, with reference to a certain custom of sailors in cases of emergency, which I will soon address, without failing to mention first that in the tradition of commentaries on the *Tale of a Tub* special attention has rarely been paid to the element of the tub. Where there are allusions to it—as a metaphor, a symbol, or an allegory, obeying the suggestions of the supposed author of the narrative—they are not systematic but merely circumstantial. But it is plausible to think that the game of this element goes through the entire story and—this is my conjecture at least—contributes essentially to determining the constructive logic of the text and its semiotic process. In order to establish this logic and process, it is necessary to pay fairly meticulous attention to the first and decisive guide for interpreting that element, which is contained in the first paragraph of the author's preface.

Faced with the threat represented by the modern wits to the already frail religious and political institutions, the grandees of these institutions have designed a huge plan. But this demands so much time and money that it is indispensable to seek a provisional expedient, an entertaining maneuver that impedes the wits from ruining all the compromised institutions. The idea of an expedient is suggested in an assembly thanks to someone's propitious reference to the sailor's custom of flinging out an empty tub to a menacing whale for its innocuous amusement so as

> to divert him from laying violent Hands upon the Ship. This parable was immediately mythologiz'd: The *Whale* was interpreted to be *Hobs's Leviathan*, which tosses and plays with all Schemes of Religion and Government, whereof a great many are hollow, and dry, and empty, and noisy, and wooden, and given to Rotation. This is the *Leviathan* whence the terrible Wits of our Age are said to borrow their Weapons. The *Ship* in danger is easily understood to be its old Antitype the *Commonwealth*. But, how to analyze the *Tub* was a Matter of difficulty; when, after long Enquiry

and Debate, the literal Meaning was preserved: And it was decreed that in order to prevent these *Leviathans* from tossing and sporting with the *Commonwealth* (which of itself is too apt to *fluctuate*) they should be diverted from that Game by a *Tale of a Tub*. And my Genius being conceived to lye not unhappily that way, I had the Honor done me to be engaged in the Performance. (25)

I guess that one cannot avoid the impression that this explanation—specifying what should be understood as the motivating conflict of the *Tale*—is not restricted to a stupendous joke but describes exactly the general strategy that governs the work's writing and fundamental implications. Setting aside the allusion to Hobbes—one of the most salient moderns that Swift has in his sights—the thing that (I presume) immediately blinds the reader with its obviousness is the scheme and the hermeneutical zeal that are responsible for the provisional solution of assuring that the modern wits waste their energies on harmless objects. The sailor's custom is understood at once as a parable, and this, in turn, is "immediately mythologiz'd," thereby establishing with utmost precision the allegorical correspondences between the parable's elements and the emergency to be coped with: the whale as Leviathan (a bidirectional image, of course), the ship as body politic. This over-symbolization, this unrestrained *allegoresis*, marks one of the essential procedures in the *Tale*'s construction and is a determinant factor in Swift's conception of "the modern." It concerns not only the application of the analogical capacities of reason, which by Swift's time had become more or less the discursive automatism of which the *Tale* provides so many instances, all with notoriously humoristic efficacy. It also concerns something that Swift understands as a general operation that sustains the diversity of performances and yields of reason, from the research into the laws of nature informing science to the attempts to order social life, the new configurations of religious beliefs, and the forms of mystical and mystifying knowledge that assure an exclusive access to mystery.[11] It is against this operation, while simultaneously using it in each of its modulations and variants, that Swift's attack is directed. Therefore, without omitting the jokes contained in the passage, what matters is discerning the moments and vectors of this strategy. It's certain: just as with the sailor's expedient, in which there must be some similitude between the ship and the carcass flung out to the whale, here, too, there must be a likeness between the emergency recourse and the religious and political schemes; the passage describes them mostly as hollow, noisy, and sclerotic, which undoubtedly is far from being a particularly auspicious judgment about the patrimony that the great lords of church and state seek to protect. But here the important thing is the representative relation that links the barrel with the vessel, the ship and the "tub," which is required in the design of such schemes: a piece without any value, dispensable, but representative. This confirms what I called an unrestrained *allegoresis*, which weaves representations in an unlimited circulation.

In this sense, it's worth considering the crucial accident in the sequence of the argument, which is a hermeneutical accident: "But how to analyze the tub was a matter of difficulty; when, after long enquiry and debate, the literal meaning was preserved" (25). What I'm calling an "accident" would appear as a sort of blocking or short-circuiting of the aforesaid circulation, were it not for the fact that the "literal meaning" turns out to be the "*Tale of a Tub*." The reader, I suppose, will not dissimulate a vague discomfiture, and Swift will have attained his first great satirical effect, which is actually—at least I'm inclined to consider it this way—the key to the procedure by which he carries out his critical dismantling of the "modern." The "accident" in question is not a blocking but a slip, a displacement, and—according to the playful puns that Swift rigorously fosters—a *rotation of the tub*. Certainly, the story, with this displacement and according to a mostly strict and scandalous forwardness that the *Tale* itself aggravates to the point of delirium, will have been charged with the same notes of hollowness, vacuity, rigidity, etcetera, that are proper to the tub-thing. And, of course, we should note that with this displacement the meaning of the colloquial phrase—this inane preaching—is confirmed. But, in addition to all this, I think it is possible that the whole design and strategy of the tale are also established with this displacement.

How can we describe the plan by which this strategy is carried out? First of all, the narrator's clumsiness is evidenced in his incapacity to retain control over his theme, his resources, his language—in the precariousness, then, not necessarily of his means but of the way in which he makes use of them, laying himself bare and betraying his intentions and, therefore, rendering them indeterminable. In order to give an account of this character on the level of strategy, critics have argued for a "technique of betrayal" (Dyson 4) and a "method of surprise" (Leavis 76),[12] meaning by that not only the constructive features of the *Tale* but also, more widely, an essential and distinctive trait of Swift's writing. The merit of these concepts—superficially considered—is at the same time their weakness: both place all or almost all the emphasis on the addressee of the discourse, on the recipient (which is obviously a fundamental pole for the satiric genre) without formalizing that which in the first case is called "technique" and in the other "method"; they neglect, in other words, the internal law of the discourse's production, for which such concepts would eventually be valid by way of approximation. So, if the main victim of "betrayal" in the *Tale* is the reader, the only possibility left is to suppose that this is so precisely because the narrator is structured as a betrayal of himself.

Indeed, if we stick to Leavis's "method of surprise," he himself recognizes the difficulty of describing such a method and, what's more, of building its model, although he says that "surprise is a perpetually varied accompaniment of the grave, dispassionate, matter-of-fact tone in which Swift delivers his intensities" (76), which paves the way for the collaboration between the intensity and energy of a blind, obsessive passion and an intelligence absorbed in pure observation as an explanatory feature of that "method." If it is true that the strategy in which I'm interested could be properly (albeit only initially) designated by Leavis's formulation (assuming the provocation involved in combining these two in principle irreconcilable terms: what would a "method of surprise" be?),[13] it would not help us to see how the literary production of surprise works. In other words, how the devices of surprise or betrayal function in Swift's writing remains hidden.

But let us focus first on what I am calling the plan of Swift's strategy. If we take up again the hermeneutical "accident," and take into account the displacement that it produces, the most salient thing to note, it seems to me, is that the supposed preservation of the literal meaning, which decides the equivalence of the tub-thing with the tub-tale or, put differently, which allows a passage from the tub of the tale to the *Tale* of the tub, has a double consequence by virtue of an exploitation of or recourse to literalness: on the one hand, it reinforces the continuum of representations; on the other, it ruins the intentions of meaning and reference of these representations and encloses them in their own circulation. I speak of *recourse* to literality (propriety and univocal meaning) that occurs beyond the letter of the text (its writing—that is, the field of the letter) and that therefore cannot be only the postulate of literality, precisely as an indication of that which remains robbed by the letter, squandered in that field.[14] I speak as well of reinforcing the circulation of representations, which is also an intensification of their intentionality: the representations that are brought into play must preserve their significance in order to guarantee the satirical and critical effects of the narration, but, at the same time and for the same purpose, they must be constitutively threatened by their own insignificance.

THE INSIGNIFICANCE

At the risk of being pedantic and thereby stumbling into one of the traps contained within the *Tale*, allow me to reconstruct the steps that I recognize in the passage of the tub, with the aim of consolidating (or irremediably weakening, as the case may be) my suggestions. Following what was previously said, I assume that it is possible to organize this passage according to the following moments:

(1) The mention (the narration, the tale) of the tub as a diverting expedient that sailors use in cases of emergency. One should think that *tub* here literally means the tub-*thing*, although displaced from its primary use or function, but the very idea of distraction already marks a duplication of meaning: if the thing can serve to distract, it is because it is a *metonymy* of the ship. The mere mention opens the hermeneutical space.

(2) The "mythologization" of the narration of this custom. The custom and any of its elements are thereby turned into *allegorical* representations and motivate the commentary according to which some religious and political schemes take on—in a *metaphorical* sense—the characteristics of a tub. We then see how the tub oscillates and rotates from one side to another, between the literal and the figurative meaning.

(3) The difficulty of finding, once the narration is mythologized, a figurative equivalent of the tub. This difficulty should surprise us if we observe that an interpretation of the implement was already insinuated, and the difficulty is also confirmed when considering that it is precisely this figurative equivalent—the religious and political schemes—that has to be saved by means of the diverting maneuver: this does not hinder one from recording a *hiatus*, a *disruption*, a *vacuum*, in the semantic play of the term *tub*.

(4) Following the aforementioned difficulty, the option in favor of the *literal* meaning of *tub*. But this supposed return, this resignation to literality has as its referent not the *tub-thing* but the *Tale of a Tub*, and in this way not only is the literality of the word *tub* driven to ambiguity; as I said, the same occurs with the meaning of the "tale," which is proposed precisely *as* the tub-thing that sailors use in order to divert.

The frenetic pace of the passage has been dismembered here and fixed into four stages that, in my hypothesis, prefigure all the satirical effects that characterize the *Tale*; these stages could be described as phases of the rotating displacement of the "tub," phases that are varying recurrences of meaning that, when one attempts to decipher them, reveal themselves as mere "noises" (you will recall that one of the attributes of the tub is that it is "noisy"). These phases are four stages in a process of (re)elaboration of the meaning of the word *tub*, which I'm inclined to call, regarding its results, an *involutionary, entropic process*. The resigned preservation of the "literal meaning" is the index of this process, to which I ascribe not a conclusive destiny, certainly, but rather a tendency, the tendency of a movement. In speaking of involution and entropy, I try to designate the *movement of a regression to literality and ultimately to insignificance*.

The semiotic play of the passage would consist, then, in the movement from one "literality" to another; the discourse passes from the literality of *tub* that signifies the tub-thing to the literality that designates the tub-tale. There's no other remedy than admitting the guideline of the hypothetical author: *Tale of a Tub* is (also) the literal meaning of the tub in the tale. But this movement renders the *semiosis* of the text radically uncertain, de-authorizing every attempt to establish fixed meanings.

And if, in turn, I talk about entropy, if I talk about interpreting the process of the elaboration of the meaning of *tub* in such a way that it can pass from one literality to the other as if it were a kind of entropic process, I'm pointing to what could be called a total *neutrality* of the signifier *tub* with respect to its possible meanings. It would be from this neutrality that such movement, such passage, becomes possible. Besides this movement, the notion of entropy is also used to suggest that this neutrality should be conceived not as a mere passivity but as a *potency* of the signifier *tub*, a potency of the text that inscribes this signifier as its principle of production, a *potency of absorption*, of reduction of all its possible meanings; it is, if I might put it this way, the image of the barrel's hole toward which all those meanings fall, as if they were magnetized: toward the *void of meaning*, toward *insignificance*.[15]

Therefore, the passage from one "literality" to the other, which is at the same time the circulation (the rotation) of meanings, generates an undecidable semiotic situation: either there is no real literality, or there is only literality. Consequently, there is no such thing as *originality* or *propriety* of meaning: any literality is figurative, but in turn any figure is the effect of the letter.

The displacement produced by mentioning the tub says, "There is no proper meaning; every meaning is figurative," *and, at the same time,* "There is no figurative meaning; all is proper meaning." Therefore, the proper meaning *is* the figurative meaning (and vice versa). The meaning of *tub* is nothing other than the *continual displacement*, the unending circulation or rotation that determines the perpetual *exchange* of the proper meaning and the figurative meaning.

To summarize, the elaboration of *tub* is an elaboration at the level of the signifier, which "produces" its possible meanings. In the passage in question, whale, tub, ship, and tale are but the tautological effects (the repetitions) of one and the same signifier: a literal *univocum*, a primordial figuration beside which all those effects appear as meanings, along with others that the *Tale* incessantly issues: the oratorial machines, the hollow of the mouth that emits the breath of the word as *flatus vocis*, the coats (or souls) bloating with inspiration and pride. I will return to this later.

For now, it is perhaps possible for me to venture from these considerations the hypothesis that the *Tale of a Tub* poses the essential problem of the *difference* between the proper and the figurative as an irresoluble problem; in sum, it poses the problem of the *origin of meaning from the void of meaning*. And, certainly, the most notable and profound aspect of the *Tale* does not lie in raising this problem—which does not obey a mere abstract formulation, for it is only approachable in writing itself—but rather in the mode of its specification, in the differentiation and circulation of meanings, and in the final direction typical for the *Tale*; that is, in the strategic proposition—the fifth and last phase of the whole process—of the void into which meaning falls as the destiny of meaning itself.

THE VOID

There is no doubt that the theme of emptiness—of a pompous emptiness—is at least one of the main axes, if not the fundamental axis, of the *Tale*. The text insists blatantly on it, evidencing the vanity and insignificance of the entire story; we have already seen some instances of this. For further clarification, in the author's preface, not far from the passage quoted above, aggravating the insanity of the beginning that multiplies proems and exordiums, we read the following on the importance of prefaces: "I am sufficiently instructed in the Principal Duty of a Preface, if my Genius were capable of arriving at it. Thrice have I forced my Imagination to make the *Tour* of my Invention, and thrice it has returned empty, the latter having been wholly drained by the following Treatise" (26).

Here, and throughout the part in which this and the previous passage are included, the aforementioned "technique of betrayal" has reached one of its sharpest points, such that the *Tale* is not presented just as emptiness and insignificance but is unmasked as a void pretext of a preface that has failed in its structure and task. Here, then, what is said is said vainly: in the vacuum of orality that draws air merely to supply its own vacuity, which breathes pointless words as instances of pure verbosity. And the oral hollowness, from which the breath of the word is issued, is also involved in this sort of implacable anti-rhetoric of the tub. For here the word is, the words are, no more than mere breath, *flatus vocis*.

This issue of breath is systematically exploited in section 8 of the *Tale*, which is devoted entirely to expounding the supposed history and doctrine of the sect of the Æolists, whose reputed founder is Jack. The point of this satirical motif is obvious: Swift has in view the eccentric doctrine of inspiration as the privileged source of the access to transcendent truths and, of course, a determining factor of various fanaticisms. Inspiration and spirit (the latter being the animating principle of the former) are understood here to the letter, according to the metaphor that has inspired their concepts: the spirit is breath; inspiration is a state of insufflation. So, the Æolists maintain "the Original Cause of all Things to be *Wind*" (99). The humoristic consequences that Swift extracts from this metaphorical regression, if I can call it that, are abundant and powerful. It is a question of lingering on them only to reproduce the doctrine's fundamental corollary: "*Words are but wind; and Learning is nothing but Words;* Ergo, *Learning is nothing but Wind*"—for which reason the teaching of the school is conducted by means of eructation (100). This type of wind, then, results in the very determination of the human being:

> Upon these Reasons and others of equal Weight, the Wise *Æolists* affirm the Gift of BELCHING to be the noblest Act of a Rational Creature. To cultivate which Art, and render it more serviceable to Mankind, they made Use of several Methods. At certain Seasons of the Year, you might behold the Priests amongst them, in vast Numbers, with their *Mouths gaping wide against a Storm*. At other times were to be seen several Hundreds link'd together in a circular Chain, with every Man a Pair of Bellows applied to his Neighbour's Breech, by which they blew up each other to the Shape and Size of a *Tun*; and for that Reason, with great Propriety of Speech, did usually call their Bodies, their *Vessels*. (100)

The theme of bodies full of air, inflated to the point of nearly bursting, the very theme of interiority as wind (belching, farting), is unmistakably Swiftian, and, if on the one hand it is to be listed under the long catalog of the dean's scatological obsessions, on the other it corresponds rigorously to the critique of the human being, which, still limited in the *Tale of a Tub*, reaches its most exacerbated point in *Gulliver's Travels*. In the passage just quoted, the depreciation of the definition of the human being from *animal rationale* to *animal eructans* is done not only to heap scorn on the conceit of "inspired" and "illuminated" men (who also used to appeal to the Æolic motif in conjunction with their "inner light"), although this is undoubtedly its principal purpose. According to Swift's most frequent strategy, which returns metaphoric expressions to their literal significations, the inspiration denounced throughout the *Tale* as the peak of madness has in the swelling of bodies its cardinal symptom. Inspiration—the pretension of a state of spiritual exaltation—is the madness of believing that man possesses a higher spiritual endowment or authority than the much more limited one bestowed upon him by mere natural reason and its use according to common sense, and it is one of the major signs of pride in the Swiftian code. (Of course, this is an eminent trait of the *Tale*'s feigned "author," who, as a character more or less endowed with coherent psychological characteristics, is a kind of coatrack on which hang—not without a peculiar coherence—attributes that are the object of satirical mockery.)

The windiness in question is, then, a sign of pride, and this is an essential item in the passionate battle that Swift leads against the modern systems of knowledge and power. But it is also more than this. In a primary sense, pride is the modern era's excessive trust in reason's power as modeler of the world and of human existence. Swift sees the most exemplary expression of such pride in utopia—that is, in the dream of reason. More radically, pride is man's original sin, conceived not as a psychological state or modification of the individual, not even as a moral flaw, but as the ontological condition of what we call "man." Put more accurately: pride is the very subjectivity of man, his subjective being.

FIGURES AND PLACES: THE RHETORIC OF THE *TALE*

Very early in the *Tale* one notices the exploitation of the symbolic, allegorical, and analogical keys. Besides the "parable" of the whale and the tub, the putative author, as soon as the introduction undertakes the explication of the theory of oratorial machines, states that there are only three such devices (the pulpit, the ladder, and the stage itinerant, all of which fulfill the condition of being "Edifices in the Air" [34] that allow the speaker to exalt himself above the host of hearers and to establish the supremacy of his voice) and reinforces his conviction by appealing to the mystic meaning of that number

> in imitation of that prudent Method observed by many other Philosophers and great Clerks, whose chief Art in Division has been to grow fond of some proper mystical Number which their imaginations have rendered Sacred, to a Degree, that they force common Reason to find room for it in every part of Nature; reducing, including, and adjusting every *Genus* and *Species* within that Compass, by coupling some against their Wills, and banishing others at any Rate. Now, among all the rest, the profound number *THREE* is that which hath most employ'd my sublimest Speculations, nor ever without wonderful Delight. (37)

What follows is the announcement of a work that develops the panegyric of the number in question. The theme of occult meanings, of arcana and mysteries, which occurs throughout the *Tale*, has its counterpart in what the quoted passage announces: the whimsical obsession that pathologically takes possession of human beings, some driven by their anxious need to believe, others because in this way they secure their dominion over the former, not to mention those who become enthusiastic with the idea of extending their dominion over the entirety of nature, which happens with philosophers and scientists. They are all related through one and the same trace of violence: a hermeneutical violence, as it were, ready to break as the most vulgar physical violence if required to do so by the corresponding fetishism.

Section 2, the first of the *Tale* properly speaking, is crystal clear in this respect through all that refers to the coarse tricks exercised by the most learned of the three brothers, who in the following section will be known as Peter, the representative of papist Catholicism. The testamentary will of the father, which stipulates the correct use of the sober garments bequeathed to his sons, is assaulted by Peter, who has recourse to various subterfuges in order to adapt the coats to the constantly shifting whims of fashion, adding ornaments and embellishments by which the coats are thoroughly adulterated.

The addition of the knots on the shoulders is justified by alleging that the testament should be read *totidem litteris*, an expedient through which one discovers in a most cabalistic way that the name of the decoration—*knot*—is encrypted in the letters of the text, the absence of the *k* explained by the fact that it was a rather unusual letter in the times when the legal instrument was composed. The golden laces are incorporated under the tutelage of Aristotelian logic, distinguishing between the written and the transmitted, both on equal footing (equality being a fundamental principle in the formation of ecclesiastical power); the flame-colored satin lining is similarly added by fabricating a codicil annexed to the testament, which obviously has the same value as the testament itself. The express prohibition of the use of silver fringes is dodged without further subtleties by arguing that "fringe" might also be interpreted as "broomstick," such that the prohibition obviously hides a mystery, the sounding out of which would amount to an irreverence. The explicit vetoes of the testament finally meet their coup de grâce when it comes to the embroidery with Indian figures of men, women, and children (which hint at the saints of the Catholic Church): there is no impediment to their use, because all "these rigorous clauses ... require some *Allowance*, and a favourable Interpretation, and ought to be understood *cum grano Salis*" (58). And in order to avoid the punctual disquisitions posed by every new demand of fashion, ever in flux, the definitive decision of the three sons, commanded by the "scholastic brother," is to store the testament in a safe place and not to consult it on every occasion.

As I was saying, Swift opposes in a most palpable way the *will* of the father to the *caprice* of the dominant son, a caprice to which the other two brothers yield at the beginning with timid resistance but in the end with willing submission. And if caprice only goes well with caprice (with the transient luster of fashion and the changeable surface of social relations and tastes), what actually moves it is *desire*, which is nothing other than the desire of *power*. When this desire becomes entirely manifest and Peter enthrones himself, the other two brothers resolve to move away from him.

The desire of power is supported by what we might call the *spirit of interpretation*, which should already be absolutely obvious as a seal of the modern that Swift consistently exploits by raising the problem of the differentiation of meanings (literal/figurative). The whole *Tale* is legible as a satire of the irrepressible drift involved in seeing signs and symbols in every twist and turn of experience, in looking behind everything in search of hidden meanings. This is, as I have proposed elsewhere (see Oyarzun, "La Cosa Que era Swift" 78–79), a *fetishism of meaning*, supportive of a narcissism of interpretation, and the document of a fateful eagerness in the domain of knowledge, which finds its strict correspondence, in the space of power, in a *spirit of exploration*, equally compulsive, that will be exposed to the insanity and irretrievability of its imperial and colonial journey in *Gulliver's Travels*.

One of the fundamental sources of the aforesaid fetishism is analogical reason, proposing multiple comparisons in order to consolidate the risky statements of the feigned author and, of course, the effects of mockery in which Swift is interested. So, for instance, when the narrator comments on the modern vein of superficiality that rejects every attempt "to inspect beyond the surface and the rind of things," being a detriment to the reception of the writings of the Grub Street society of which he himself claims to be a member, he says,

> *Wisdom* is a *Fox* who after long hunting, will at last cost you the Pains to dig out. 'Tis a *Cheese* which, by how much the richer, has the thicker, the homelier, and the coarser Coat; and whereof, to a judicious Palate, the *Maggots* are the best. 'Tis a *Sack-Posset*, wherein the deeper you go you will find it the sweeter. *Wisdom* is a *Hen*, whose *cackling* we must value and consider, because it is attended with an *Egg*. But then lastly 'tis a *Nut*, which unless you chuse with Judgment, may cost you a Tooth, and pay you with nothing but a *Worm*. (41–42)[16]

What follows is the explanation that, given these circumstances, the sages of the society in question have constantly made use of "the Vehicles of Types and Fables" (42). The devastation of meaning suggested by passages like this one appears throughout the *Tale* and is reinforced by extravagant or moody metaphors and by the very profusion of figures and allegories frequently granted doctrinal weight. This is the general design that the "author" describes in the conclusion: "In my Disposure of Employments of the Brain, I have thought fit to make *Invention* the *Master*, and to give *Method* and *Reason*, the Office of its *Laquays*" (*Tale* 136).

Modern imagination (and one should say that the modern itself is nothing other than a product of imagination, an invention) is a "converting" imagination, operating everywhere with representations: Jack is the paradigmatic case, and the narrator, scrupulously insisting on the issue, wants to satisfy those "whose converting Imaginations dispose them to reduce all Things into *Types*; who can make *Shadows*, no thanks to the Sun; and then mould them into Substances, no thanks to Philosophy; whose peculiar Talent lies in fixing Tropes and Allegories to the *Letter*, and refining what is Literal into Figure and Mystery" (123).

A profusion of allegories and figures, I say, all of them giving off the stench of the esoteric and always completely distorted in their applications: besides the "oratorial machines," if the motif of the coats that the father bequeaths to his sons is outlandish, how much more so is the teaching—pertaining to the cult of the tailor-god—of suits as animals, man being the suit of the most refined species; nevertheless, this motif has its cutting edge, for in the end (as the text immediately notes) garments are the mark of social identity for people, such that the cult of the tailor-god is nothing other than the "religion" of fashion, which is in turn a fundamental signifier of modernity.

Swift's satirical ways, such as can be deduced from the allegory of the suits and from so many other instances, are always double-edged, and they give no place for a univocal reading, because they always (and usually where the figurative delirium reaches its peak) show a side that not only ridicules the hectic storyteller but also seriously attacks the established customs and institutions. In this sense, Phiddian has argued that Swift's parody is an anarchic one, de-authorizing every authority instead of restricting itself to blaming an identifiable victim; particularly, the "personification" of *this* victim by the hypothetical author is actually the vertiginous abyss toward which all the themes and behaviors touched by the parody plunge (cf. 140, 145, 171).

For this end, Swift has recourse to a precise rhetorical procedure: the figures, allegories, and metaphors that proliferate in the *Tale* are governed from the standpoint of certain eminent "places," all of them articulated in terms of oppositions whose extremes cannot be decided either in their possible mutual exclusion or in their relative hierarchy. I have already mentioned the oppositions of beginnings and ends, heads and tails, tips and stumps, entries and exits. Perhaps the most important of all is that of interiors and exteriors, associated with that of surfaces and depths, which Swift wields to such effect in satirizing modern science in the form of anatomy: "Last Week I saw a Woman *flay'd*, and you will hardly believe how much it altered her Person for the worse" (112). The line reveals the narrator, and the natural conclusion is that outsides are much better than insides. The same oppositions are already condensed in the tub, which, as a receptacle, is defined by its void, and the void separates space from space, as a mere surface (like the garments), in the fashion of an osmotic membrane that facilitates the exchange between both spaces—that is, in what amounts to the dialectics of meanings, the exchange between an *inside* that in principle is the proper (or the soul) and an *outside* that in principle is the figurative (or the body), but in such a way that the inversion of order is inexorable because of the circulation of meanings on which I commented earlier. At any rate, the point is that the text does not offer a pinnacle from which it would be feasible to set stable meanings or valuations: it does not provide a *criterion*. The text, as well as its unadvised "author," is radically stupid.

It would be necessary to rigorously construct the rhetoric of the *Tale*. It is not in vain that the first section begins with the exposition of oratorial receptacles on the premise that being heard and persuading others always demands an eminence and a proper altitude; these receptacles are rhetorical machines (implying a pleonasm based on the old and pejorative idea of rhetoric as a machine). In a certain way, it concerns a peculiar meta-rhetoric that, insofar as it overlaps with the rhetoric of interpretive devices, of the mechanisms for the production of (non)sense that define the systems of knowledge (and power) criticized in the *Tale*, lays open not only the procedures of those systems but also their entire structure and, with it, the vectors that determine their historical destination. This is perhaps the thing that, on a second viewing, might most surprise the reader of today, who, like Swift's contemporaries, has to take into account that everything making up the content of the *Tale* is insistently and insidiously accompanied by a *tua res agitur*, even if today's reader counts on a perspective of three centuries that tends to corroborate, in terms of prognosis, the structure as well as the vectors of those systems. The meta-rhetoric that I'm talking about (and that I equate with the character of Swiftian satire), starting from the "places" mentioned and in view of their undecidability, applies those devices to themselves, carrying out their reduction *ad absurdum*. But, again, this reduction does not suppress them; it is, so to speak, the incitement that promotes them to the extreme of nonsense: to madness. This is what the ninth section of the *Tale*, which is in a certain way the climax, teaches, because in it, by way of digression and under the auspices of "my *phenomenon* of *vapours*" (80), as the narrator says, madness is celebrated as the highest endowment of man, from which there can spring only beneficial contributions to the commonwealth. There, in a long paragraph that has been quoted thousands of times—for it is probably one of the paramount specimens of irony in all of literature—a paragraph that defends credulity and the advantage of epidermic outsides over inner depths, there follows a conclusion with a forceful analogy:

> Yesterday I ordered the Carcass of a *Beau* to be stripped in my Presence; when we were all amazed to find so many unsuspected Faults under one Suit of Clothes: Then I laid open his *Brain*, his *Heart*, and his *Spleen*; But

> I plainly perceived at every Operation that the farther we proceeded, we found the Defects increase upon us in Number and Bulk: from all which, I justly formed this Conclusion to myself; That whatever Philosopher or Projector can find out an Art to sodder and patch up the Flaws and Imperfections of Nature will deserve much better of Mankind, and teach us a more useful Science, than that so much in present Esteem, of widening and exposing them (like him who held *Anatomy* to be the ultimate end of *Physick*.) And he whose Fortunes and Dispositions have placed him in a convenient Station to enjoy the Fruits of this noble Art; He that can with *Epicurus* content his ideas with the *Films* and *Images* that fly off upon his Senses from the *Superficies* of Things; Such a Man, truly wise, creams off Nature, leaving the Sour and the Dregs for Philosophy and Reason to lap up. This is the sublime and refined point of Felicity, called, *the Possession of being well deceived*; The Serene Peaceful State, of being a Fool among Knaves. (112)

This "rhetoric of surfaces," as Phiddian calls it (166), accumulating parodic targets among which Epicurus's head peaks out, is driven helter-skelter toward the muddy ground of ridicule. But the mockery does not justify any option in favor of a "rhetoric of depths," which also gets its share in the *Tale*. The device of "places" forms a tangle in which are unfailingly trapped all the precepts, all the axioms and corollaries, all the operations and metaphors through which the ridiculed systems seek to state their authority. But the harassment to which they are submitted does not deactivate them. The sharpest point of Swiftian satire consists in showing that the keys according to which these systems are organized are not objectifiable by means of a simple critical assault; they don't become stiff when identified, but change and combine, permanently producing new alternatives of interpretation, an assured destiny that is one and the same with their origin: delirium. And as the systems in question are also systems of control, of power, of dominion over nature and fellow human beings, to live a life in deception might be in the end the best choice in a world that does not cease to be built and rebuilt with those same keys. The ridiculous and fateful game of interpretations lead to a continual contest among them, a permanent and mutual displacement, entwining them until they form a dense web (the tangle in which the text consists), where the only relations we can establish are the same ones with which the text has been woven and continues to be woven. Modernity is this progressive densification of the web. Its deactivation demands more drastic measures, unheard-of measures. That's what Swift teaches.

COMMON SENSE

Drastic, unheard-of measures, I say. Maybe some of the *Tale*'s readers would share with me the impression of a vehement, violent movement, as if the narrator's irrepressible stream would be pushing everything to an end from which, by virtue of a kind of bounce, things, their meanings confused, all tolerance of thought and speech surpassed, would claim from us a minimal restraint, a safeguard. Call it something we all have (should have) in common, a sense for sense, a common sense.

Swift has a word on this. The requirement of common sense in his oeuvre does not have foundations that were exclusively epistemological or pragmatic: it is a political-religious, a theological-political requirement. In fact, the expression "common sense" is found mainly in papers related to such connection. This also seems to be at the center of the *Tale*'s polemical strategy and of the multiple ruses that make its plot. Those foundations are related to a great quarrel in the seventeenth century, which precedes the quarrel of ancients and moderns: the one that confronts Anglicans and Catholics. The *Tale* reflects this conflict in a most visible manner when it comes to the testament in which the father specifies the instructions for the good use and preservation of the marvelous coats that he bequeaths to his sons. In the same vein, further evidence can be gathered from the various distortions imposed on the text of the testament in order to spuriously authorize the add-ons applied to the clothes according to the dictates of fashion. These distortions, scandalous as they are, constitute overt aggressions against the "common sense" of words (Swift employs this turn more than once). In short, it may be spoken of as hermeneutical violence. Well, by the time Swift was working on his first masterpiece—and also earlier—the Anglicans indicted the Catholic Church for exercising this kind of violence; they maintained that the Catholic defense of oral tradition had as its true aim to secure the supremacy and sovereignty of the spiritual as well as secular authority attributed to papal power. Instead, Catholics affirmed that the origin of Christian tradition was the unwritten magisterial word of Jesus, which gave the spoken word preeminence over the written word. This is the same distinction that Peter draws in section 2: "of Wills, duo sunt genera, nuncupatory and scriptory," he says, with which he follows, once the absence of any qualification concerning golden lace in the written testament that the brothers possess is granted, a contemptible excuse that invokes mere rumors: "For Brothers, if you remember, we heard a Fellow say when we were boys, that he heard my Father's Man say, that he heard my Father say, that he would advice his Sons to get Gold Lace on their Coats, as soon as ever they could procure Money to buy it" (55). The Roman idea of a continuum of oral tradition as a warrant of the evangelic command's consistency is downgraded to the most infamous of hearsays.

But if the argument supported by the proponents of an embattled Catholic worldview advocated for the innermost and ineradicable vulnerability of the written word—the uncertainties of its transcription or translation, of its many ambiguities—Anglicans based their argument precisely on the firmness, a firmness approaching inalterability, of what has been recorded in writing. Catholics argued—almost as an echo of Plato's condemnation of logography in *Phaedrus*—that the written word is not only liable to be expropriated, but that it is already born as expropriated; and although they had to count on it as the indispensable source of the Gospel's good news despite its undeniable lability, it is the spoken word credited by the church alone that allows them to retrieve that which is truly *meant* by it. It is interesting to mention that one of the Anglican advocates, John Tillotson, who became archbishop of Canterbury (and author of a text against transubstantiation, a doctrine that the *Tale* ridicules in the story of the lamb thigh that is everything to everybody), explained the trustworthiness of writing by alluding to the example of a father who, having his testament orally communicated to his sons, would need, at the hour of his death, to put it in written form so that on this basis any controversies that might henceforth arise could be settled.[17]

However, the recourse to writing required a criterion and a control. Anglicanism was threatened on two fronts: Catholicism was one, the diverse dissident sects the other. Good polemical reason had the Anglican representatives denouncing the extreme subjectivism of some of those sects, which entrusted the insight into the Bible's teaching to an alleged inner light: radical spiritualism led to a sort of privatization of the evangelical message, with all the pernicious effects that assuredly would follow. The need for a guide was therefore obvious. We already know that the Anglican response to both threats was the affirmation of the primacy of writing with respect to tradition as well as to the allegedly illuminated exegeses. But this had a twofold implication: on the one hand, it entails that the biblical text delivers Christian doctrine in an intelligible manner with no additional support; on the other, that its expression can be comprehended with no other help than that of sound human understanding. These are indeed two different things, and the difference between them is glaring, by contrast, with respect to Catholic premises, which presuppose the need not just for specific aids and supplements, but also for what could be termed the institution of meaning; according to those premises, it is not only impossible to rely simply on the existence of a text, no matter that its genuine provenance might be ensured, but it is definitively troublesome to entrust the comprehension of the evangelical message to mere human discernment. There has to be an ultimate power entitled to establish norms of interpretation and to control the observance of these norms; and this is the papal power. This is fundamentally what the Anglican argument opposes. In a similar way, the idea of a general accessibility of the text, and of a human capacity that makes this access generally possible, sets a wall of contention against the sectarian claim to a mystical principle of comprehension.

The *Tale* distinctly reflects the first of these two aspects of the argument in the description of the testament that the father gives to his sons: it is plain and clear-cut, just as the clothes he bequeaths them, and just as Swift's ideal seems to have been. Certainly, the *Tale* stands in direct opposition to this simplicity: the seven commentaries that seven deepest scholars would produce locked up in seven rooms during seven years could not contain anything that was not inferable from its variegated text.[18] This, of course, is a statement of total ambiguity, and it involves the absolute futility of the work. Such a flagrant opposition supports the Anglican concept, as the apologist wants the *Tale* to be read. However, the testament's declared simplicity has no guarantee of its own. It remains exposed to the most gratuitous semantic abuses, as we already know. Each of these abuses gets farther and farther away from the ideal of language that the document embodies: notwithstanding its name, the *copia vera* that John and Martin seize from the safe where Peter had deposited the manuscript in order to avoid consulting it again, cannot be endorsed either: the explanatory note that supplements the passage indicates that the use of the copy represents the translation of the scriptures into the vulgar tongues; and certainly, the translatability of the testament is perhaps the most emphatic proof of its hermeneutic vulnerability. One need only think of the document's *pendant* in the form of the famous coats: unrecoverable in their primitive integrity, they likewise represent the definitive loss of the testament's pristine condition.

So, the Anglican assertion of simplicity, of plainness, has its complexities, for it is necessary to have recourse to premises that aren't minor in any respect.

On the one hand, a strict concept of the written text is needed; on the other, one must assume (in a coherent and verifiable manner) a universal capacity of comprehension that corresponds to the meaning of the text so conceptualized. As regards the first, John Wilson formulated the premises with all desirable clarity: The scriptures "have a true Sense *Originally* and *Essentially* in themselves, given them by their Author when they were first indited"; "the Sense of Scripture is fixt and immutable, not varying with the times ... not other than it always had, and ever will have to the Worlds end"; "the Rule of Interpretation is that which gives us the objective Evidence by which the true Sense of Scripture is discern'd."[19] In reading assertions of this tenor together with the *Tale*, one can have a rough idea of Swift's intention in producing a text whose author does not at any moment possess the meaning of what he is actually saying—in other words, a text that is radically unstable, eliciting interpretation with no other outcome than proving its inanity. To that extent, a good reason speaks in favor of those who maintain that Swift proceeded here, as a determined Anglican, in defense of the high church,[20] and Swift himself seemed to want to be esteemed in such a capacity. But the point is precisely that, in order to strengthen the Anglican premises, it was needed to bring to light the ultimate consequences of their omission, which would fatally occasion the annihilation of authorship, sense, and permanence; at least Swift may have considered it imperative. Nevertheless, these extreme consequences betray a concealed mistrust in those premises: they cannot sustain themselves on their own, but can only be demonstrated dialectically; or, to put this differently, the worst would ensue if they were renounced. As seen from this rather gloomy point of view, it is as if the truth was at any given moment suspended on the brink of its abolition.[21] Therefore, the second point that Anglicanism was in need of securing was the original sympathy of human understanding toward the univocal determination of meaning. Certainly, this is also a strong thesis, for it appeals to a congenital affinity with and understanding of all the conditions that the text should meet in view of having full and unique meaning, while many things seem to speak against it. At any rate, the second thesis can only be sustained in tension with its total opposite: madness. It is as if one would say: if there is not *one* meaning, there is only nonsense.

Undoubtedly, it is not a question of each utterance having a unique meaning (although this would be ideal): equivocacy is ineradicable from the medium through which we make those utterances. What is required is that in each case, regarding each utterance, it should be possible to *decide* the relevant meaning; it is a matter of criterion. In other words, the affinity between understanding and univocal meaning is only possible if there is a criterion inherent in human understanding that might allow us to discern in each case the corresponding meaning. This criterion is the heart of healthy human understanding—it is the capacity to identify just *one* meaning amid a possible proliferation of meanings, it is the intimate conviction that this unique and truthful meaning is a sense that should be common to all people, and the ignorance of which or deviation from is ascertainable only as nonsense and madness (moral or intellectual). Therefore, the prerequisite of the criterion, which is articulated on the basis of an exigency of comprehension that conditions the validation of any utterance, is not merely formal: its total scope is political, insofar as common sense, properly understood, is the precondition for community itself. If there is not *one* meaning—that is, a meaning in common—there is no community.

It is, then, as if the preservation—or otherwise the establishment—of the semiotic order is the guarantee of public order. The central problem lies in the complexity of Swift's operation concerning that semiotic order. I was alluding to the inescapable equivocacy of the medium in and through which we make our utterances. The problem consists in the fact that Swift gives free rein to the multiple possibilities of the medium, he emancipates it, so to speak. In this respect, one can recall what Wittgenstein says about the dead end of philosophical conundrums, which arise "when *language goes on holiday*."[22] This holiday, as a matter of fact, is wonderfully described in chapter 11, regarding the analogy between writing and riding: "For in Writing it is as in Travelling" (Swift, *Tale* 122), which promotes the idea that the proper and pleasurable act of writing is digression, and we well know that the text in its entirety perfectly matches such idea; in fact, digression is its principle of construction. Only one thing should be set apart: for, unlike the spirited traveler, who enjoys free time and pampers his companions at every turn of the road, Swift provokes and challenges his reader, embarrassing her or him, offering her or him one of three not very promising options: "the superficial, the ignorant, and the learned" (119).[23] Such embarrassment may be seen as the pendant of the assurance of the essential vulnerability of anything that could be codified in language. In the end, the reader has to decide meaning without a guide or yardstick: she or he has to *produce* meaning.

Swift's operation is highly complex, I say. Let us take account of this complexity. On the one hand, there is a series of oppositions. Duality governs all of them under the sign of the irreconcilable. I say *duality*, because in these oppositions, although there is always a third party in conflict, it is systematically excluded. The flagrant proof is the aforesaid *querelle* between Anglicans, Catholics, and dissidents: it is always one against another. And this is, nevertheless, precisely the problem: although they are three parties, the fundamental twist is to reduce them to two, attempting to resolve the conflict by setting aside a third party who will, nevertheless, remain a sort of haunting, peripheral threat. Furthermore, and maybe for the same reason (and perhaps because this reason is the secret cue of everything else, in politics, knowledge, and letters), we find triads swarming everywhere; indeed, they make up the tropology of the *Tale*. Everything—or almost everything—is played out between a binary logic of critical oppositions and a triadic rhetoric that complicates and undermines those oppositions.

I was talking about taking account of this complexity; in fact, it is more about counting. In order to ponder the difference between logic and rhetoric in the *Tale* the aid of a peculiar kind of arithmetic of additions and subtractions is required. To determine the outcome of these additions and subtractions it seems appropriate to listen to the declaration of the apologist in the edition of 1710. There he argues that the accusation of sacrilegious abuse against the dogma of the Trinity owes to the many mutilations suffered by his manuscript at the hands of others. He claims that he would not have the number three as a target—that he in fact aimed at the number four, a figure "much more Cabalistick" and suitable to make a mockery of the numerological superstition (8).[24] The outcome at issue in the aforesaid arithmetic is, then, number four; by this I mean that wherever the meaning splits into opposing segments (or sects), and one tries to make two out of three, the result will inevitably be four, and it is up to the reader to get this result, provided that she or he counts well—in other words, that she or he has a well-balanced mind in order not to be at a loss when counting. A fourth sense hovers over the conflicting three (meanings) that are continually and obsessively reduced to two. This fourth sense, the fugitive and as it were asymptotic verso of the author's derangement, is common sense. And, in a sort of negative suggestion, the text seems to hint at it as a sense that maintains balance amid the vortex.[25]

This hint occurs in the passage I have already quoted in extenso, which brings to its conclusion a disquisition in favor of the science of superficies and against the philosophy of profundity, praising the art of patching up the flaws of nature. Let us get back to the passage's closing:

> And he whose Fortunes and Dispositions have placed him in a convenient Station to enjoy the Fruits of this noble Art; He that can with *Epicurus*

content his ideas with the *Films* and *Images* that fly off upon his Senses from the *Superficies* of Things; Such a Man, truly wise, creams off Nature, leaving the Sour and the Dregs for Philosophy and Reason to lap up. This is the sublime and refined point of Felicity, called, *the Possession of being well deceived*; The Serene Peaceful State, of being a Fool among Knaves. (112)

The negative hint to which I refer is this fool. I know that the passage, and most particularly its ending, have been copiously discussed and interpreted in terms of an *ironic* trap: that point at which the reader, after being vertiginously driven by the meanderings of the preceding discourse, finds her- or himself in a wasteland, caught in the miserable alternative of being either a fool or a knave. Surely, this alternative is not possible without the exclusion of a third party, which is the very fount of the discourse, who pronounces here a eulogy of madness, being himself a Bedlamite.[26] His exclusion is in fact a self-imposed one, and it might not be a folly to say that this self-exclusion is the *cogito* of madness. But let me get to the point: the passage, no doubt, is awfully ambiguous. Yet I take recourse to this ambiguity (so characteristic of everything that Swift wrote, by the way) to suggest that the passage does not end simply in a booby-trap.[27] I take recourse to this ambiguity in order to assume that Swift, under the mask of his raving narrator, mutters here—as he does throughout his work, I would say—that meaning is never a given, that there is nothing resembling a gift, a donation of meaning, that if there ever was one, an original donation, our primal eradication from that scene has deprived us forever of this gift. Swift would mutter, I suggest, that the meaning and the sense are not given, that the presumption that they would be given is sheer precipice, because it invites and urges us to seek meaning and sense everywhere; he would mutter that seeking them, obsessively, frantically, and at last violently, is the major foolishness of the human being, that it is, in a word, madness. For madness is twofold: to believe that sense and meaning are given (that the world is full of itself, that there is no contingency at all); and to believe that everything has sense and meaning. Well, in the end both beliefs are one and the same.

SATIRE AND SKEPTICISM

Swift exposes sound human understanding to the extreme test of its alleged health, obliging it to go into the Babelic labyrinth of convulsive discourses (of any kind and origin) that are the expression of a society in the course of acute historical change. Nothing of what those discourses say may be used as a criterion, not even provisional, in order to tackle the current disorders, for they momentaneously emerge from these very disorders and, after a short life, sink again into them, no matter the label: religion, morals, science, literature, politics, economy. Nor are there any supports in tradition, for the changes and what they have occasioned in people and discourses push it to the limbo of a deplorable obsolescence that can only be seen (if one does not pertain to the party of the moderns) with excruciating nostalgia. You cannot believe anything, you cannot trust in anything: that seems to be the *Tale*'s lesson. You cannot believe anything straightaway, and it is perfectly probable that your state of mind will remain the same after the issue that has been presented to you (deceptively, for sure) has been put to the test. Therefore, the demand for a criterion is so radical in Swift; therefore, the measures he adopts are so extreme. It is as if common sense were the eye of calm in the center of the hurricane-force delirium that has set out to conquer heaven.

I have said that the pair of fools and knaves and the corollary reduction of humankind to this odious alternative depend on the exclusion of the madman. This operation, the form of which is everywhere present in Swift's work, this formal operation that is perhaps essential to Swiftian satire, brings with it a product, or at least the possibility of a product. For you do not unavoidably have to be a fool or a knave—or a madman. The former two are what they are by virtue of the exclusion of the latter; they are inextricably associated with him in a way that links all of them intimately.[28] Recall that the famous passage, and to a large extent the whole chapter to which it belongs, formulates the panegyric of credulity and of the perpetual "*Possession of being well deceived*" as the quintessence of happiness; the three of them are bound together by credulity: fools, because they swallow everything that is said or presented to them; knaves, because they profit from the credulity of others and lucratively parasitize it; madmen, because they are captives of the credulity they offer to themselves. Therefore, you are not inevitably condemned to be a fool, a knave, or a madman. You can be incredulous; you can be prudent. You can, on every occasion (but not in general), produce common sense, provided you don't yield to the seduction of believing (which is the seduction of believing that sense is already given). And this is the product that is made possible by the aforementioned operation.

On this basis, I don't think it out of order to relate Swiftian satire to Pyrrhonic skepticism. With regard to the Swiftian strategy I've been trying to describe, I think it could be argued, from a formal point of view, that it has an affinity with the skeptical eradication of dogmatic judgments and prejudices. In addition, one could expand this affinity toward a general relation between skepticism and satire by considering the procedure by which satire is enacted, which lies in inverting the value of established customs, opinions, and beliefs that the satirist proposes to criticize by turning them against themselves. Also in formal terms, the skeptical procedure consists in the production of negative arguments that rebut the existence of a rational justification for dogmatic assertions. Here, certainly, it is not the *contents* of determinate opinions or beliefs but the *forms* of their validation by means of rational expedients that are turned against themselves, which makes their accreditation unsustainable in terms that would allow us to take them as conclusive truths. Within the skeptical tradition, this is the critical point of the five "logical" tropes of Agrippa—discrepancy, regress *ad infinitum*, relativity, hypothesis, and circular reasoning—as distinguished from the casuistry of the ten "classical" modes.[29] I would like to see these tropes matched with the "places" (*topoi*) to which I was referring. Skeptics and satirists—if you don't find this generalization too awkward—coincide in abstaining from the introduction of new principles or theses, either in the cognitive or in the moral order; they dismantle the pretensions of their adversaries from their own foundations, turning them against themselves; and, finally, both seek the restitution of a psychological and behavioral equilibrium, which has the ordinary individual of everyday life as its subject and plain common sense as the criterion for living.

In a certain way, if the skeptic carries out his undermining work on the epistemological terrain, the satirist does the same on the moral. The satirist is interested not so much in the validity of a corpus of opinions and beliefs tested for their cognitive scope as in the reliability of the premises and consequences of determinate social customs and behaviors. The satiric treatment of these premises (which are, of course, opinions and beliefs) and of the implications of such customs points to a denunciation of their radical incoherence with respect to their ethical validation. Just as the skeptic, with recourse to the means of accreditation that rational argumentation provides, proves the dogmatist's epistemological position untenable on the rational grounds that he himself claims, the satirist proves his addressee's ethical position—the way in which he conducts his life—not only untenable on but also in direct contradiction of the moral grounds that he himself avows when urged to justify his behavior, and this the satirist does by appealing precisely to the means of rational justification that would be alleged in order to provide sound credentials to that position.

Finally, there is also an affinity in a principal trait of the respective strategies. I have spoken of satire's homeopathic guideline (*similia similibus curantur*, the cure of evil by evil, if you like), which in Swift reaches an unsurpassed expression.[30] This expression assigns to satire and to its entire linguistic and representational economy a cathartic, purgative function. I recall on this point the self-refuting character that Sextus Empiricus attributes to the formulae by means of which the skeptic declares his forbearance in judging and concluding. These formulae suppress themselves to the extent that "they themselves are included in the things to which their doubt applies" (206), as in, for instance, "All things are undetermined" (198), "All things are non-apprehensible" (200), or "To Every Argument an Equal Argument Is Opposed" (202)—formulae that are not categorical but merely restrict themselves to announcing the state of mind in which the skeptic finds himself at a certain point in the course of his inquiry. Sextus says that these expressions work "just as aperient drugs [*tà kathartiká*] [that] do not merely eliminate the humours from the body, but also expel themselves along with the humours" (206). The *Tale* shows blatant proofs of a similar cathartic strategy. Its ferocious prototype will be promoted in *Gulliver's Travels* as a kind of panacea: when the rational horses of the Fourth Voyage need to cure the repulsive Yahoos—who are something like crude human beings, in the most rudimentary state of nature—they force them to swallow a mixture of their own dung and urine (Swift, *Gulliver's Travels* 394).

Of course, the outcome of Swift's satiric critique differs from the result of the skeptical dismantling of dogmatic attitudes. One could not say that Swift's labor ends with something of a serenity of mind, a state of *ataraxia* like the tranquility in which the mature skeptic allegedly finds himself once his adversaries' pretensions to knowledge are scrupulously examined and tested. I have spoken of the anxious condition that characterizes the narrating self in the *Tale*, of the persistent uncertainty to which the reader is exposed when trying to determine what, precisely, has been meant here, of the substantive difficulty of discerning what could have been the intention of the covert author of the text (that is, of Swift himself): all that seems, rather, to emphasize the aspects of the stress that would be typical of this writing. And, nevertheless, the neutrality in which its tensions result, the laughable disqualification of the pretensions of reason and faith wherever these arise and wherever one of them tries to fill up the deficiencies of the other, the removal of the hermeneutical eagerness through the evidence of its futility—all suggest a desistance whose emancipating aspect is perhaps no different from that which skepticism promises.

Chapter Three

On the Insignificant

FIGURES OF LICHTENBERG

To discover a thought such that anyone,
upon hearing it, would laugh themselves to death.
—G. C. LICHTENBERG, *The Waste Books*

IT IS CURIOUS that the Spanish word *nimio* (insignificant) originally meant exactly the opposite of what we normally understand it to mean, being related to the negligible, the bagatelle, and the trifle. The word is a composition of the negation *ne* (not) and *mei-* (little), which sprouts from the root *meion* in Greek and *minus*, *minuō* (diminish), *minimus* and *minister* (servant) in Latin. Consequently, *nimio* is the negation of the little: *nimius* properly means "excessive," "too much." The dictionary attributes the usual meaning to a wrong interpretation of phrases like *cuidado nimio* (excessive care). This contradiction, tied around the same word, recalls the issue of the antithetical meanings of primitive terms, to which Freud devotes a brief discussion, alleging that they—connected to the semantic economy of dreams—provide a clue for the operation of the unconscious, and to which he appeals on several occasions. Of course, here it is a different matter, because the antithesis is not located in a single word but is due to an error of comprehension, which modifies the use of the term. Nevertheless, it could be possible to think that the distance is not so great, because, in the end, it is precisely the word's life in its use, determined by the intentions and comprehensions of speakers, that is at stake in both cases.

What is the point of this preamble? What is the point, I ask, if it is clear that I'm going to take the word *nimio* in the sense of "unimportant," "trivial," and the like? Surely, this is what interests me here: to discuss the role of trifle in the production and the effects of humor. This has its reason. There is a relation to laughter that could somehow be brought to an analogy with tickling. We know by experience that tickling, in its convulsive and unbearable delight, does not know the dividing line between the minimum and the absolutely excessive, to the point that cases have been recording of people dying because of it. So, considering the very ambiguity of that line, my intention consists in granting the insignificant a peculiar power with respect to humor.

It seems to me that in the theories of laughter and the comic there is little space for the acknowledgment of such power. Those theories are perhaps too dominated by the effects of meaning that provoke hilarity. According to these theories, the insignificant makes us laugh not just by itself but by the effect it produces when it is part of a chain of meaning. It could be as Kant and Schopenhauer say, assuming that one bursts out laughing when the expectation of meaning turns into nothing; its logical structure would correspond to incongruity. But there is also relief as an alternative explanation (this is the catharsis theory): that is to say, the insignificant being in the end the meaning of what is said, the relief results from an economization of the effort suggested to be necessary to understand it. In all these cases, the insignificant is always thought of from the point of view of meaning, either because of the expectation it awakes or for the benefit it provides. I mean that it is not considered in itself: it is not conceived as an interruption of the logical causality opening to something different. This interruption would be what happens at the dividing line, which, being diffuse, no longer divides but rather opens a passage between trifle and excess. I'm going to talk about something like an *economy of surplus*.

Anyway, with respect to the insignificant in its usual sense but seen from the perspective of philosophical implications, there are, I suppose, two matrices: one is the concentration of totality in one of its constitutive atoms. It is the insignificant as an unnoticed clue to the universe. The other is the residual, which does not enter into a coherent system or agree with anything else but remains incompossible, lacking sense and value. It is the trifle as mere insignificance.

Is it possible to conceive of a theory of the trifle? This seems to contradict the very notion of theory. A theory is governed by an interest. This is the interest of knowing, which in turn may be—and regularly is—coordinated with other interests, particularly the one that seeks to exercise control over our relations and interventions in reality. This interest demands that everything susceptible to being theorized should be interesting to the same extent.

I will begin with a classical instance of such an interest, precisely an instance that shows how the interest of theory—and its coordination with other interests—ought not simply discard the insignificant.

From a methodological point of view, the issue of the little and the insignificant, of what at first sight, and rashly, would be considered unworthy of theoretical attention, is a relevant theme in philosophy. Plato gives the earliest evidence: from the standpoint of dialectics, the insignificant cannot be neglected. The *Sophist* has an emphatic passage in this respect, which I quote *in extenso*:

> STR. Very good; you can decide about that for yourself as we proceed. Meanwhile you and I will begin together and enquire into the nature of the Sophist, first of the three: I should like you to make out what he is and bring him to light in a discussion; for at present we are only agreed about the name, but of the thing to which we both apply the name possibly you have one notion and I another; whereas we ought always to come to an understanding about the thing itself in terms of a definition, and not merely about the name minus the definition. Now the tribe of Sophists which we are investigating is not easily caught or defined; and the world has long ago agreed, that if great subjects are to be adequately treated, they must be studied in the lesser and easier instances of them [*en smikrois kai rhaosin*] before we proceed to the greatest of all [*en autois tois megistois*]. And as I know that the tribe of Sophists is troublesome and hard to be caught, I should recommend that we practise beforehand the method [*ten methodon*] which is to be applied to him on some simple and smaller thing, unless you can suggest a better way.
>
> THEAET. Indeed I cannot.
>
> STR. Then suppose that we work out some lesser example [*paradeigma*] which will be a pattern of the greater?
>
> THEAET. Good.

STR. What is there which is well known and not great [*eugnoston men kai smikron*], and is yet as susceptible [*medenos elattonta*] of definition as any larger thing [*tôn meizonon*]? Shall I say an angler [*aspalieutes*]? He is familiar to all of us, and not a very interesting or important person [*spoudes ou pany*]. (218b–e)

The strategic recommendation of the Stranger is explicitly directed toward a matter of method. The correlation between the little and the great is not based, at least in principle, on an affinity of content linking both but on the power of dialectics to administer and subject them to its economy, no matter the intrinsic value that could be attributed to them. From the point of view of method, there's neither better nor worse: all things are equal before its tribunal. This is so as long as we take for granted that the axiological (and ontological) abstinence of the dialectical method is straightforward and simple, as long we do not realize the ironical mood, of Socratic roots, that continues to inhabit it. For Plato does not restrict himself to crediting its procedure exclusively in methodological, formal terms. In addition to the schematic correlation of the little and the great, there is a surreptitious connection between both, which is no longer subordinated to form but concerns the very substance (or insubstantiality) of the object under examination. It will be recalled that in the *Republic*, on premises that are certainly very different from those that are beginning to show here, attention is paid to the macroscopy of the *polis* and its structure in order to get a clear picture permitting us to discern the miniature of the soul and to settle the question of justice. The big picture favors the inspection of the thumbnail sketch, inasmuch as there is an essential affinity between both, a structural homology. Here, instead, the typological survey of the fishermen (which is in every respect a minor and unworthy issue) does not seem to imply anything for the actual object of inquiry. Nevertheless, the ironic torsion to which I was referring has its point. The example of the angler (and this also entails the question of the example as such) must give occasion for a game of capture in which, in the end, all are involved: the humble fishermen, the arrogant sophists, and the inquisitors themselves, the latter by way of bloodhounds at the service of *logos*. Certainly, they do not all share one and the same essence, but they are related to each other by their activity and their zeal.

But not everything is exhausted by methodological eagerness, which in the end is perfectly explainable. The point is not to validate littleness by itself.

The panoramic grandeur of the method must encompass everything, and, as the *Sophist* states, the application of its procedures to the little (in onto-axiological terms) might provide largely significant lessons for the inspection of things that are really hard to decipher, just as the details of the internal constitution of an object that is large enough to be perspicuous might serve as a guide to discover the structure of a similar thing that, because littler (in terms of magnitude), does not reveal at first sight its own structure, provided that there is a real homology between both.

Not everything ends here, I say. Plato also opens the way to asking about the essential possibility of a *theory* of the insignificant. The most delightful moment in this respect can be found in the *Parmenides*, in the perplexity and embarrassment of young Socrates when submitted to interrogation by the Stranger from Elea as soon as he has exposed the first noble fruits of the theory of ideas. Are there ideas of insignificant things?

> While Socrates was speaking, Pythodorus thought that Parmenides and Zeno were not altogether pleased at the successive steps of the argument; but still they gave the closest attention, and often looked at one another, and smiled as if in admiration of him. When he had finished, Parmenides expressed their feelings in the following words:
>
> Socrates, he said, I admire the bent of your mind towards philosophy; tell me now, was this your own distinction between ideas in themselves and the things which partake of them [*charis men eide auta atta, kharis eè ta touton au metechonta*] and do you think that there is an idea of likeness apart from the likeness which we possess, and of the one and many, and of the other things which Zeno mentioned?
>
> I think that there are such ideas, said Socrates.
>
> Parmenides proceeded: And would you also make absolute ideas [*ti eidos auto kath'auto*] of the just and the beautiful and the good, and of all that class?
>
> Yes, he said, I should.
>
> And would you make an idea of man apart from us and from all other human creatures, or of fire and water?
>
> I am often undecided, Parmenides, as to whether I ought to include them or not.
>
> And would you feel equally undecided, Socrates, about things of which the mention may provoke a smile [*geloia*]?—I mean such things as hair,

mud, dirt, or anything else which is vile and paltry [*atimotaton te kai phaulotaton*]; would you suppose that each of these has an idea distinct from the actual objects with which we come into contact, or not?

Certainly not, said Socrates; visible things like these are such as they appear to us, and I am afraid that there would be an absurdity in assuming any idea of them, although I sometimes get disturbed, and begin to think that there is nothing without an idea; but then again, when I have taken up this position, I run away, because I am afraid that I may fall into a bottomless pit of nonsense [*eis tin abuthon phlyarian*], and perish; and so I return to the ideas of which I was just now speaking, and occupy myself with them.

Yes, Socrates, said Parmenides; that is because you are still young; the time will come, if I am not mistaken, when philosophy will have a firmer grasp of you, and then you will not despise even the meanest things; at your age, you are too much disposed to regard opinions of men. (130a–e)

The uneasiness confessed by young Socrates does not attenuate the humorous effect of Parmenides's remark. The possibility of postulating ideas for contemptible things is a pitfall into which the grandiose theory of ideas threatens to sink. The result would be a strict and total duplication of everything sensible, a sort of perverse mirror, definitively useless from the standpoint of the claim for the intelligibility of the real that commands the doctrine. It is this mirror, which reverses the derivation of all that appears in this world from corresponding intelligible paradigms and makes of them an endless number of futile reflections of sensible things, that Socrates brands as "a bottomless pit of nonsense," an abyss of pure and simple verbosity (*phlyaria*). Gazing at the edge of the precipice, the youthful enthusiasm of the inquirer collapses, and he finds no resort other than running away, looking for shelter in the ideas of worthy things.

But here, too, Parmenides's warning (notice that in both cases it's about the Eleatics, as if Plato wished to save something decisive of their teaching) is directed toward the contempt for the little only because it does not seem to be worthy of inquiry, and here it is necessary to add what the master from Elea says: it seems unworthy only to the "opinions of men." With philosophy it should be different. Similar to the argument in the *Sophist*, here, too, the right of the insignificant to be considered is claimed, not for itself (its lack of value continues to be stated, and, although this statement has its ironic side, it also has a serious and utterly determined one), but on behalf of method, on behalf of dialectics. The difficulties imposed by its conception seem to be the best gymnasium for the philosopher's training, to such an extent that at last he ends up understanding that "there is no science of the individual."

And yet, and yet.

The little haunts philosophy. It frequently becomes the touchstone of the discipline's aspirations, a factor of philosophical self-critique, which so many philosophers (among them Pascal, for instance)[1] have put forward tenaciously and sharply. It could be said that the trifle, the insignificant, and the little represent for philosophy the absolute limit of the concept: they are, in their paltry nature and their opacity, the proof of the *un-conceptual*.

So, is it possible to think of a theory of the insignificant?

Although many witnesses who come from the field of philosophy could be called to testify in this respect, I want to invoke here Georg Christoph Lichtenberg (1742–1799), this flamboyant child of the Enlightenment, hunchbacked and hypochondriac, who was trained in natural science and mathematics but kept throughout his life a close relation to philosophy and literature and established between the two an unheard-of connection.

The question of the little fills his writings in many different keys. There is the importance of the little, for instance, which is confirmed through a historical observation, as it were: the proclivity of men to deem little things important has produced many big things (G 234).[2] Insofar as one learns this lesson thoroughly, the aforesaid importance has, then, the stature of an epistemological principle: "Ask yourself whether you can explain the insignificant details; this is the only means to create an accurate system, probe its strengths, and put your readings to use" (KA 296).[3]

A related note indicates that the main difficulty in the "study of a profound philosophy" is the habit of considering that many things are so simple, easy, and natural that it is not possible to think that they could be otherwise, whereas it is necessary to know how to give importance to those "trivial things ... in order then to explain what is pronounced *difficult* about them.... To find these simple things difficult reveals no marginal progress in philosophy" (K 65).[4]

At this point, it is worth warning the reader that, whatever our opinion about what Lichtenberg is saying in these few notes, it sounds principally like a confirmation of the precept on which I was commenting—namely, that there is an epistemological significance that has to be granted to the little and the trivial in the search for truth but only for the sake of methodology and in view of the truly important things that we desire to know. As if little things couldn't be true. As if there were no universality in the small, in the little. In a certain sense, it is peculiar that we tend to confound the big or the great with the universal. It is something like supposing that only huge things can be sublime, a prejudice of which even Kant is guilty. Anyway, it has to be said that the importance of the insignificant for theory is not the same as a theory of the insignificant. It is true that there is a certain nuance in the tone and tenor, in the dull insistence of these notes, that seems to suggest something more than mere methodological prudence, something that has to do, I would say, with valuing the insignificance of the insignificant, not merely to assign it an illustrative or propaedeutic function in the strategy of knowledge, but to learn that the truth for which one is searching might be discreetly contained in those insignificances. The same implication becomes more evident with respect to the moral key:

> To the wise, nothing is immeasurable and nothing insignificant, especially when he is doing philosophy—assuming he is not hungry or thirsty or has not forgotten his snuff if he uses it. In this case, I believe he could compose an essay on keyholes, which would sound as important as one on *jus naturae* and be equally as enlightening. As only few sages well know, in minor everyday occurrences one can discover a moral principle just as readily as in the major ones. A raindrop contains so many good and artistic things that it should not be sold in a pharmacy for less than half a florin. (B 195)

And this is clearly something different from the purely methodological validation of the little; Lichtenberg advocates its autonomous significance. The way in which he does so is telling: in this sort of curious density of minimal events, of the raindrop, for instance, the universality and richness are described by way of analogy to the minimum and the maximum, which, more than an analogy, is actually a virtually constant exchange between the universe and the individual or, in any case, something like an invagination of worlds inside worlds:

> What will become of this species before it extinguishes? The world can continue turning easily for a million years as it has until now, in which case 5,000 years would be exactly what 1/4 of a year is in the life of a man of 50, hardly 1/12 of our time at a university. What have I done in my last quarter of year? Ate, drank, conducted electrical experiments, made a

calendar, laughed at a kitten, played with little girls, and so 5,000 years of this little world that I am went by. (F 541)

Small things, little things, have something to do with random things. Seen through metaphysical lenses, they all share the condition of being nothing momentous, of being nothing substantial—that is, of being accidents. I think that the invagination I mentioned is a frequent mode of being for accidents precisely because they do not obey a strict law of causality and don't need to stand in line waiting for their turn to happen. Or, if you prefer, it's a distinct manner in which the law of causality functions. Seen from this other side, it's because of this invagination that the random event has the magnitude of a determining cause, and this by virtue of linking causes and effects in detail, somehow in the manner of what today is promoted under the auspices of the theory of chaos known as the "butterfly effect":

> If I had not written this book, a thousand years from now, between six and seven in the evening, people would in many towns in Germany be talking about quite different things from what they will in fact be talking about. If I had thrown in Vardöhus a cherry kernel to the sea, the Mynheer at the cape would not have wiped the drop of seawater from exactly the same place on his nose. (D 55)

And there are many other pieces and scraps that cover an ample spectrum of tonalities, from joking or claiming to provocation or irony and even poetry on everyday trifles.

As is well known, Lichtenberg's fundamental philosophical-literary legacy is a massive collection of notes recorded in several notebooks, which he himself named *Sudelbücher* (remnant books), in which he wrote down notes of any sort from the age of twenty-three almost until the day of his death. These annotations are usually placed under the general heading of aphorisms, which is a concept that I'm afraid does not fit here. Aphorisms are defined as brief sentences of doctrinaire character and of a personal stamp; they differ from maxims, because the latter are the expression of an established and shared wisdom: aphorisms, instead, are at best candidates for maxims, if they do not straightforwardly discuss or challenge a common legacy from the standpoint of the peculiar experience and wit of the author. Lichtenberg's notes are, of course, mostly peculiar. But they are far from the character of an aphorism. Their briefness does not obey a zeal of synthesis or epitome but are frequently unfinished or do not advance beyond mere sketches. They teach neither doctrines nor lessons, but they express intermittently, and always under a shadow of doubt and hesitation, what could be termed the pulse of Lichtenberg's thinking. If one considers his scientific education and activity, it would be possible to speak of "intellectual experiments," but this is still far from their specific nature. "Remnants" is perhaps the most faithful translation.

The denomination is explained by an analogy with the procedure of shopkeepers and what they do for their bookkeeping:

> Merchants and traders have a waste book (*Sudelbuch, Klitterbuch* in German I believe) in which they enter daily everything they purchase and sell, messily, without order. From this, it is transferred to their journal, where everything appears more systematic, and finally to a ledger, in double entry after the Italian manner of bookkeeping, where one settles accounts with each man, once as debtor and then as creditor. This deserves to be imitated by scholars. First it should be entered in a book in which I record everything as I see it or as it is given to me in my thoughts; then it may be entered in another book in which the material is more separated and ordered, and the ledger might then contain, in an ordered expression, the connections and explanations of the material that flow from it. (E 46)[5]

More emphatically, another note—which certainly does not employ the same term but, rather, "draft"—registers the idea, raising it to the paradoxical dignity of a method: "The method of the rough draft notebook [*Schmierbuch*] is highly commendable. No turn of phrase, no expression, left unwritten. One also becomes wealthy by saving penny-truths [*durch Ersparung der Pfennigs-Wahrheiten*]" (F 1219). "Penny-truths," truths that are worth a penny, says the sketch: truths, in the end. This would be the quality of all the notes, and, in due correspondence to this encompassing character, it makes sense to speak of a method. Nevertheless, it would be worth asking what, in sum, a heap of fragments might be, when each fragment, no matter its weight, scope, or its very condition (reflection or record, remark *en passant* or piece of narrative, ironic aggression or moral critique, phrases that are kept for some further use), when each fragment, as I say, has a pretension to truth. Meanwhile, this could give occasion to speak of a theory of the insignificant by way of a "theory of remnants." Its essential concern, like that of any theory, would be truth. But what kind of truth? One could imagine something of a *big bang* that would have affected *the* truth from the beginning of time and forever after, in which case the "remnants" would be nothing but the vertiginous splinters that are the innumerable and inexhaustible traces of this primordial event, without order or concert. One would be inclined to say that this is the mode in which Lichtenberg maintains an epistemological standpoint that is difficult to name anything but skeptical because of its visceral rejection of the structure of the treatise and the systematic exposition of knowledge, a rejection that at the same time rescues in its detail, through the chance of witty ideas, the dispersion of events. Yes, for each one of these "truths that are worth a penny" is precisely that, an event: nothing fixed and nothing solid.

(Let me return to Spanish, by way of an aside: for the English words *remnant* or *balance* we have *saldo*, which derives from the verb *saldar* and means "settling an account," "paying a debt"; its primary meaning has to do with integrity, as it comes, through Italian, from the Latin *solidus*; although it normally designates not the sum total but the remnant quantity that is left after having accomplished all the operations of an account, as when one speaks of a positive balance, a surplus, or a negative balance, an overdraft. You see that the economy of the surplus, to which I called attention when treating the semantics of *nimio*, shows up here again.)

I was saying: nothing fixed and nothing solid. "Stop your chattering [*Schwätzt doch nicht*]. What do you want? If the stars are no longer fixed in their places, how can you continue to say that truth is still truth [*daß alles Wahre wahr ist*]?" (E 139). No doubt, one can ask how those penny-truths go together with this contestation of the true. No doubt, also, Lichtenberg's notes—which are humoristic not only because of their laughable or disturbing effects but also because of the changes of humor (good mood, bad mood, weariness, anxiety, indifference), pivoting upon that conditioning of knowledge and truth that Nietzsche pointed out with his warning about the important fact that there are good and bad days—these notes, I argue, are susceptible to more than one reading because of the disturbing and surprising reactions they provoke in the reader and because of the fact that the latter is also subject to those changes, the lesson he deduces today not necessarily being the same as the one that he could have deduced yesterday or the one that he might deduce tomorrow. And maybe for this same reason, paradoxically, this annotation lends itself to a singular and exact reading: just like the stars, truth and the true are not fixed or sealed once and for all, but rather fluctuate. This is the idea I meant to invoke when I spoke of the penny-truths as events—that is, as what we call in Spanish *ocurrencias* in both senses of the word (a witty remark *and* an occurrence, an incident). Therefore, their record, their inspection, demands something like a method, and it is to this method that I now turn.

As you know, there are so-called Lichtenberg figures. Obsessed with electric phenomena, he made a discovery by chance, as often happens: an open electrophorus on which a resinous paste was warmed up, when in contact with the air, caused electrified dust particles to be deposited onto the glass sheet in such a way as to form figures similar to stars and trees. Lichtenberg tried to explain the event (once he could reproduce it at will) in terms of positive and negative electricity, but he lacked the knowledge of electrons and positive ions. The little constellations captivated the interest of the members of the scientific community, among whom were celebrities like Alessandro Volta, and no doubt caused the astonishment of Lichtenberg's Göttingen neighbors.

What I wish to propose here is a game-like exercise whose outcome I do not intend to be systematic. My guess is that, revising Lichtenberg's original "waste books," one could gather, without any hope of wholeness, a set of thought figures, something like logical figures, that could give an account of the outer edges and meanderings of their author's musings.[6] Of course, in addition to the foolish eagerness of attempting to be exhaustive in such matters, there cannot be any hope that the figures do not interweave and contaminate each other. The same applies to the characteristic of those "figures": to pretend that an irrefutable index could be established is sheer nonsense. Everyone can proceed at his own ease. Here, I will simply follow the influence of my own proclivities and my scarce ingenuity. Nothing would be more naive than to think it possible to follow a secure direction when the very firmament that would serve as one's guide is the result of an explosion of systems and constellations in infinite expansion—"An entire milky way of witty ideas [*Eine ganze Milchstraße von Einfällen*]" (J 344)—and in which one finds oneself presently lost. But it could so happen that, at the end of this exercise, we come to guess something of the thinking that attains its own figure in that myriadic expansion.[7]

I'm going to start from something that could be a kind of principle of Lichtenberg's ponderings, something like a principle of relativity, a principle of subjectivity, according to which the big and the little essentially, or perhaps exclusively, depend on the *look* that perceives them:

> If sharpness [*Scharfsinn*] is a magnifying glass [*Vergrößrungs-Glas*], wit [*Witz*] is a lens of reduction [*Verkleinerungs-Glas*]. Or do you think perhaps

that discoveries can only be made with magnifying glasses? I believe that in the intellectual world more discoveries have probably been made with lenses of reduction or at least with similar instruments. Through an inverted eyeglass the moon looks like Venus and, to the naked eye, like Venus through a good eyeglass in the right position. Through common binoculars the Pleiades would seem like a nebula. The world, so beautifully covered with trees and grass, might for this very reason seem moldy to a being superior to us. The most beautiful starry sky seems empty to us through an inverted telescope. (D 469)[8]

You can have "new looks through old holes" (F 879) and vice versa; the present case seems to be the inverse of the inverse, new looks through new holes (without forgetting the fundamental fact that "the most important things are accomplished through holes in the world" [C 252]); Lichtenberg plays on both sides of the alternative; old for new and old for old were not part of his priorities, so he always tried to think by himself.

This play of *inversions of the gaze* (here we have a first figure), as well as the experiment of the *look from outside* (and a second, closely related to the first—a figure that is also present in this text), seems to me substantial in Lichtenberg. Take for instance this example of inversion: "The American who first discovered Columbus made a bad discovery" (G 183). And also: "As foolish as it must seem to the crab when he sees man walking forwards" (D 125). When it comes to walking, the latter is connected with what follows: "If walking on two legs is not natural to man, it is certainly an invention that does him credit" (J 226). As you can easily see here, the inversion of the gaze implies in a most natural manner the look from outside: "That man is the noblest creature on earth can be deduced from the fact that no other creature has challenged him" (D 331). There is also the following note anticipating certain Borgesian ironies on the attribution of our existence and the world's to a clumsy intermediate demon: "I doubt it will ever be possible to prove we are the work of a supreme being and not rather fabricated for its own amusement by a very imperfect one" (D 412).[9] Resorting again to the idea of a superior being (not God himself but one who has sight, an ear, or an intelligence superior to ours), there is a note that turns the point upside down again, to the praise—a little doubtful—of poets:

> The nightingales sing and have no idea of the fuss poets and lovers create over their song, or that there exists a whole society of higher beings who entertain themselves solely with Philomena and her complaints. Perhaps

a higher race of spirits regards our poets as we do canaries and nightingales: they enjoy their song precisely because they find no rational sense in it [*weil sie keinen Verstand darin finden*]. (G 141)

The inversion of the gaze is frequently due to rapid changes of position. We would do well to remember that this is the gymnastics commended most by critics of overly rigid philosophies and creeds and that the mood that enlivens this exhortation is, in one way or another, one of skepticism. It is about emancipating the spirit from the rigidity and the obfuscation that produce in it the persistence of unquestioned certitudes, whose real value is no different from the value of prejudice or superstition. This emancipation clears up the perception of things and opens up room for understanding. Therefore, in the end, the inversion of the gaze always connects with the look from outside.

In this endeavor, the technical devices that help and modify the perceptive operations, and for which new uses or paradoxical functions can be imagined, have a considerable significance. This explains Lichtenberg's interest in conceiving what could be called the *marvelous apparatus* (and here we have yet another figure). In addition to playing with optical instruments, in addition to Lichtenberg's obsession with Franklin's lightning conductor (near the end of the century he managed to have one installed at the University of Göttingen), the epoch's fascination with mechanisms, particularly those related to clockwork, leads him to imagine objects as peculiar as, for instance, a "clock that every quarter of an hour says to its proprietor *You* ... at half an hour *You are* ... at three quarters of an hour *You are a* ... and when it strikes the hour: *You are a man*" (D 59). (Of course, this memento has its counterpart: "Hour-glasses remind us, not only of how time flies, but at the same time of the dust into which we shall one day decay" [C 27].) Or again, a clock that allows those in its presence "to smell what time it is—a peculiar clock indeed" (J 468). Perhaps the most curious thing about these artifices is that, if we let the one hand turn, we find them again on the other hand in nature: "A measure of cares, *mensura curarum*. My face is one" (J 1079).

But there is no apparatus as marvelous as the *machine of language*, and, to a certain extent, one could say that this is the figure of all figures. And perhaps we cannot find a better and more exact formula to indicate that language is the pivot around which everything rotates than the one that says, "The world of words [*Die Wörter-Welt*]" (J 357).

Lichtenberg practices permanently the critique of language, which is at the same time a critique of human knowledge. It is as if this admirer of Kant had fulfilled precisely that which is missing in Kant's critique; maybe this is one of the main reasons why Wittgenstein included Lichtenberg in his meager philosophical pantheon. For you will not deny how comfortable the author of the *Tractatus* would have been when reading this note:

> *I* and *myself*. *I* feel *myself*—these are two things. Our false philosophy is embodied in our entire language; we cannot reason, so to speak, without reasoning falsely. We fail to consider that speaking, regardless of what, is philosophy. Anyone who speaks German is a folk philosopher, and our academic philosophy consists in qualifications of this common philosophy. All our philosophy is the correction of linguistic use, that is, the correction of a philosophy, our most common one. But only this common philosophy has the advantage of possessing declinations and conjugations. Thus true philosophy is always taught in the language of false philosophy. Defining words does not help, for in defining them we do not alter the pronouns and their declinations. (H 146)

Yes, I know that I am attributing to Wittgenstein an assent to these terms that he could not have accepted without further consideration.[10] The terms are indeed ambivalent, for on the one hand they propose the substantial idea of a properly philosophic character of language, and on the other hand they distribute values of truth and falsity among common or vulgar philosophy—the one spontaneously spoken—and academic philosophy; it is true that Wittgenstein, as author of the *Tractatus*, might have sympathized with the issue of rectifying ordinary language, but certainly not the Wittgenstein of the *Philosophical Investigations*. Anyway, what surely interested Lichtenberg was underscoring the debt that the discourse of philosophy incurs because of its having to inevitably resort to what we call natural language. "Language originated," he says in a passage not very far from the one we are reading, "prior to philosophy, and that is what makes philosophy difficult, especially when it is a matter of making it clear to those who do not themselves reflect very much. When philosophy speaks, it is always compelled to express itself in the language of nonphilosophy [*Unphilosophie*]" (H 151).

The point is that language is a structure, one that regulates certain internal operations over which we have no control: the grammatical automatisms are at once our prison and our refuge. Just like "the fly that does not want to be swatted is safest when it sits on the fly swatter" (J 415), the human being reposes on grammar—if we might put it that way—in order to gain confidence: grammar provides him with the grounds and bases for his beliefs. And it would almost be possible to say that there is a deep grammar, which has to do with the structure of the human subject itself, just as happens with the grammar of causality: "We must believe that everything has a cause, just as the spider spins its web to catch flies. It does this before it knows flies exist" (H 25).

In fact, the subject of knowledge, without necessarily ceasing to be a fly, is also a peculiar kind of spider trapped in its own web of representations (*Vorstellungen*). This is one of the sharper points of the critique of knowledge, as seen in the following quotation, one that compliments what we have just read:

> With just the same degree of certainty with which we are convinced that something occurs *within us*, we are also convinced that something occurs *outside us*. We understand the words *inside* and *outside* very well. There can be no one in this world and unlikely one born who would not sense this *difference*; and for philosophy that is sufficient. It should not go beyond this; to do so would be wasted effort and lost time. For whatever the things might be, it is agreed that we can know absolutely nothing of them except what lies in our representations. In this regard, which I believe is correct, the question as to whether the things really are outside of us and really are as we see them is utterly without sense. Is it not peculiar that man absolutely demands to have things twice when once would have been sufficient and necessarily must be sufficient since there exists no bridge from our representations to their causes? We cannot think of anything as existing without a cause, but where then lies this necessity? The answer again is *within us*, inasmuch as it is completely impossible for us to go outside of ourselves. (L 811)

Trapped in its web of representations, yes, and in the weft of its beliefs (*Glauben*). The point of all this is that human beings (this is so Anglo-Saxon, so evocative of empiricism and of its skeptical mood, that one is tempted to say, "Humean" beings) are dominated by a practical necessity, no different from the one that impels them to say "I" (we shall see this promptly). Lichtenberg writes, "First we must believe, and then we believe" (K 136). A force, which proceeds from our own nature, imposes belief upon us, be it in God, immortality, or causality. And this infiltrates our cognitive power: "We cannot say how anything would have turned out but only how we believe it would have turned out [*nur wie sie meinen, daß sie sich zugetragen hätte*]" (C 375). This necessity is determinant to such a degree that, "with most people, disbelief in one thing is founded on blind belief in another" (L 674).

Against this incarcerating imposition the motto and the insistent exercise of *thinking by oneself* (which would also be another figure) thrive and work, and language plays a leading role therein. And this is something that has the air of a paradox, for the same absolute indifference of language with respect to all our semiotic intentions is what can free us from that imposition, however much that imposition is itself nourished by such indifference. Let me try to explain this.

What one might call, using a word that I've already employed, "the automatism of language" (I have the impression that Lichtenberg could be described as one of the fundamental precursors of the acknowledgment of this interesting trait, not in the sense in which Breton deemed to understand it but in the neighborhood of Kleist) gives occasion to many of Lichtenberg's most disturbing, disconcerting, or simply paradoxical annotations. It is what I would like to name the figure of the *aboli bibelot*. This expression, taken from a sonnet by Mallarmé, although it surely points to something very different, attracts me as a way of designating something like the entropy of meaning caused by the imperturbable functioning of language, completely apart from the *intention* of the speaker. (Similarly, *aboli bibelot*, I suppose, does not *describe* a disintegrated trinket so much as *accomplish* the abolition in the expression itself, in that sort of spiral that withdraws toward itself, in itself—"spiral aspired" is the translation that occurred to Octavio Paz for Mallarmé's peculiar expression.)

The paradigm of all this is well known: "A *knife without blade*, from which the handle is missing";[11] or another comes near: "A screw without a beginning" (J 434), which brings us back to the spiral. In the series administrated by this putative figure, I will simply catalog a small collection of pieces, without further commentary. I begin with some that, in various ways, touch on the theme of death (although, in saying it this way, I confess, I'm guilty of a gross simplification):

> In the end, a tomb is always the best fortress against the storms of destiny. (D 143)

> Undoubtedly, the strangest thing about this thought is that if he had it a half minute later, he would have had it after his death. (G 186)

> An autopsy cannot uncover those faults that end with death. (J 382)

One should also include in the catalog this discrete derision of the usually unnoticed inertias of language, which perhaps reveals something of what we read before under the heading of "common philosophy":

> When our late cow still lived, a lady once said in Göttingen. (G 198)

More malicious is the following:

> Due to his peculiar head, the little brother got a little position in the *Theatro anatomico* of G.... Namely, he came into the world dead, and now he is stored there in alcohol. (UB 14)[12]

Or consider the nonsense of religion and eschatology, carried along the rail of exorbitant analogies:

> Just as they paint a zero over the heads of saints. (F 167)

> Church steeples, reversed funnels to conduct prayer to heaven. (UB 8)

> There lie the potatoes now, and they sleep with their back turned to their resurrection. (G 191)

And to these samples of language's anomalous functioning, favored by a peculiar kind of aphasia—if I may express myself in these terms—because they mark the disorder between the linguistic performance, the intellectual exercise, and the very conditions of comprehension, I add these other absurdities *sine glossa*:

> A fish that drowned in air. (J 469)

> If you can hit a judicious man and turn him stupid, I don't see why one cannot hit a stupid man and turn him smart. (G 222)

> He fell in love with the beloved God. (J 158)

> He who is in love with himself has in his love at least the advantage that he will not have many rivals. (H 31)

Or finally, this one, which I especially like:

> The performances of those born blind are proof of how far the spirit can go when it encounters difficulties. (D 296)

All of these, I think, are short circuits of meaning (and I guess that this description should fit a man who was an electrician), short circuits that are flagrant infractions of both logic and common sense (I say "both," for it is well known that logic and common sense are not always compatible). These short circuits of meaning are possible because of the linguistic mechanism, the automatism of language, that happens either because of the inertia of grammatical or syntactical structures against the grain of what is said or because of the persistence of rhetorical codifications, turns of phrase, collisions, or abrupt discords between things invoked or suggested by the discourse—that is, collisions or divorces between the reference, the referent, and the way of referring. The curious thing about all this is that it does not have to do merely with incongruities that one could put aside in a fit of anger or with a condescending smile; rather, in the style of the "new looks through old holes," the incongruities have about them the air of a radical emancipation, one that frees the rebellious swarm of possibilities from the more or less stagnant ground of our representations, uses, and relations.[13] This is what I called the "economy of the surplus."

The point is that language, independently from us and from our will of meaning (which is frequently willfulness), is a store, as it were, of *unthought* riches. The following note, which suggests this, delighted Heidegger, who chose it as an epigraph for a late essay: "Those who think a great deal for themselves will find much wisdom recorded in language. We probably do not add it all ourselves, but much wisdom does reside there, just as in proverbs" (J 443).[14] This would be, then, the specific turn of the enlightened "to think by oneself," an exhortation that Lichtenberg advances in his most peculiar style: to open oneself to the *unthought*.[15] (And I am tempted to say that this figure of the *unthought* is the counter-figure or the *pendant* of language.) This is the corrective that he applies to the privilege of reason as the principle and faculty of the Enlightenment's program (acknowledging its limitations) and that makes place, without losing the prerogatives of thought, for the density and the original strangeness of that "self" that is existence and body. Therefore, to think by oneself has the character of a *cogito interruptus*. I suggest, then, this other figure, if you'll pardon my use of such a hackneyed formula, only with the intention of proposing the idea of an interruption in the course and discourse of thinking. This is perhaps the very nature of what I referred to above as an *ocurrencia* and of its multiple appearances in Lichtenberg's *Waste Books*.[16] Wherever there is interruption, there is also something that interrupts, or at least something that makes itself known by virtue of the interruption: I would dare to say that this is existence, experienced in a manner suggested by the following passage: "a profound philosophy is often required to restore to our feelings their initial state of innocence: to extricate one's *self* [*sich*] from the detritus of alien ideas [*fremder Dinge*], to begin to feel for one*self* [*selbst*], to speak for one*self*, and, I might almost say, to exist for oneself [*auch einmal selbst zu existieren*]" (B 264).

It is a matter, then, of a *cogito* that bursts in the sudden incident of the "it occurs to me ... ," making thinking and existence briefly coincide. It is somewhat odd—assuming I've grasped the issue—that it is precisely language that permits this sudden coincidence, but perhaps it receives the necessary force from its peculiar anteriority with respect to everyone that could be conceived as an already-constituted human being. In a certain way, it might be possible to maintain that Lichtenberg belongs to that lineage of cavillous men who have felt the inhumanity of language, its radical *impersonality*. For, after all, the aforesaid *cogito* occurs outside the self, or at least it has the curious virtue of producing what could be called a diminishing of the self, slimming it and pushing it to the surface and, in the end, proving its merely hypothetical nature.

> We become conscious of certain representations that are not dependent upon us; others, at least we believe, are dependent upon us; where is the boundary? We know only the existence of our sensations, representations, and thoughts. *It thinks* [*es denkt*], we should say, just as one says, *it lightnings* [*es blitzt*]. To say *cogito* is already too much if we translate it as *I think*. To assume the *I*, to postulate it, is a practical necessity. (K 76)

In this primordial state of innocence, thinking is not something we possess; it's something that happens to us, almost as a natural phenomenon. "All motion in the world has its cause in something that is not motion; why, then, should the universal force not just as well be the cause of my thoughts as it is of fermentation?" (E 32).

It may seem strange that the sharpest point of individuation in thinking and in language coincides entirely with something that, if it is not straightforwardly impersonal, assumes a quality very similar to it.[17] This, which is perhaps the most original skeptical trait in Lichtenberg, is also what confers the highest importance upon the effort toward a progressive reduction of intentional knowledge, a return, so to speak, to innocence, from which the veridical determination of *the condition of the human being* might also be drawn: "Every moment we do things of which we are unaware, and this ability continues to grow; in the end, man will do everything without knowing it and will literally become a rational *animal*. Reason approaches animality" (F 424).

Perhaps this is what identifies *dreams* (this will be my last figure) as a conspicuous model of such a *cogito*. The experience of dreams was decisive for Lichtenberg for many reasons. He was a hypochondriac (he used to say that the only part of the world on which thoughts have an influence is one's own body) and, in attempting to get rid of his sufferings, asked for the help of a Jewish doctor named Amschel, who considered that the only cure possible was to bring to consciousness what unconsciously unsettled the patient.

> I once again commend dreams. In dreams we live and perceive no less than while awake, and one is just as important as the other. It is among the virtues of man that he dreams *and knows it*. But we have yet scarcely made best use of this. The dream is a life which, combined with our remaining life, constitutes what we call human life. Our dreaming merges gradually into our waking life so that we cannot tell where waking life begins. (F 743)

So, then, is it possible to think a theory of the insignificant? It would be something like a "theory of the folds in a pillow [*Theorie der Falten in dem Kopfkissen*]" (L 476).

Chapter Four

Kleist, the Puppets, and the Vanishing Point of Meaning

AT THE BEGINNING OF THE SECOND SECTION of Sigmund Freud's essay on "The Uncanny," the founder of psychoanalysis alludes critically to the interpretation of this affect proposed by the psychologist Eduard Jentsch, which states (in Freud's word's) that the paradigmatic case concerns "doubts [over] whether an apparently animate being is really alive; or conversely, whether a lifeless object might not be in fact animate" (244/226).[1] The theoretical matrix of this interpretation attributes this strange feeling, which is in the end the most radical feeling of strangeness, to a condition of intellectual uncertainty—that is, to a state of insurmountable perplexity about the identity and ontological status of an object, phenomenon, or situation. It is well known that Freud's interest concerns here his conviction that the roots of the uncanny lie deeper in psychic life and that the affect cannot be reduced to intellectual confusion. However, his refusal of Jentsch's explanation, repeatedly pronounced in the essay, is marked by signs of vivid hesitation,[2] as if Freud himself suffered an "intellectual uncertainty" concerning the theoretical localization of the uncanny.

Soon after registering his doubt about the thesis of perplexity, Freud invokes the cases that Jentsch presents as typical or, at least, as effective illustrations of the feeling: "waxwork figures, ingeniously constructed dolls and automata" (244/226). The impression that these artifacts provoke is comparable to the one produced by "epileptic fits, and . . . manifestations of insanity, because these excite in the spectator the impression of automatic, mechanical processes at work behind the ordinary appearance of mental activity" (244/226). Freud's reticence and disbelief notwithstanding (he invokes Jentsch's writing "without entirely accepting this author's view" [244/226]), his examination in the second section, which forms the center of the essay, will be initiated with recourse to E. T. A. Hoffmann, the same master of the uncanny mentioned by Jentsch, and to his tale "The Sand-Man." We know Freud's argument: the puppet Olympia, an automaton with which the unfortunate Nathaniel falls in love and an object of dispute between Professor Spalanzani and the optician Coppola, cannot be the main cause of the tale's uncanny effect; rather, this has to be found in the motif itself of the "sand-man" and the atavistic anxiety associated with it. Discarding the puppet, further stimulated by the "satiric" turn of the "episode of Olympia,"[3] does not prevent Freud from disclosing its meaning in a lengthy footnote, with the diagnosis that it is nothing more than "the materialization of Nathaniel's feminine attitude towards his father in his infancy" and that the obsessive love that the protagonist feels for Olympia is due to a narcissistic complex (249n1/232n1).

However, the exclusion is not as total as it would seem to be. Apart from the fact that the diagnosis reinserts the puppet into the series of constituents responsible for the uncanny effect, one also has to pay attention to the weight that Freud assigns to the motif of the double among the factors of *das Unheimliche*, a motif whose discernment starts precisely from a consideration of the child's wish to see the puppet from his or her play become a living creature. Olympia's reinsertion is characteristic of the essay's tortuous course and of Freud's discussion with Jentsch, which betrays a certain difficulty. And one should not fail to recognize the link that connects the structure of the double to the operation of return that Freud privileges in explaining the feeling of the uncanny: the return necessarily brings about (or is caused by) an effect of splitting.

Surely, one could not exclude from the domain of the uncanny the puppet, the automaton, the living device, and all those other uncomfortable apparatuses that fluctuate between the natural and the artificial, the biological and the technical, the archaic and the modern. Romantic fantasy and its wealth of images have filled literature with figures that have been deeply engraved in our collective imagination: Hoffmann's Olympia has been followed by Dr. Frankenstein's monster in Mary Shelley's novel, Auguste de Villiers de L'Isle-Adam's *L'Ève future*, Gustav Meyrinck's *The Golem*, and, marking an ironic turn, Marcel Duchamp's *The Bride Stripped Bare by Her Bachelors, Even*. And all of this without mentioning the crowd of ill-fated freaks scattered throughout hundreds of narratives in the late nineteenth and early twentieth centuries, who, headed by the patchwork monster and the hemophilic count, find their true glory in the horror films of the past century or the hybridizations and hyper-technological products of the present, cyborgs included.

My interest here is to add a figure that precedes all of them, a figure to which in a certain sense all of them could be traced back.

A CURIOUS TEXT

Heinrich von Kleist (1777–1811) writes in 1810 a little text entitled "On the Theater of Marionettes" ("Über das Marionettentheater").[4] The text is a sort of a puzzle for interpreters and commentators and has accumulated a burden of secondary literature that reflects very well the difficulties of comprehension that it poses. Such difficulties have nothing to do with obscurities but concern the formal and thematic determinations of the story, peculiarly reluctant to a univocal reading.

Therefore, the most conspicuous question that can be addressed to this brief narrative is, *what, in the end, is it about?* The story begins conventionally ("Als ich ... "—"When I ... one evening ... " [555/264]), not promising much more than an anecdote about a certain character, Mr. C, a successful dancer. But it rapidly turns into a dialogue that, alternating between direct and indirect discourse, revolves around Mr. C's bold opinion about puppets' incomparable dancing grace. The very rhythm of the narrative, which at the beginning seems to advance very swiftly, slows down as soon as the narrator says that he has the feeling that his partner's opinion is something more than merely incidental: "Since, by the way he said it, the remark seemed to me more than the stuff of idle fancy [*ein bloßer Einfall*], I sat down with him [*ließ ich mich bei ihm nieder*] to learn more about the underlying premises for such an extraordinary statement" (556/264). Hereafter, the sedentary stance will be, as it were, the solid basis for all the things that will be said.

Of course, the dancer's opinion has an aesthetic connotation, but he backs it with ingenious geometrical and mechanical explanations that have at their core the law of gravity. To these explanations—which aside from being ingenious are captious too—is added, by way of token or example, a remark on the prostheses with which the unfortunate who have lost their limbs manage to make gracious movements. Yet precisely at the moment when the dialogue seems to reach its natural conclusion, something more remains to be cleared up—"but I sensed that he still had more on his mind, and bid him continue" (556/269)—and the conversation goes further toward new dimensions with the introduction of the difference between puppet, man, and God and with the postulation of an identical grace at both ends to the detriment of human virtue. The aesthetic meaning of the term *grace* extends or changes to attain theological scope, and gravity, as a law that governs physical bodies, drifts onto the theological concept of the fall and the loss of the paradisiacal condition; the fall and this loss are inseparably related to the function of consciousness, which spoils natural grace. This is the *thesis*—though not necessarily the thesis of the story, or of Kleist himself, but the thesis of which the dancer is spokesman and the narrator accomplice; it is also ours, as readers, as long as we grant it provisional credit in order to follow the thread. (For, being a matter of puppets, this seems to be the point.) At this moment, the narrator, who wants to show his clear awareness about the inconvenience that is consciousness itself, tells an anecdote that, if not a direct proof of the new assertions, nevertheless has the capacity to offer its timely illustration. His partner replies by telling another anecdote that, according to his own statement, must have a clear relationship with the former. The narrator's anecdote serves to make evident the extent to which the person who is conscious of his or her own elegance suffers irreparable damages to his or her grace for this very reason. In turn, the dancer's story introduces another figure to the ball: animal nature, embodied by a bear who happens to be unrivaled in fencing. As soon as the story's credibility is established, the conclusion rushes in: consciousness being the constitutive hindrance to grace, the latter is recovered if consciousness becomes infinite. If man eats again from the Tree of Knowledge, innocence is regained, and this is, as the dancer notes with a definitive tone, "the final chapter of the history of the world" (563/273, translation modified). In the most expeditious manner, totality is shown to us in abbreviation.

What is this narrative about? I asked. Is it a reflection on aesthetics supported by speculative reinforcements? The parade of almost all the arts seems to give occasion for thinking that this is the case: dance, theater, painting, and sculpture (not to forget fencing) form a sort of frieze supported by the literary space. But the speculations on grace, consciousness, and loss (and possible recovery) of innocence suggest another register. Is it, then, the sketch of a theological or metaphysical treatise, projected onto a scenario enlivened by artistic motives? Is it a parable of the human condition? Before answering such questions (and there are many others we could add), these alternatives suggest that the first of them, notwithstanding its apparent cautiousness, perhaps takes for granted something that is by no means guaranteed. Is it truly a narrative? We should in the first place determine whether the piece we are reading is a story, a tale, or something else that is invested with narrative traits. Is it a divertimento whose virtue lies in the plays of fiction, or does it, rather, have a pretension to truth? There is in the first place, then, the question of form. The issue of whether the piece is a narrative or a treatise, an allegory or a parable, is not innocuous, because it affects another question, which is one not of form but of content: What is the intention that governs this discourse? Is what is said a joke or serious? More briefly: What is its discursive status?

For all these reasons, any hypothesis would certainly be premature if one does not first examine the diverse elements that converge in the text. To begin, let us talk simply of the *figures* that are invoked in it, of the *faculties* or *gifts* that it recognizes, and of the *themes* to which it alludes. The figures were already mentioned: the puppet, the human being, the animal (the bear), and God (or a god); the gifts: grace and innocence confronted with consciousness, reflection, and knowledge; the themes: the aesthetic, the geometrical, the technical, and the theological. One is tempted to draw a chart on which to specify the places that those elements would occupy, but, before undertaking such an illustration, one might realize the complexity of the task; indeed, one would be inclined to anticipate its total failure. The overdetermination of each of the elements is such that none of them could be univocally specified, and the displacements of meaning that affect the terms implied (and they do not concern only the eminent pair *grace* and *gravity*, which I shall soon approach) are so acute that their reduction to a unique sequence does not seem to be possible: a more precise inspection of the text shows that, despite appearances, it does not entail an *argument* that permits proving the *conclusion* to which it arrives. For the same reason, it would be difficult to read the assumed "conclusion" as the assertion or set of assertions that are logically required and logically enforced by the preceding development. Indeed, with its peculiar and almost apocalyptical tenor, it seems to be stated *on the other side* of what is said, as if it were coming back from the reverse of the text, similar to the lines and specular images that Mr. C describes, in this final stage, as going to the infinite and unexpectedly returning from it.

In a certain way, the assumed "conclusion" is the vanishing point of the text, from which its meaning(s) is (are) constituted and toward which it (they) at the same time is (are) driven, so that this is precisely a text that runs off, so to speak, *vanishings of meaning*. But the peculiarity of these vanishings has nothing to do with suppressions or providential hiatuses; quite the contrary, we constantly have in view the meanings that are vanishing, and we can follow those meanings with apparent continuity and consequence (and this amounts to the argumentative appearance of the text) up to the moment when suddenly, by virtue of an unexpected slip, which we nevertheless cannot attribute to negligence or abuse, they change their aspect entirely, become averse to any administration, or bring along with them a shadow that we cannot determine. My efforts will lie mainly in providing not proofs but at least some traces of plausibility for this idea, turning back on the issues that I have already sketched and bringing on some new ones.

An addendum on the peculiarity of this text might still be a useful addition to in this preamble. I have spoken of "vanishing": a stubborn logician could not fault Kleist for having composed the piece by sheer force of rhetoric, at least not in the usual sense, which empowers rhetoric to cover the gaps of an argument or, rather (to speak with Plato and Aristotle and the ancient treatises), to invest a certain discourse with the seeming aspect of an argument that actually is not one. Quite the contrary, in Kleist's text, which undoubtedly obeys an astounding rhetorical construction (for it involves—from an exemplary point of view—*all* types of discourse and *all* tropes), the gaps, hiatuses, and slips are in full view. The question *what is this story about?* probably cannot be tackled—let alone resolved—if one does not ask at the same time, *what kind of text is this?* For it isn't clear that it is a story at all.

GRAVITY AND GRACE

Let us begin with the most notorious point: I was talking about the change of meaning of the words *grace* and *gravity*. The first appearance of the former term (*graziös*) openly proclaims its pertinence to the vocabulary of aesthetics, and with this meaning it governs the entire first half of the story until the entrance of the speculations about the puppet, man, and God. *Anmut*, which is often translated as "grace," is another important word invoked by Mr. C, and one cannot avoid recalling Schiller's essay "On Grace and Dignity" ("Über Anmut und Würde"), which formally establishes the aesthetic relevance of the term, referring it closely to beauty, unlike dignity, which belongs to the rule of the sublime. Indeed, Paul de Man, who on several occasions mentions

Schiller as the initiator of "aesthetic ideology," reads "On the Marionette Theatre" to a large extent as a deconstruction of that ideology, and of course the word *Anmut*, with its meaning pattern belonging to the great project of "aesthetic education," is for that purpose specifically cited.[5] It is precisely in the more or less extensive passage in which the theme of the Tree of Knowledge and the loss of innocence is introduce that, one witnesses the displacement by which the text slips from aesthetic meaning to theological meaning: as the dancer recalls the third chapter of Genesis—the one that tells the story of the primordial Fall—as an indispensable premise for adequate comprehension of what he is saying, the narrator answers that he "know[s] all too well what a mess consciousness had made of the natural grace [*in der natürlichen Grazie*] of Man" (560/270).[6] From now on, the theological meaning will prevail in the argument, notwithstanding its persistent contamination by the aesthetic meaning. One should ask which kind of contamination this is and, in the first place, if it is one at all. For I guess it would not be a mistake to think that during the eighteenth and early nineteenth centuries the discourse of aesthetics was, to a large extent, a secularization of theology and a sensibilization of metaphysics, the yields of which are collected and capitalized in the domains of ethics and politics. If such a hypothesis were valid, it would not be adequate to read the change of meaning on which I am commenting as a capricious slip; rather, it is a clear hint to the essential connivance between aesthetics and theology.[7]

Anyway, the arrangements of this first "vanishing point," this first "leak" of meaning, are not to be overlooked. When exposing the geometrical-mechanical characteristics that explain the peculiar "grace" of the puppet's movements, and referring to the line determined by the center of gravity—which, as is well known, is the authentic key of the whole matter—Mr. C notes that this line, as considered from this point of view, is entirely simple and obvious but that, from another point of view, it is "something very mysterious [*etwas sehr Geheimnisvolles*]," for "it was nothing less than *the pathway of the dancer's soul*" (557/266, emphasis added), which seems to demand from the puppeteer not only a certain knowledge but mainly an appropriate attitude and dancing skill. It is true that this requisite is quickly discarded, at least by way of hypothesis, but the mention of the "soul [*Seele*]," of "sensibility [*Empfindung*]" (557/266), of the "*spirit* [*Geist*]" (559/269), which are all values that lay the foundations of beauty and aesthetic grace, brings along with these values something that seems to be incommensurable with mere mechanism and, along those lines, something that is determinant of aesthetic manifestation. Nevertheless, we will not look very far to find a reason for its hypothetical exclusion: the negative advantage that the puppets have over human beings lies in the fact that the former lack every affectation (*Ziererei*), which consists in the disagreement between the soul and the point of gravity. It is because human dancers do not have their soul hanging by a thread, or perhaps because they have it so all the time, that the accident—the constant proclivity to fall, if I may use this pleonasm—is for them the rule; they lose foot and step in comparison to the borrowed skill of the puppets. What appears in this way on the surface of the text is a paradox, which could appropriately be called the paradox of art.

This brings us to the second advantage, which is positive, and, along with it, to the theme of gravity. Puppets, argues Mr. C, "have the advantage in that they are gravity-defiant" (559/269), because they are moved by a stronger force than the one that binds them to earth. Because the souls of these anthropomorphic dolls hang by a thread, because they have neither soul nor spirit, or because they have a borrowed soul that is nothing other than the prolongation of the thread, they are paradoxically endowed with a lissomeness that no human being can defy. "The puppets only need the ground, as do the elves, to graze it [*streifen*], and thereby to reanimate [*neu zu beleben*] the swing of their limbs against the momentary resistance; we need it to rest [*ruhen*] on it and recuperate from the strain of the dance: for us the moment of contact clearly plays no part in the dance and we have no other recourse but to get it over and done with as quickly as possible" (559–60/269). That is, certainly, in order to hide it from others' eyes, which is a fundamental concern of the dancer, but also to hide it from oneself: there is no doubt that in the *rest* that we imperiously need lies death concealed, the definitive accident; the mere mention of life concerning the puppet's motions, and its omission in the case of humans, should induce us to ponder the issue, and Kleist is certainly sharpening the paradox.

Of course, the text does not accomplish the journey from mechanical to theological meaning (it would be redundant), from grace to the original Fall, but this is precisely the sense in which it teaches us to understand the handicap of human beings. An additional paradox? The bear, which is a symbol of strength and heaviness, is the consummate fencer; it does not require anything other than the unhurried skill dictated by its nature with neither delay nor hesitation, because that skill is absolute when compared with the abilities of any human opponent.

INTERLUDE: ABOUT FALLING

The fall, physical or metaphysical, is thus at the story's center of gravity. De Man, among others, reasonably calls attention to the many variations of the German terms *Fall* and *fallen* that happen in the opuscule.[8] In this interlude I will just point them out.

Fall, the noun, as is known, designates the fall (*casus*) and also the incidence, the incident, the case: in this text it is employed with this meaning when Mr. C offers his geometrical explanation of the puppet's mechanical movements and once again in the story of the bear. The verb *fallen* means "to fall." Both noun and verb are capital members of a large family that Kleist exploits with as much sharpness as moderation. First, there is the sudden idea (*Einfall*): we saw that the storyteller warns us that Mr. C's opinion about the excellence of the puppets is not a mere idea that he improvises; what he says must have more weight. Then there is, without any need to utter the term, everything that marks the human inferiority compared to the peculiar weightlessness of the little dolls, which are always lighter than the force impelling and raising them, because it is not that the puppet simply has no weight or that it is miraculously alien to the all-embracing law of gravity, which admits of no exemption in the physical world: the point is that we fall inversely to the puppet's motion, that is to say, *downwards*; this is our fatal automatism. As a corollary we can infer that, if we could reverse our fall, we would be back in grace. To put it differently, gravity is perhaps nothing more than the manifestation or the reflection of grace in a fallen world.

A third item: the incident (*Vorfall*) that robs the beautiful ephebe of his innocence and his paradise and that, as we shall see, is something of a parodic duplicate of the original sin (and for this the German tongue has *Sündenfall*). Fourth, if we leave out the use of the verb *fallen* to describe the unfruitful assaults that the dancer launches against the undaunted fencing beast, there is the applause (*Beifall*) with which the narrator receives the story of the bear, declaring his full faith in its veracity.

Lastly, at the end of the text, the term figures with a new variation in the final question that the narrator addresses to his partner: "In which case ... would we then have to eat of the fruit of the tree of knowledge again to fall back [*zurückzufallen*] into the state of innocence?" (563/273). To fall backwards, then, back to innocence, to come back—but, we know, only if the knowledge that hinders us has passed through infinity—to a time before the first Fall, which is only possible by virtue of an infinite afterwards, which leaves us back—and this is a second fall—in that absolute before that is grace itself. How can we read this relapse (*Zurückfallen*), how to think of this relapse? How can the fall be reversed? How to fall inversely? Perhaps all these questions are one and the same question; perhaps the answer—which is not given here and is therefore deferred—is the entire text.[9]

BAD CONSCIOUSNESS

"Such missteps," says Mr. C, referring to the reason for which poor human dancers have to yield to the invincible supremacy of his admired puppets, "are unavoidable ever since we ate of the fruit of the tree of knowledge. But Paradise is bolted shut and the cherub is on our tail; we are obliged to circle the globe and go around to the other side to see if perhaps there's a back way in" (559/269). I will not dwell upon the Kafkaesque resemblance of this commentary; my aim is to underline that this is a notorious twist—in a text made up of twists and breaks—that preludes the theory with which Mr. C supports his daring opinion. A theory, that is to say, that considers knowledge to be a condemnation and that is widely known in all its aspects, a topic of Romanticism mainly in what concerns the hypothesis on the "last chapter" about which the text's last phrase speaks: the fortunate recovery of innocence at the end of the journey through the infinity of knowledge—or, if you prefer, the journey of knowledge to the infinite.[10] Anyway, it is the narrator that introduces the word *consciousness*: "I responded that I did, indeed, know all too well what a mess consciousness had made of the natural grace of Man" (560/270). Consciousness is above all the consciousness of oneself, self-consciousness, the constitutive fold that consciousness is in and of itself and without which there is no consciousness at all. Puppets are exempt from it, and they owe to this prerogative their perfect dexterity in dance. So, the designation of consciousness (of self-consciousness) as a hindrance is something like the epistemological, metaphysical formalization of those two traits that, not present in puppets, bother human beings: psychologically, the affectation; physically, the weight. And these are paradoxical nuisances because the soul, excessively attentive to itself, weighs more than the body by virtue of affection, and consciousness weighs more by virtue of the gravity of the body in that it fears the fall through which, as I said, death makes its dull repercussion heard.

Well, then, in order to win credit, the narrator tells the story of a candid young man who lost his innocence due to a remark that made him notice his natural grace, which he lost from that very moment on, becoming ever more obsessed with himself. It is worth recalling the passage *in extenso*:

> "Some three years ago," I recounted, "I happened to be bathing beside a young man, blessed at the time with an astounding beauty. He must have been about sixteen years old, and manifested only the faintest first traces of vanity fostered by the favor of women. It so happened that we had both shortly before seen the young man pulling the thorn out of his foot in Paris; a copy of that famous sculpture can be found in most German collections. A glance he cast into a large mirror at the very same moment at which he set his foot on a stool to dry it reminded him of it; he smiled and remarked that he had just made a discovery. In fact, I had at that same moment made the same association; but, whether to test that his innate grace was still intact, or to put a healthy damper on his vanity, I laughed and told him he was seeing things! He blushed and raised the foot again, to show me; but, as one might well have predicted, the attempt failed. Befuddled, he raised his foot a third and fourth time, indeed he raised it ten more times: but for naught! He was simply unable to repeat the same movement—and what's more, the movements that he did manage to make looked so comic that I was hard pressed to restrain my laughter."
>
> "From that day, indeed, as it were, from that moment on, the young man underwent an incomprehensible transformation. He began to stand for days at a time in front of the mirror; and he lost one charm after another. An invisible and inconceivable force, like an iron net, seemed to settle over and impinge upon the free play of movements, and after a year had gone by, not a trace could be found of the charming allure that had once entranced all those whose eyes fell upon him. I know another living soul who witnessed that strange and unfortunate incident, and could confirm, word for word, my account." (560–61/270–71)

The story is loaded with too many implications—almost every word in it carries grave associations and echoes—to attempt a commentary that could take into account its multiple intentions. It is indeed a sort of *Urszene* of the birth of consciousness (a birth that certainly could not take place if there were in its imminent bearer no traces of it, and these are those embryonic vestiges of vanity), which replicates in a different setting that other primordial scene of the Fall, seduction included. (And this retrospective leak or vanishing point might be suggested by the curious detail concerning the witness who could confirm what is told: a man who is still "living," witness to an incident that happened only three years ago.) Needless to say, this evocation is complicated by the inevitable allusion to the myth of Narcissus.

For this is undoubtedly a scene of mirrors. Busy with drying himself after the bath (and nudity is not a minor detail in this scene), the beautiful boy gazes at his own figure in a mirror, and he recognizes the resemblance to the effigy of the Roman bronze called the *Spinario*, which shows a gentle ephebe who is trying to take a thorn out of his right foot.[11] The calamitous instant will cause this youngster to be a captive from now on of the reflected image, at the cost of all his charms. What I have called seduction mediates between one mirroring and the other. The narrator, who certainly has made the same recognition, puts him to the test (*um die Sicherheit der Grazie, die ihm beiwohnte, zu prüfen*) or seeks to mend his incipient vanity. It is this provocation that injects the adolescent with poison, and he is forced to react by searching in the eyes of his companion for another mirror, a third one, apart from the mirror in which he sees himself and apart from his own gaze on the reflecting surface, which could close and certify the image's circuit: as long as the testimony is not guaranteed, all confidence in his own grace is affected by a helpless fragility.[12] We already know that the results of this effort are the catastrophe of grace, ridicule and melancholy, and condemnation to a fourth mirror, abyssal and sterile, all signs of the authentication of consciousness. But, for this, that third instance and the deliberate blindness of the third mirror have been necessary. (This multiplication of mirrors is precisely what one could call a "logic of the double," which is perfectly uncanny.) Although the premonitory traces of vanity are already present, a consciousness is not born without the intervention of this third instance that, withdrawing from the circle of identity, incites it. Put otherwise, a consciousness is not born without the prosthesis of consciousness, without this other that unhappily prescribes for it the *autos* of self-consciousness. It is the thorn that splits consciousness and hurts it without fail, as the one and only stipulation of identity.

AN ART OF BEARS?

Without any mediation, Mr. C pays for his partner's story with another anecdote from his own experience. I say he pays for it, and this is already a way of interpreting a step that is not transparent at all. "In this context" or "in such a case [*Bei dieser Gelegenheit*]," says the dancer, "I must tell you another story [*muß ich Ihnen eine andere Geschichte erzählen*]" (560/271). It is not easy to understand why—or how—one story should give occasion to the other, on what account telling a second story would be something of a necessity, an obligation: as if with the first one a contract had been established that now has to be fulfilled. What's more, in hearing the story, one understands that the intimation—"you will immediately comprehend the connection" (560/271)—is abusive, if not for the alleged fittingness, at least for the supposed easiness.

To the story, then. During a visit to the estate of a wealthy aristocrat, the dancer is challenged by the aristocrat's elder son to a duel with rapiers; although the son judges himself dexterous in fencing, the dancer has a clear advantage and defeats him. The young man declares that he has found his master, and, in retribution, he, his brothers, and the father himself lead Mr. C to a shed so that the dancer can meet his own master:

> When I appeared before him in stunned amazement, the bear stood upright on its hind legs, with his back to a post to which he was attached, his right paw raised and ready to strike, looking me straight in the eye: this was his fencing position. And finding myself face to face with such an opponent, I did not know if I was dreaming; but Sir von G ... egged me on: 'Thrust man! Thrust!' he said. See if you can teach him a thing or two! And having gotten over my initial amazement, I lunged with my rapier; the bear made a very slight movement with his paw and parried my thrust. I tried with feints to trick him; the bear did not budge. And once again I lunged with a nimble stroke that would have pierced without fail any human breast; but the bear made a very slight motion with its paw and parried the thrust. Now I was almost as befuddled as had been the young Sir von G. ... The bear's perfect calm helped rob me of my own composure, I varied thrusts and feints, sweat dripped from my brow: for naught! Not only did the bear, like the foremost fencer in the world, parry all my thrusts; but, unlike any human counterpart would have done, not a single time did he go for my feints: Looking at me eye to eye, as if he could read my soul, he stood stock still, paw raised and ready, and if my thrusts were ruses, he did not even budge. (562/272)

Leaving aside the doubts about the significance of this story in the sequence of the text (you might recall that it is in no way easy to determine the statute of the latter, whether it is a narrative or an essay, whether it belongs to the field of fiction or of knowledge), this scene, taken by itself, has something that, in spite of its verisimilitude, diffuses a mist of suspicion around it. This is perhaps the effect of the absolute economy of the situation, the unmediated confrontation between play and seriousness, between art and nature, effort and facility, cunning and simplicity, waste and calmness, simulation and knowledge. This economy, this freedom from traits and events, shorn of every accessory and adornment, invites an allegorical reading, as if what is at stake in this incident were something more, much more, than the incident itself—say, a truth. But what would be the key for deciphering the allegory? I guess we would seek it in vain outside the text. The problem is that, if it has to do with an allegory here, it has only those keys that the text itself, as text, provides, and the text is a system of displacements, so that a fixed key—a univocal and stable principle of meaning—is not something to which we could aspire. There is no dominant meaning to which we could appeal in order to control the text; quite the contrary, the text is the a priori of its meaning. But this also means that the a priori has fallen here right into contingency. The commerce between truth and lie is as fluent as it is ungovernable; if it is an allegory, it is an allegory in closed circuit.

If I'm not mistaken, de Man reads the text in this way and posits that Kleist "puts his own text *en abŷme* in the figure of the super-reader or super-author made invincible by his ability to know feint from what is so aptly called, in German, *Ernstfall*" (*Rhetoric* 282). So, the story becomes an allegory of writing, and fencing is certainly a good metaphor for the latter and for the inevitably elusive game between what is mere play and what is serious, which only a super-reader or a super-author could administrate, with the additional proviso that this perfect administration implies the end of the game in the still center of death—that is, of pure seriousness.

I was talking about displacements. Notwithstanding the analytic perspicacity of de Man, let me add some elements. I said that one does not quite comprehend, at least immediately, the relation between this story and the preceding one or the connection it could have with all that comes before it. If one examines the matter more closely, one can notice certain signs, but they are precisely signs of displacement—that is, signs that are not to be understood in terms of axiomatic contents but rather to be analyzed following the transformation to which they are subjected. The bear: it lies in the antipodes of puppets; if the latter are lissome, light, agile, the former is a symbol of gravity—in both senses: by virtue of its bulk and weight and of its seriousness and circumspection—and remains almost motionless, in addition to being chained to a post. And, nevertheless, this opposing figure ratifies the human disadvantage. This figure and the previous ones share that disturbing automatism that bestows upon them infallibility. If those little dolls, which are pure artifice, pure technical device, can beat with their astounding turns the most distinguished human dancer, the bear, which is pure nature, can humiliate with its dauntlessness the most skillful swordsman. It is tempting to think that the human being is kept as a fixed point of reference. But it isn't so: herein lies the connection with the previous story. You can observe that the victim of the bear is the artist, that is to say, the human being assisted—and this also means enhanced—by art. In the ephebe's anecdote, art is the first mirror in which he gazes at his own figure; it is his model, as the image is repeated by the actual mirror in which the young man discovers the resemblance. The older man who escorts him is the third mirror, the guarantee of resemblance, but the kid, who has scarcely begun to train his natural gifts, lacks art: his resemblance is by chance; he cannot simulate it; he has no management of the feint and succumbs to his own anxiety. The image of Narcissus becomes distorted and dissipates on the surface. It remains the case that the artist finds his master, which has to be—an ironical thrust directed at the heart of Romanticism—nature. And nature is now (you will notice the detail in the scene: face-to-face, looking each other in the eyes) a lucid mirror, an impenetrable gaze, and therefore absolute: "Looking at me eye to eye, as if he could read my soul, he stood stock still." It is another specular scene, which, notwithstanding its playful character, is as ill-starred as the former.

And this scene, like the former, needs to be proved as true. In the same way that the narrator of the first scene was prompted to invoke the testimony of a man who could testify to what he told, the narrator of the second immediately begs his listener's faith: "Do you believe this story [*Glauben Sie diese Geschichte*]?" (563/272). It is a strange question, one that seems to expect from that credit something more than what the contract of conversation demands, something like a seal of truth, which disturbs again every opinion about the status of the text. Stranger, perhaps, is the answer, fired with no delay and giving, more than credit, a devoted credulity: "'Absolutely!' I replied with cheerful applause; 'I'd believe it from the lips of any stranger; all the more so from you!'" (563/272).[13]

ANOTHER INTERLUDE: THE RETURN OF THE IMAGE

The text comes to its end. If we can believe—with a faith similar to the faith the narrator declares—that Mr. C's apparently passing remark involves a doctrine, if, moreover, we can believe that this doctrine would be the *thesis* of the text, it is now time to make the point. And it is apparently in these terms that the dancer's conclusive words might be understood. What at the beginning could have seemed to his amazed interlocutor a simple, witty idea shows up now with consequences that, even on the explanation of the mechanical rudiments of the puppet's elegance, he could not have anticipated:

> "Well then, my fine friend," said Mr. C . . . , "you now have all the knowledge you need to grasp my meaning. We see that in the organic world, to the same degree that reflection gets darker and weaker, grace grows ever more radiant and dominant. But just as two lines intersect on one side of a point, and after passing through infinity, suddenly come together again on the other side; or the image in a concave mirror suddenly reappears before us after drawing away into the infinite distance, so, too, does grace return once perception, as it were, has traversed the infinite—such that it simultaneously appears the purest in human bodily structures that are either devoid of consciousness or which possess an infinite consciousness, such as in the jointed manikin or the god." (563/272–73).

We are brought back to geometry, and, of course, everything turns upon the concept of the infinite, the projection onto the infinite, and the return from the infinite. We are back in geometry, with a complement of optics, which repeats the theme of the mirror precisely in the key of the infinite, and the use of the term *Reflexion*, no doubt, equivocally plays between the order of the mind's operations and that of optical relations, according to a metaphor that is at least as old as the modern age and that is exposed here to its constitutive difficulty (think of the case of the ephebe). With both illustrative instances, what I have called, in a deliberately hesitating manner, the "thesis" of the text is reinforced: if human consciousness, human knowledge, would have likewise (*gleichsam*) "traversed the infinite [*durch ein Unendliches gegangen*]," the grace originally lost would be re-encountered, regained.[14] It isn't clear if this would be to go around the world, entering paradise by the back door, but we have sufficient grounds to guess.

I speak of the thesis *in* the text and not of the text's thesis, because we are not to believe that the great Romantic and idealist promise of redemption, which this passage formulates, is being said straightforwardly, with neither irony nor paradox. But the "thesis" in the text is also the "thesis" in which the text reflects itself, in both senses of the word. This would be the "design" or the "outline" of the text: two lines (two intentions, maybe?) intersecting on one side, going to infinity, and coming back on the reverse side. The return of the image is the return of the text; the truth of the text (if there is one) is encountered in the guise of the infinite that is the text itself, and it is encountered, as we shall see immediately, in an absentminded and prosthetic way and cannot possibly be contained in any consciousness at all, at least not in a consciousness that would be present to itself.

THE PROSTHESIS

I've talked about the exemplary figures of this narration, all of which, according to Mr. C's approach, coincide in the accusation of human deficiency, the handicap that is caused in us by consciousness: the marionette, the bear, God (or a god). But we are forgetting a figure that briefly traverses the story, a human being, a *handicapé* among human beings, for he has suffered the amputation of his legs. And this figure, increasing the narrator's astonishment, also crosses the scene with the utmost grace:

> "Have you," he asked, upon noticing me cast my gaze in silence to the ground, "have you heard of those mechanical limbs that English artists had fashioned for those poor unfortunates who'd lost their own?"
>
> "No," I said. I had never laid eyes on such a thing.
>
> "What a shame," he replied; "for if I told you that these poor unfortunates could dance with them, I almost fear you would not believe it.—Well not exactly dancing! The sphere of their movements is indeed limited; but those movements which they are able to command are executed with a lightness, a serenity, and a gracefulness [*Ruhe, Leichtigkeit und Anmut*] that makes every thinking person stand in awe." (558/267, translation modified)

It isn't without reason that these strangely graceful beings appear precisely here, in almost the exact middle of the story. Of course, they give support to the bold hypothesis of the unrivaled mechanical dancer and, I would confidently say, the hypothesis of the absolute marionette. But they bring along something more as well. The substitute that technology has provided for their missing limbs almost seems to be the supplement that the irrevocably finite consciousness of human beings would require to avoid the hindrance and the clumsiness brought about by their own disposition. It is another instance, inscribed in and in between the lines of the text: if it is not the epic of consciousness, accomplishing from itself, from its principles and conditions, endogenously, as it were, its journey through infinity, it is at least (or solely) the technology or orthopedics that by exogenous means not only substitutes for what is lacking but also (and this is the decisive point) replaces by way of a mechanism what the mind's spontaneity can only ruin;[15] if it is not eschatological consummation, it is at least (or solely) a borrowed redemption. This is the virtue of the prosthesis.

Of course, nobody would believe that this case, which Mr. C invokes in order to foster his hypothesis, also supplies the basis or the key for a supposed thesis of the text, no more than the concluding statement concerning what I've just called the epic of consciousness. No, this resort, this pretext concerning prostheses and their curious therapeutic virtue (which not only substitutes the lack but also cures us of the spirit), is the prosthesis of every thesis of and in the text. And if the text reflects (upon) itself, then what is said here cannot be read only referentially, as if it concerned the case that the dancer brings up or as if it were another tale inside the tale; what is being said here speaks simultaneously of the very form of the text. (We should indeed recognize that every tale that is told in the text speaks, in many different ways, of the same form.)

Maybe this is precisely the "grace" of this text. Maybe its strange, uncanny "grace" consists in its self-reflection, which neither happens nor realizes its truest form without the rupture or the lack for which a prosthesis comes to substitute—not in a particular neuralgic point but in all the points, because they all are neuralgic here—conferring on it that curious movement of a mind that is at every moment *absent*. I guess that it wouldn't be at all inappropriate to maintain that the text itself displays that sort of automatism that it seems to celebrate. After all, the partners appear as if they were manipulated by stage directions in their dialogue (brief indications describing little gestures: to sit down, to look down, to inhale a bit of *rapé*, etc.), indications that, cutting them out like manufactured figures that the author delivers to an exchange that is at once time accidental and mechanical, almost make them marionettes—which are, don't forget, devices made out of prostheses. Maybe the "grace" of this text consists precisely in its prosthetic structure, or, to put it differently, "grace" is prosthesis.

Therefore, this "grace" no longer belongs to the human order. It is, just as the text reiterates in different ways, a post-human "grace" that is here, for a human being, only hinted at, with the insinuation of a latency of all powers of negativity, and this latency—in the figure of this text—is enough to bring about the crisis of the human.

END OF (HI)STORY

The text comes to its end. In addition to Mr. C's closing words, there are still a few things left, the conclusion, let us say. The listener must still prove that he fully understands the issue. (This is also a curiosity of the text, filled with so many instances of proof.) But there is no doubt that the "conclusion" offers obvious anomalies.

The narrator draws it ("then") *absent-mindedly*, "somewhat amused," "a little inattentive [*ein wenig zerstreut*]," and he offers it in addition in the form of a question, which, because the moment of a final assertion, must be a rhetorical one: "In which case . . . would we then have to eat of the fruit of the tree of knowledge again to fall back [*zurückzufallen*] into the state of innocence?" (563/273). But what does it mean to draw a conclusion in the half-abandoned state of inattentiveness? Above all, what does it mean with respect to the *truth* of the text? This is a relevant question, if we have admitted that the piece we are reading might be something more than a mere story, a fictitious divertimento, that it might have a *claim* to truth, notwithstanding the fact that we haven't established the character and statute of this "truth." A first possibility: perhaps there are truths at which one can arrive or of which one can know only in an *absentminded* way, and this would be a different form, a *divergent* form, as it were, with respect to the logical procedure of the "argument." A second possibility, more abrupt: maybe *every* truth is the involuntary product of inattentiveness, and the logic and reliability of argument, in cases in which they aren't a protection *against* truth, are at best an indirect, collateral expedient with respect to its discovery. And a third possibility, which is in some way prepared by the previous one: perhaps it is not only that truth might be found absentmindedly, like a fleeting idea (the *Einfall* that assaults us when we deliver ourselves to the autonomous and automatic machine of language), but also that truth is inattentiveness in itself, the anomaly of discourse, that which can never coincide with itself *in a discourse*, that which can only announce itself in the leaks of the meaning (the absentminded moments) of a discourse. Whatever it may be, it remains the peculiar figure of this *Zerstreuung*, and, if in it truth or a truth is at stake, one could suspect that this isn't something that is at the disposal of someone who is in full control of his faculties and means: not at the disposal of a subject, but something that comes up to the surface in the interstices of his dispersion—or of his dismemberment.

Yes, because *zerstreut*, the term that I read in the first place as "absentminded," also means dismembered; de Man makes the point well. And I should not omit that "marionette" is called in German—besides *Marionette*, which was borrowed from French—*Gliedermann*, "articulate man," a "man (composed) of members (*Glieder*)," members that are all—and we should have learned this by now—prostheses.[16] This is perhaps the secret of the mannequin, of the automaton, of the vast modern ancestry that reaches back to the cyborgs.

And there is still the final phrase, which implies not only an affirmative answer to the concluding question but also long developments that should support the unheard-of magnitude of what is said: "'In any case [*Allerdings*],' he replied, 'and that is the final chapter [*das letzte Kapitel*] in the history of the world'" (563/273, translation modified).

With its warning tone ("in any case"), with a rare weight in its finishing touch, alien to any conjecture, to any conditional, extenuating circumstance ("that is," not "that would be," "it may be considered as," etc.), the final phrase, with a sort of apocalyptic scope that I judge fair to attribute to it, at least upon a first hearing, is evidently incommensurable with all the discourse that precedes it. It is true that it has been anticipated in the story: two times by the narrator himself ("I did not then and there have the slightest inkling of the conclusions which he would subsequently derive from it" [557/265]; "I sensed that he still had more on his mind, and bid him continue" [559/269]), and once, more clearly, by the dancer ("It appears ... that I had not read carefully enough the third chapter of the first Book of Moses; and it would be impossible to confer with a man who was unfamiliar with the first period of human refinement concerning the subsequent periods, let alone concerning the last" [560/270]). But the anticipations don't give the measure. The phrase is incommensurable with all that is previously said, and it can only be stated as a prosthesis of the discourse. Not as a conclusion but as an ending, though an excessive ending. An end of what? Should we say an end of the "history of the world," or an end of this text? Or an end of the "history of the world" as text? For "history," the "history of the world," is vertiginously summarized and read here also as a "narration," as a "story." Does the history of the world have an argument? Is history an absentmindedness of God?

Chapter Five

Kafka and Skepticism

A NOTE

IS THERE ANY RELATIONSHIP between Kafka (1883–1924) and skepticism?

I believe that it could be argued that there are two central issues in Kafka's work and thinking that may be considered in this context.

I present the first issue by way of a starting point: it touches what we could call the human situation in Kafka's universe. This situation determines for human being the closure of transcendence. But this is not a total closure, for it continues to have an effect on human life. It is a closure affecting everything that could be known about transcendence, except for the infinite distance that separates human life from it; it is a closure, moreover, regarding the possibility of knowing with certainty that there is transcendence at all. Human being is denied access to transcendence, but, in a way similar to the peasant that comes to the doors of the law, he or she has a faint glimmer of it. This glimpse teaches him or her that transcendence is inaccessible, even if he or she is destined to it, and it teaches that it is inaccessible, even if it is determined for him or her. This glimpse is a kind of knowledge. It is a knowledge only about the essential inaccessibility of transcendence and, insofar as transcendence is the only thing that should be known, it defines knowledge as such, for which its inner coherence is not enough, for which it needs to know (about) the other—it is a knowledge about its own futility, a knowledge about itself as non-knowing. Knowledge that knows about itself as non-knowing transcendence would be the mode (at least a first mode) of skepticism in Kafka. In this non-knowing, however, transcendence remains in force and rules in the form of the "non." This non-knowing is not a deficiency attributable to human faculties, and possible knowledge is not knowledge due to the operation of a cognitive faculty. Transcendence is known or not known in existence, through existence, and by existence. Therefore, this knowledge is anterior to everything we could call knowledge according to our usual standards; it is primitively inscribed in human nature almost as an instinct, or else in the way instincts reveal themselves in us: as a sentiment. The mark of this sentiment is belief. Knowledge of transcendence expresses itself in the mode of belief, but precisely as a conflict between knowledge and belief. From this point of view, it could be called an epistemological conflict. But with a caveat: the knowledge that is primarily at stake is neither a particular knowledge, however relevant it might be, nor the sum of all knowledge, but, rather, an original knowledge about good and evil, with an addendum: on this knowledge all others depend.

Transcendence is meaning. But it is not conjectural, hypothetical meaning subject to hermeneutical conflict; it is meaning whose truth is immediate. This immediacy is not just the immediacy of comprehension: it is an absolute exigency of realization, of accomplishment. To that extent, writing (literature, art) always has for Kafka an ambivalent character. On the one hand, it is weakness, impotence, the culpable absence of action, the disavowed or explicit renunciation of transcendence, of truth, the problematic production of meaning that cannot be redeemed from its controvertible condition; on the other hand, as the mode of existence that is irretrievably, inalienably Kafka's own, it cannot but be exercised as the only way—the only weapon—that permits him to respond to that absolute exigency.

This remark allows us to move to the other issue that I deem determinant in the hypothetical relation between Kafka and skepticism. This element has to do with a basic unease.

As is well known, skepticism's purpose—referring here to ancient skepticism, codified by Sextus Empiricus—is the release from the disquiet that provokes doubt about phenomena and impressions (what, why, how, etc.). Apparently, the only way to resolve the doubt is to acquire the knowledge that is pertinent in each case. More emphatically, if it is possible to think that knowledge may be coordinated and prioritized, it is also possible to aspire to a master knowledge upon which all others would depend. This is the philosophical stance that the dogmatist adopts with all the variants and all the nuances possible. As opposed to the dogmatist, the skeptic understands that any intended knowledge that may appease the disquiet is vulnerable, always susceptible to controversy. Doubt does not die out, but it eventually increases, and the skeptic counts on the means to activate doubt by opposing—as Sextus succinctly says—phenomena and thoughts.[1] Consequently, instead of rashly laying down as true an opinion that is debatable, the skeptic suspends judgment and happily finds that his or her abstinence is followed at once by a state of spiritual calm.

With Kafka you can permanently feel the unease. Its origin is guilt. However, not guilt as a moral or religious fact but, rather, guilt as a debt of being, as infinite distance from what could lend consistency to one's being. This painful condition induces the human to interpret what being might be in his or her case and to believe that it may be overcome by way of knowledge; of course, both inducements are one and the same. Nevertheless, the debt cannot be settled through knowledge, because the latter is inseparable from the condition of owing: we have eaten from the Tree of Knowledge and, if this was not the cause of the expulsion from paradise ("Why do we harp on about Original Sin? It wasn't on its account that we were expelled from Paradise, but because of the Tree of Life, lest we eat of its fruit" [Kafka, *Zürau* 82]),[2] it is in any case a primary and inseparable determination and endowment of the creature we are. Contrary to appearances, Kafka is not a religious thinker. It is evident that you can find in him a constant recourse to motifs that have their root in Jewish (and Christian) religion, and the book of Genesis occupies a preeminent place among the texts of the scripture. These motifs are not articles of faith but, rather, metaphors (if I can say so) for the fundamental conflict. Knowledge does not settle the debt, just as the consciousness of guilt is not self-sufficient either. Guilt is nothing other than an exigency, and this exigency demands—immediately—to be fulfilled in existence. Guilt can only be paid with existence and through existence. It demands action, realization in which the whole of existence is committed. But in turn the exigency announces itself in knowledge, and precisely in the knowledge of good and evil. This occasions something that has the appearance of an insoluble contradiction. Knowledge (of good and evil) notifies us of the exigency that is imposed upon us, but it is not in this knowledge's capacity to satisfy the exigency and, as we know about the exigency through knowledge, we attribute to knowledge a force that it does not possess. An aphorism phrases it with all desirable clarity:

> Ever since Original Sin, we are basically all alike in our ability to know Good and Evil; even so, this is where we seek a particular advantage. Actually, it's only after knowledge that the real differences begin. The appearance to the contrary is provoked in the following way: No one can be satisfied with understanding alone but must make an effort to act in accordance with it. He lacks the strength to do so; therefore he must destroy himself, even at the risk of not receiving the necessary strength; it is simply that he has no option other than to undertake this final effort. (This is the meaning of the penalty of death for eating of the Tree of Knowledge; it may also be the original meaning of natural death.) The effort is daunting; one would rather reverse the original knowledge of Good and Evil; (the term "Original Sin" refers to this fear) but what was done cannot be undone, only muddied. To this end motivations appear. The entire world is full of them—yes, the whole visible world may be nothing more than a motivation of a man wanting to rest for a moment. An attempt to forge the fact of knowledge, to make of the knowledge an end in itself. (*Zürau* 86)

We *want to believe* that knowledge is or has a peculiar force. What force? The force to attend and to resolve the primary demand: to act according to knowledge. Let us call it responsibility. Yet, knowledge is in itself an aporia. It gives notice about the essential, and at the same time it makes the essential inaccessible through its own means. Hence, the gravitational center of this aphorism is located in the idea of destruction. However, it is not knowledge that should be obliterated; rather, it is the knower who has to destroy him- or herself under the demand of acting in conformity to it. A similar lesson is offered in an entry from Notebook G:

> "If—, thou shalt die" means: knowledge of Good and Evil is both a step leading up to eternal life and an obstacle in the way. If you want to attain eternal life after having gained knowledge—and you will not be able to do otherwise than want it, for knowledge of Good and Evil *is* this will— you will have to destroy yourself, the obstacle, in order to build the step, which is the destruction. Expulsion from Paradise was thus not an act but a happening. (Kafka, *Schriften* 78/*Blue* 40)

Destruction is not a symbolic act or process: the instance of death determines it beyond doubt. Yet, this destruction—or more precisely, this self-destruction—does not have the character of suicide.[3] It is the sole effective effort that is reserved for the knower as a response to the demand, an effort that does not guarantee the effectiveness of the response. In a certain sense, one could say that this self-destruction is the only way in which the knower or the human being, succumbing, can prove to him- or herself that there is the indestructible, for in this way he or she realizes his or her absolute singularity and, at the same time, what may be called his or her intimate human solidarity: "The indestructible is one thing; at one and the same time it is each individual, and it is something common to all; hence the uniquely indissoluble connection among mankind" (Kafka, *Zürau* 70/71). Yet, the fear of this effort, of this kind of active abdication, exceeds all evidence and seeks to revert evidence, to turn back what is unfailingly known into ignorance, into innocence, which is impossible: therefore the need for an alibi, a justification, a subterfuge, a *Motivation*, as Kafka calls it. Subterfuge is a kind of substitution of an ineradicable knowledge (the knowledge of good and evil, which cannot be undone) by a pretended knowledge, which elaborates a chain of causes and motives that could justify the condition and place in which one finds oneself and one's disposition in the given circumstance. This is still an effect of knowledge as an original and destined endowment of human being; it amounts either to reverting to knowledge itself in order to feign a force that is absent and that is probably impossible to reach or else to hiding the demand; therefore, it is a literally perverse effect because, instead of assuming that endowment as the means toward a full realization, it is postulated and simulated as an end. Yet, the aporia resonates here: simulation and postulation of knowledge as an end are (or become), against all evidence, against all truth, the truth of our existence; they are not the truth of error but, rather, the error of error.

Certainly, nothing and nobody urges the demand; there is neither a god nor a superior being that is its primary source. In fact, the idea of a personal god (or else of a domestic god) would be a *Motivation*, a subterfuge to foster confidence in the indestructible, as one of the aphorisms states.[4] The demand determines human being as such; it has no content, but it is sheer exigency, and therefore it can be experienced—and in fact is experienced—as a mandate, as law. One knows about it in and through responsibility, through the exigency to respond to the exigency. It is this circularity that evinces and confirms it as law.[5] But responsibility is too heavy a burden or, otherwise said, it is a task whose imposition is accompanied by the certitude that it cannot be definitively fulfilled. It is a task (*Aufgabe*) that is life itself,[6] the most ominous gift (*Gabe*), for it inherently brings along the constitutive possibility and, given the lack of force, the irrepressible tendency to renounce (*aufgeben*): "You are the exercise, the task. No student far and wide" (*Zürau* 22), says one of the aphorisms.

The law is known in the mode of a responsibility that knowledge reinforces, because the latter is nothing other than the knowledge of the exigency, and the exigency can be met only at the expense of oneself. This is not a conflict between belief and knowledge; it is a conflict between knowledge and existence, something we used to call a moral conflict that in this case, notwithstanding the fact that it concerns will and duty, involves existence in its totality in terms of being, good, and meaning.

One might think that what I have tried to discern as the two issues I deem pertinent in order to pose the hypothetical relation between Kafka and skepticism, assuming they are appropriate as descriptions, correspond to a weltanschauung, to Kafka's worldview. This is not my intention. Indeed, it does not seem to me that something like a "worldview" can be attributed to Kafka insofar as a view of this kind, disregarding actual gaps and incongruities, presupposes an aim of integrity and coherence. By contrast, Kafka places himself in the blind spot of any "view," in all that resists integration, all that disavows any purported coherence, all that reveals the claim to truth as mere claim and as alibi. Therefore, evincing a conflict is essential, along with the determination of this conflict as irresolvable.

I mentioned a double conflict: epistemological and moral, to use the conventional terms. So, the total scope of what is known under the name of skepticism (concerning not only pretensions of human knowledge but also the radical doubt about the criterion of duty) thus remains involved. This is possible because of the inseparable link that Kafka establishes between knowledge and existence, certainly not in the guise of an opposition or a contradiction (Kafka's thinking is not dialectic), but as a structure of scissions that impact one another and call into crisis (but do not annul) the possibility of meaning.

Well then: Kafka makes us feel this conflict in his writing and through it. This is a decisive point, for it is not about exposing or arguing against the conflict but, rather, about inscribing it in ourselves (just as punishment operates in Kafka's "Penal Colony"), a conflict that marks in turn another knowledge, another feeling, though no longer another belief. It is about engraving in ourselves this conflict or, if allowed, of bringing out in ourselves, in Kafka's writing and through it, the atavistic, immemorial inscription of the conflict as something that preexists us insofar as it is our constitutive condition. Nevertheless, the mode in which this writing operates does not have to do with provoking commotions or strong affects. There is always in Kafka an air of neutrality that disquiets, even where it seems to express states of mind in an immediate manner, because this expression is generally associated with objective description and ratiocination. In this sense, it is fundamental to construing the logic of the Kafkan text in order to understand how the structure of scissions to which I referred instantiates itself in it. And it is the reciprocal impact of scissions and their reversal that interests me when I speak about a logic of the Kafkan text.

The necessity I have outlined has to be considered, however, as an excessive pretension. The construction of the aforesaid logic exceeds almost infinitely the limits within which the present argument can be developed, and, even under conditions that may be judged optimal, it is probably a desperate enterprise. It should not be desperate because it is impossible but, rather, because Kafka's writing could hardly provide assurance for the conclusions to which the quest may lead. In question is not only its complexity, the frequently unsuspected—and literarily unprecedented—ways in which the narratological procedures relate, combine, or mix with the forms of ideation. These ways essentially affect the effects of texts' meaning and putative intention; in question is not only the ideological components that may come together in this writing but also, and most notably, the fact that in the latter there reigns a peculiar principle of indetermination, according to which the comprehension of the sign—that is, of the literalness of the text in any of its phases—allows one to determine precisely its position in the ideal sequence of discourse while, at the same time, rendering all the more indeterminate the meaning that is to be attributed to that literalness—that is, its insertion in a wider order of sense that would allow one to establish with certainty what the discourse means as a whole. The issue is that the Kafkan narrative brings about a proliferation of signs and traces that point to that sense of totality; one could speak of an allegorical writing. Formulated otherwise, in abbreviated fashion, the comprehension of a narrative by Kafka is incompossible with the comprehension of the narrative's meaning, to the point that this meaning is precisely that incompossibility. So, what we call meaning is shifted asymptotically, becoming the horizon onto which the narrative opens itself without, however, indicating the corresponding orientation, not for lack of hints but, rather, for multiplication and overdetermination of spurs.

I leave this model—for in a way what I have just described would have this character—somewhat on its own. If it does not merit conviction, I suppose at least that the point of indetermination is very much marked when reading

Kafka and that it is, one way or another, an essential *affect* of that reading. Yet, this affect is not simply an *impression* that the reading provokes, something like a vague sense of suspicion, as it were, which leaves behind a trace of unease and fascination in the reader. This affect is not the effect produced by the narrative, once concluded in its peculiar un-conclusion of meaning, but rather the process of comprehension and ideation to which the reader is subject. Consequently, if I am talking about logic, it is because the forms and operations of Kafka's writing are not merely rhetorical resources to attract the reader's attention and favor throughout the narrative and in its denouement, to foster the concatenation of events, or any other reason we may adduce. To put it in other terms: the rhetoric of this writing is immediately a logic; its rhetorical tropes are immediately logical tropes. Ancient skeptics practiced what they themselves called "tropes" (or modes) with argumentative and controversial purposes. At times, I think that many of the aphorisms and similes, many of Kafka's parables and loose annotations, have an air and an efficacy that ancient skeptics would have wished for themselves and that this has to do precisely with the peculiar schematism to which I am referring when I speak about tropes. It is in this sense that I believe that one can attempt to bring Kafka and skepticism together, insofar as one tries to discern and, so to speak, categorize these logical figures.

Of course, this may not seem sufficient for securing such a relation. But I think that to follow this path may be worthwhile.

I have said that any attempt to render a rigorous and exhaustive account of the logic of Kafka's text surpasses by far my present purpose and that it surely, in another context and with better equipment, would still remain exposed to the unsettling efficacy of his writing. Here, I will restrict myself to a brief sketch that seems to me not at all irrelevant. I take as my reference—indeed, I was already doing so—a number of entries scattered throughout many notebooks that Kafka selected and copied, gathering them into a collection of aphorisms with a thematic kinship. With regard to this idea, Kafka's friend and posthumous editor Max Brod assigned them the title "Reflections on Sin, Suffering, Hope, and the True Way" (Kafka, *Zürau* 1–108). They are known as the *Zürau Aphorisms*, Zürau being the place where Kafka wrote down these notes between September 1917 and the beginning of 1918. Of course, I cannot limit myself only to these aphorisms (I will also refer to a number of entries from the *Blue Octavo Notebooks*, as I have already done), but they will be my fundamental background.[7]

I have the impression that what primarily jumps out when reading these aphorisms is something similar to a stasis, an abrupt cognitive standstill. And this is the first trait that I am interested in highlighting: the aphorisms do not benefit from the artistic resources and capacities of language; they neither arouse metaphorical astonishment nor abuse synecdoche to attain their peculiar effect. They operate in the field of thinking and, as I said, inflict upon it something that alters it essentially. What could have been their predictable course, routed by sequences and the continuum of causes and motivations, suffers a collapse that does not stem from anything other than this very course; it is a sort of assault coming not from irrational zones but, rather, from its own tension, occasioned by the excessive attempt to think the (absolute) other. It could be said that it is the strenuous effort to attain of itself, as I suggested before, a meaning whose truth could be immediate. This is precisely what writing *cannot* do. This impotence, then, is processed by writing, which suffers from an impotence that is greater, because it is guilty. Writing is guilty, for it happens in the place where the right action should be performed according to the knowledge of good and evil. Writing's fundamental duty, in this trance, consists in its fidelity to the evidence of that collapse. Writing itself has to bring it to light.

The stasis to which I referred a moment ago—this sort of paralysis of thinking that has so much to do with paradox but is not to be confused with it, this *paranoesis*, if I may say so—is an essential requisite for Kafka, not just in what concerns dealing with his own experience, but in a general sense that touches the condition and destiny of the human being. It is true that, even in his aphorisms and in the entries that contain assertions about this condition and destiny, Kafka constantly strives to be a faithful witness to himself and to a truth that—quoting Blanchot—"was despairing only for him" (58n1, translation modified). Yet, there is no doubt that what he says about sin, pain, salvation, about good and evil, as well as the admonitions and intimations addressed to a "you" that is he himself but that engages the reader in a relationship that, in other places, expresses itself in the anxious solidarity of a "we," are all interpellations of that condition, that destiny.

Just as I have pointed out what I consider the two issues that would give verisimilitude to the alleged relation between Kafka and skepticism, I have also talked about two sets of immediacy: of meaning and truth, of knowledge and action—that is to say, in the latter case, the immediate need to do what is necessary according to the exigency of the knowledge of good and evil. Well then: the human condition consists in the distance and the deferral that splits one immediacy from the other. Such a condition is what Kafka qualifies with his constant recourse to the concept of sin, in the same sense as the pain of scission reveals itself with extreme anguish in the excruciating longing for salvation.

What seems to me particularly relevant is that sin and salvation do not have here a primarily religious value. It is true that one can speak of a certain religiousness in Kafka; as I said before, a very important sector of his vocabulary and his array of figures and images has an unequivocal religious provenance. I am trying to say that those concepts do not have a religious value in the confessional sense of the word, notwithstanding that a different and necessarily more original sense of "religion" may be argued in this context: "Writing as a form a prayer" (Kafka, *Schriften* 354) could be one of the keys for that purpose. To that extent, it could be said that those notions have in Kafka a signification anterior to any religious codification. Therefore, faith itself acquires the character of a symptom of the human condition, not of an original determination, although it is to a certain extent the measure of this condition. This anteriority presupposes a radical accentuation of the experience of what we call sin and of the hope for salvation, and this accentuation is inseparable from the irrepressible and indisputable literary destiny of Kafka. Indeed, writing tends to aggravate the distance and deferral I mentioned, introducing the demon of misunderstanding and the idol of imagery between meaning and truth and offering a questionable substitute for action in the form of a "talking about" what knowledge of good and evil demands as an unavoidable exigency. Writing was experienced by Kafka as a destiny; he himself named it as his most intimate being, his "writerly being [*Schriftstellersein*]" (cited in Corngold, *Lambent* 11). Thus, Kafka's problem was also how to render account in writing and by it—that is, *through* the experience of writing, of the supreme exigency, of a justified life, with which writing itself is in a fundamental tension. This is not possible without opening a breach in writing, without splitting writing itself, opening a gap, and impeding its self-enclosure in the accomplished roundness of the work of art, which nevertheless weighs heavily as another demand that cannot be ignored once writing is unleashed.

In this context, it seems to me suitable to speak about tropes of Kafkan writing, which have a certain affinity with skeptical tropes; or maybe I should correct myself here: not with such and such a skeptical trope, but with the mode of their operation, their efficacy. I think that this is so precisely inasmuch as this mode prevents thinking from closing upon itself in the dogmatic and unjustified assurance of some certitude, always untimely, whatever that certitude might be.

I said that (re)constructing the logic of the Kafkan text is a desperate endeavor. I have to confess, too, that I would not know how to sketch a catalogue raisonné of the (alleged) tropes that Kafka would apply in his aphorisms. It may be argued that this is a sufficient proof of the preposterous character of my hypothesis. However, it seems to me indisputable that in many of those entries it is possible to recognize certain recurrent figures and a general mode of, say, its functioning. In what follows I will briefly review some of the figures that I think I can identify, and subsequently I will suggest something about that mode.

Let the first be the figure (the trope) of the *confusion of opposites*.[8] We read in aphorism 86 that, "ever since Original Sin, we are basically all alike in our ability to know Good and Evil." The affirmation is followed by two cardinal warnings. According to the first, "even so, this is where we seek a particular advantage [*unsere besondere Vorzüge*]." The second states: "Actually, it's only after knowledge that the real differences [*die wahren Verschiedenheiten*] begin." This second warning, which is particularly emphatic, bluntly prepares what will be said immediately after: the "real differences" consist in the fact that knowledge of good and evil—we paid attention to this point—unfailingly brings about a practical exigency that exceeds all the capacity and force of mere knowledge. Knowledge of good and evil, which is the knowledge of the *difference* between good and evil, demands *making* the difference—that is, *acting* according to this knowledge: to do right.[9] The first warning outlines the manner in which human beings resist the force of the exigency by subterfuges through which, insofar as they seek to extract "particular advantage[s]" from the capacity to know good and evil, they hope to meet these advantages in knowledge itself. The latter, however, is unable to *make* the difference. Left to its own strength, it reveals its proximity to evil: "Evil knows of the Good, but Good does not know of Evil" (*Schriften* 48/*Blue* 24). Hence, the knowledge we have results entirely in the exigency and not in knowledge itself: "Knowledge we *have*. Anyone who strives for it with particular intensity is suspect of striving against it" (76/39). The consequence is a radical limitation of knowledge: good, the reality of the good, contains, exhausts, and suppresses knowledge, which therefore can be neither independent nor autonomous.[10] Simply on its own, knowledge is confusion, nurtured by a multiplicity of subterfuges.

With regard to the double immediacy to which I referred previously, the right understanding of these subterfuges (the *Motivationen* of the great aphorism that I took as my starting point) is decisive. It is decisive because, although subterfuges establish distance and deferral, they are not engaged with an explicit consciousness of mediation but, rather, as the postulation of a false immediacy, a *different* one, spurious, which betrays what ought to be the original calling of knowledge, to know the *other*, and which in this way offers itself as a surrogate of true immediacy. Herein takes root what Kafka considers the capital human sin: impatience (*Ungeduld*).

> There are two cardinal human vices, from which all the others derive their being: impatience and carelessness. Impatience got people evicted from Paradise; carelessness kept them from making their way back there. Or perhaps there is only one cardinal vice: impatience. Impatience got people evicted, and impatience kept them from making their way back. (*Zürau* 3)[11]

Kafka says that impatience is the source of "all human errors" (2), and I think that the reason thereof does not lie in the fact that impatience itself is an error but, rather, in the fact that the purpose that guides its unease and its urgency is, *a contrario sensu*, to avoid any kind of error. It is "the premature breaking off of what is methodical" (to which it has for this very reason proximity, maybe the closest proximity),[12] and it is a closure within appearance. One might think that this is a most precise characteristic of what skeptics call the dogmatic frame of mind. At the dead ends of a search that never seems to land on firm ground and to attain unshakeable certitude, exasperation leads to quitting its methodical continuation and to terminating it, retaining only that which has an appearance of truth due to its relative and temporary solvency. Moreover, if it is possible to suggest a relation between this aphorism and the one that precedes it and opens the entire series, with its ironical image of the true path as a rope strung "just over the ground" that seems rather to be "destined to make one stumble" (*Zürau* 1),[13] it would be possible to infer that to follow the course of the true path means nothing less than exposing oneself to the constant risk of misstepping, to error (therefore, "what we refer to as way is hesitation" [26 bis]). If the "world is our errancy [*Verirrung*],"[14] and if we are inevitably in it, then to err is the only way to access truth.[15]

With its urge, its unawareness of the difference between the mediate and the immediate (which amounts to making knowledge an end), impatience is also liable for the confusions of good and evil that have seduction as their efficient center:

> A. is terribly puffed up, he considers himself very advanced in goodness, since he feels himself magnetically attracting to himself an ever greater array of temptations, from quarters with which he was previously wholly unacquainted. The true explanation for his condition, however, is that a great devil has taken up residence within him, and an endless stream of smaller devils and deviltons are coming to offer the great one their services. (*Zürau* 10)

From seduction derives something that I would like to call a subordinated trope, which I will term the trope of the *guile deceived*. I am not going to linger on it. I will only indicate that subterfuges are measures of cunning to which we appeal, insofar as we are faced with a life whose adversity, be it stealthy or manifest, is in the end unfathomable for us. Wherever a final instance of comprehension or knowledge is lacking, guile takes its place. But for Kafka this cannot be anything other than an intensification of impatience, whether guile pretends to anticipate evil eliciting its secrets (*Zürau* 19), or to win the bet presuming that it is possible to pay evil in installments (39), or else, so to speak, to set negotiable conditions within the context of generalized deceit (55).[16] Another aphorism categorically seals the destiny of guile, pointing out its fundament:

> The reservations with which you take Evil into yourself are not yours, but those of Evil. (29)

This hesitant acceptance, in any of its forms and in any of its degrees, is everything that is needed for total surrender: "Once we have taken Evil into ourselves, it no longer insists that we believe in it" (28). I leave here my first item.

I will call the second trope *suppression by contrariness*. I see that my title is not transparent, but what I am trying to suggest is a certain procedure by virtue of which Kafka proposes a relationship between contraries that annul one another by their very opposition. Contrasting with what I have done in my previous sketch, I will begin by what may be a subordinate trope—namely, the trope of *inversion*. Here are two instances:

> A cage went in search of a bird. (*Zürau* 16)

> Martyrs do not underestimate the body, they allow it to be hoisted up onto the cross. In that way they are like their enemies. (33)

Of course, these are two instances of a very different kind. The first has an air of fable, or of parable (I will return to this), in extreme abbreviation. The second aphorism rectifies a topic that is taken for granted, more or less similar to the way in which the skeptic punishes rash judgments through a counterargument that implies not a commitment to what he or she enounces but, rather, precisely an abstention regarding any definitive pronouncement. If in the first aphorism terms are inverted, in the second it is judgment that is inverted. A question of force underlies both cases. (One has to recall the significance of this concept concerning the exigency of acting in accordance with the knowledge of good and evil.) The cage is stronger than the bird: it is intended to be its prison, just as the bird—which we usually see as an image of freedom—is designed to be a prisoner; it is a mutual destiny (like that of paradise and human being),[17] in which the cage outweighs, forcing the inversion. And the body (which belongs to the realm of facts, whose right Kafka always recognized) is stronger than whatever structure of meaning to which it could be subjected, even if this structure has the exorbitant sublimity of sacrifice; therefore, the inversion of fact and meaning is forced in this case too. However, this inversion does not merely turn related terms around; it results in a distinctive effect of neutralization. It would be possible to adduce here the skeptic motto of *isosthenia*, the equipollence of reasons (in Kafka's aphorisms, of course, it is not just about the mere indication of force but also its discursive operationalization), which leads to the suspension of judgment. Therefore, not even with respect to oneself is it possible to exert sufficient force, if not by counter-effect and passively (with a passivity that is not idleness but patience):

> I do not strive for self-mastery. Self-mastery is the desire—within the endless emanations of my intellectual life—to be effective at a certain radius. But if I am made to describe circles around me, then I had better do it without action: merely contemplating the whole extraordinary complex and taking nothing away with me but the strength that such an aspect—*e contrario*—would give me. (*Zürau* 31)

As I said, my brief comment about inversion is meant to introduce the trope of suppression by contrariety. I have the impression that this trope gathers much of what may be considered Kafka's peculiar style of thinking. In this sense, it concentrates a main part of what at first sight is perceived as the paradoxical turns typical of the "Kafkaesque." However, it is recommendable to maintain a dose of reservation with regard to the use of the term *paradox* in the examination of these aphorisms and of Kafka's work in general.[18] I begin with a concise conditional:

> If it had been possible to build the Tower of Babel without having to climb it, that would have been sanctioned. (*Zürau* 18)

The image of the tower is eminent in Kafka. Like other pieces of the scripture's grand repertoire, it belongs to his fundamental symbolic stock. Seen from one angle, it is also a figure of impatience: the figure of the assault on heaven that attempts to abolish all mediation, though on the condition of counting on the earth as ground.[19] The contrariety of heaven and earth is at its center. This contrariety becomes efficacious precisely with the exacerbated task of the colossal building's construction: there is no way of carrying it out without the gradual expansion and entrenchment of the foundation, whose ultimate impossibility must be recognized. Yet, this impossibility would be precisely its sole possibility: the tower remains as a ruined image of such (im)possibility, and this mode of (im)possibility is a Kafkan mode, if not *the* Kafkan mode. While the tower remains as such image, it has a supplementary inverse, which specifies and literally deepens the (im)possibility with an impressing counterimage: "We are digging the pit of Babel" (*Schriften* 484).[20] The erection of the tower, the higher it reaches, presupposes (and here, too, literally) the equivalent digging of the ground on which it rests in order to give it unlimited (and for that reason impossible) founding; otherwise said, to found is indiscernibly to un-found.

My second instance is a parable:

> The crows like to insist a single crow is enough to destroy heaven. This is incontestably true, but it says nothing about heaven, because heaven is just another way of saying: the impossibility of crows. (*Zürau* 32)

In one way or another, this is also an assault on heaven, which should be the most powerful of all, since it would bring about heaven's destruction. However, it is inane. The contrariety of crows and heaven reverses (and this is a mode of suppression) in mutual exclusion. Yet, since all starts with the crows' boast and its innocuousness, at stake is the major force: the force of possibility. Here, it is also transformed into (im)possibility and stopped in its very announcement, in infinite suspense. Suppression is not annihilation but, rather, precisely this suspense, and this suspense, this (im)possibility, is the only glimpse of transcendence. The trope I am suggesting would have to do with this motif, which was essentially involved in my first element in the relation between Kafka and skepticism. According to it, the place that knowledge occupies in skepticism should be assigned in Kafka's work to freedom, the practical principle par excellence precisely because freedom is the only endowment or condition that would permit in its own right the passage from the knowledge of good and evil to the realization of good. It is maintained with good reason, from a theological perspective, that together with that knowledge freedom of choice was given to us.

In this sense, it would be plausible to think that what I am calling *(im)possibility* determines what may be understood as freedom in Kafkan terms. This is the lesson of two aphorisms that I deem pertinent to my second trope. This is the first one:

> He is a free and secure citizen of the world because he is on a chain that is long enough to allow him access to all parts of the earth, and yet not so long that he could be swept over the edge of it. At the same time he is also a free and secure citizen of heaven because he is also attached to a similar heavenly chain. If he wants to go to earth, the heavenly manacles will throttle him, if he wants to go to heaven, the earthly manacles will. But for all that, all possibilities are open to him, as he is well aware, yes, he even refuses to believe the whole thing is predicated on a mistake going back to the time of his first enchainment. (*Zürau* 66)

This aphorism speaks of two different kinds of freedom, terrestrial and heavenly. Both are plenary in their respective realms. However, as soon as you want to exert the freedom you enjoy in one realm in order to pass to the other, strict jurisdiction impedes it. They are, then, incompossible kinds of freedom. All possibilities are given, and the subject can already count on them in the privacy of his sentiment. But the restraint imposed every time the chained man or woman wants to trespass certain bounds makes the sentiment but a futile presentiment. Thus forked, freedom becomes innocuous, nullified. The last sentence—which, unsurprisingly, alludes to a reluctance to commit an error and the difficulty of enduring it, that is, the lack of patience—marks the force that silently imposes this annulation: it could be called the force of gravity.[21] Let us read the second aphorism:

> Man has free will, and of three sorts:
>
> First he was free when he wanted this life; now admittedly he cannot take back his decision, because he is no longer the one who wanted it then, he must do his own will then by living.

Second he is free inasmuch as he can choose the pace and the course of his life.

Third he is free in that as the person he will one day be, he has the will to go through life under any condition and so come to himself, on some path of his own choosing, albeit sufficiently labyrinthine that it leaves no little spot of life untouched.

This is the triple nature of free will, but being simultaneous, it is also single, and is in fact so utterly single that it has no room for a will at all, whether free or unfree. (*Zürau* 104)

This aphorism is a typical sample of Kafkan ratiocination. Between the two extreme sorts of free will, each of which signals a limitation of freedom—life that once was desired is already irreversible, and there is no other option than to live it; the path that leads back to oneself (to the one who wanted this life, perhaps), through multiple circumstances and under multiple conditions, modifies this life down to the finest detail without any intervention of the will—between these two sorts there is the only sort that seems to be an unrestricted exercise of free will, which certainly is nothing but the freedom to choose. (Here, one could think, "all possibilities" are given, as the previous aphorism states.) However, the three modes are simultaneous, such that this freedom remains gripped by restrictions, and "free will," in the end, is no more than the whimsical title that is given, from the narrow perspective of the individual subject, to the inexorable. It is, if one might say so, the efficacy of another force of gravity, to which we usually give the name of "destiny" and, if we want to attribute its determination to heaven (that is to say, to the figure that each and every life traces from a universal point of view), then it will be a celestial force of gravity. The exposition of the triple mode of freedom suppresses precisely the will in which we wish to find its principle housed and, confronted with the aspect of an accomplished fact that everyone's life acquires for that reason, freedom takes on the character of a mere belief, a presumption, a subterfuge.

Suppression, I said, is not annihilation but suspension. The latter, in turn, temporally interpreted, is as it were an effect of eternity (or of indefinite suspension, if you will), which we know well from certain eminent pieces of Kafkan narrative, like *A Country Doctor*, and which has that implacable appearance of perdition or condemnation. The use of freedom remains marked by that effect: "The dogs are still playing in the yard, but the quarry will not escape them, never mind how fast it is running through the forest already"

(*Zürau* 43). Freedom here seems to be but flight without hope, for its point—its vanishing point—is already fixed. Nevertheless, I do not believe that this should necessarily be Kafka's *position*—that is, a *thesis* from him. Rather, I understand it as a radical corrective imposed on what I just called "belief," on the helpless assumptions with which we organize our lives, taking them for granted due to the necessity of counting on something to which we could attribute the quality of a firm ground. Lastly, of all that the aphorisms contain concerning the issue of beliefs and faith, I glean the following:

> "It cannot be claimed that we are lacking in belief. The mere fact of our being alive is an inexhaustible font of belief."
> "The fact of our being alive a font of belief? But what else can we do but live?"
> "It's in that 'what else' that the immense force of belief resides: it is the exclusion that gives it its form." (109)

There is no thesis in Kafka; there is neither stance nor position that may be taken as a stronghold (conviction, principle, precept). Kafka's thinking is, it seems to me, essentially a-thetic, proper to a man who said that one form of happiness consists in the fact that "the ground on which you stand cannot be any bigger than the two feet planted on it" (*Zürau* 24), which certainly does not define a position but, rather, a passage. This narrowness, which does not coincide with anything but one's own corporeal existence, concentrates "all possibilities" on the (im)possibility that we are. I say narrowness with the fundamental aspect of Kafkan writing in mind: *Angst*, anguish, anxiety, and the constriction of existence to its bare *factum*. The force of this *Angst* consists in the fact that it does not draw comfort from any of the subterfuges, that it, so to speak, defends itself against them, that it cannot be compensated by any belief whatsoever. I assume that this is the way in which an entry from Notebook G could be understood, an entry that indicates the only acceptance of "to believe" that has a positive signification for Kafka: "Believing means liberating the indestructible element in oneself, or, more accurately, liberating oneself, or, more accurately, being indestructible, or, more accurately, being" (*Schriften* 55/*Blue* 27).[22]

In this entry, the fundamental word is stamped: "the indestructible." I mean fundamental, because I think that it is at the center of the aphorisms, which is not a novel observation, for this has been said more than once (for instance, Bloom 454).[23] This word's link here with belief and faith could be judged the touchstone of every assessment of Kafka in skeptical terms, whatever the inflection of these terms, taking into account that it is precisely here that its limit seems to be reached. In the collection of aphorisms I have been consulting, the word figures in four of them (*Zürau* 50, 69, 70/71, and 74), and in each it has a kind of prominent seriousness, beginning with the aphorism that specifies the concept (I quoted it before): "the indestructible" is the most intimate core of the human being, I will not say its essence, but its *secret*, which is that to which I have been referring in talking about (im)possibility: "The indestructible is one thing; at one and the same time it is each individual, and it is something common to all; hence the uniquely indissoluble connection among mankind" (70/71). In a particular manner, the following (to which I previously alluded) speaks about the need of a faith in the indestructible:

> A man cannot live without a steady faith in something indestructible within him, though both the faith and the indestructible thing may remain permanently concealed from him. One of the forms of this concealment is the belief in a personal god. (50)

This aphorism seems to say that it is impossible to live without faith or belief, such that when the fundamental belief is absent—when human being escapes from itself—the subject substitutes it with another belief, another faith, transferring the indestructible to an exterior and higher being, who in some way is endowed with what distinguishes us humans. But, in fact, the idea of a belief that overshadows a basal trust (a faith), the idea of an alienation of what is most intimate and endogenous to oneself by attributing it to a higher entity, the idea, lastly, that there is no proper life without such a trust and that, nevertheless, it is possible to live ignoring both trust and alienation by hiding them from oneself, this idea points to an essentially problematic status of faith and belief, as if precisely in the latter were staged the unbearable tension of the exigency to the point of provoking the crisis of belief itself.[24] This crisis tints belief with a shade of deceit, especially where it ought to maintain a reference to the essential: "If what was supposed to be destroyed in Paradise was destructible, then it can't have been decisive; however, if it was indestructible, then we are living in a false belief" (74). In any case, the problem of this status impinges without fail on the relations between belief and knowing, starting with the mutual exclusion of these concepts (and of both subjective states): what is believed is not known; what is known is not believed. Yet, this mutual exclusion—which is trivial and, as regards its principal part, merely semantic—is determined by the aforementioned *isosthenia*, the equipollence of both terms, a parity of forces that marks in the end the *asthenia* of both, their weakness, as confronted with the supreme exigency.[25] Put differently, just as knowledge is irrelevant in view of this exigency, of which we are nevertheless notified by virtue of knowledge itself, so, too, is belief, without which, however, life is in fact unbearable: impossible. If the link between the indestructible and belief is the touchstone of Kafka's putative skepticism, the indestructible in turn is the trial by fire of faith, which only leaves us its ashes.

I have said that Kafka's writing engraves on its readers the essential conflict of knowledge and existence, of exigency and freedom. There are two things that remain to consider. One of them was already announced: What might be the general mode of skeptical efficacy or, if you prefer, the principle that governs the tropological diversity in Kafka's writing? The other remaining consideration obviously stems from the fact that literary writing—art—is only the space and operation in which that efficacy deploys itself: consequences for the status of the literary and art cannot but derive from this. In this final part of my attempt, I will begin with the latter issue.

What is said about knowledge is in a certain way also said about art, as I suggested already. The aforementioned uncontrollable tendency to renounce (to avoid, to defer) the responsibility that the exigency demands—the exigency of acting according to the law, that is to say, of being accountable to the law—has the character of art too, and it is felt most strongly in the irresistible proclivity to write. However, writing brings along its own demand and, as the title of one of Blanchot's essays on Kafka reads, in the most vigorous manner another exigency acts in him, namely, "the work's demand" (57–83). "I am nothing but literature and can and want to be nothing else" (Kafka, *Tagebücher* 579/*Diaries* 230): this is one of Kafka's decisive pronouncements, and it is beyond doubt that there is nothing in these words that could be heard as a boast or declamation; it is, rather, the acknowledgment of a condition and of an inexorable destiny.[26] The point is that this exigency, which can be assumed in so many other writers, great or humble, with more or less emphasis, with diverse nuances, coexists in Kafka with the other exigency, which has the name of salvation or justification of existence (ethical or religious exigency, whatever the name, as long as one does not yield to the trivial connotations we give to these terms), with an intensity and an equality of strength perhaps never before seen in the history of literature. It is this intensity that confers upon Kafka's text its unique physiognomy and effect. And, again, this means that, in Kafka's work, only writing can take this intensity and its conflict on as its charge and that, in spite of the insurmountable difference between the life and the oeuvre to which Kafka permanently bears witness, writing has the character of existence and remains for that very reason branded to its innermost core by the (im)possibility. Whence also the difference between writing and art; such, perhaps, is one of the principal meanings of the following aphorism: "Our art is an art that is dazzled by truth: the light shed on the rapidly fleeing grimace is true—nothing else is" (*Zürau* 63).[27]

Writing, then, assumes an essential character. Maybe there is no better image of it than the one offered by a diary entry from January 16, 1922, in which Kafka speaks of a total "breakdown" marked by the violent rupture between the interior and the exterior clock: "the inner one runs crazily on [*jagt*] at a devilish or demoniac or in any case inhuman pace, the outer one limps along [*stockend*] at its usual speed" (*Tagebücher* 877/*Diaries* 399). It is the image, then, of persecution:

> There are doubtless several reasons for the wild tempo of the inner process; the most obvious one is introspection [*Selbstbeobachtung*], which will suffer no idea to sink tranquilly to rest but must pursue [*emporjagt*] each one into consciousness, only itself to become an idea, in turn to be pursued by renewed introspection.... This pursuit [*Jagen*], originating in the midst of men, carries one in a direction away from them. The solitude that for the most part has been forced on me, in part voluntarily sought by me—but what was this if not compulsion too?—is now losing all its ambiguity and approaches its dénouement. Where is it leading? The strongest likelihood is, that it may lead to madness [*Irrsinn*]; there is nothing more to say, the pursuit goes right through me and rends me asunder. Or I can—can I?—manage to keep my feet somewhat and be carried along in the wild pursuit. Where, then, shall I be brought? "Pursuit" [*Jagd*], indeed, is only a metaphor. I can also say, "assault on the last earthly frontier [*Ansturm gegen die letzte irdische Grenze*]," an assault, moreover, launched from below, from mankind, and since this too is a metaphor, I can replace it by the metaphor of an assault from above, aimed at me from above (877–78/399).

Without considering the relativization of the image, this "assault on the last earthly frontier" is the very nature of Kafka's writing, the way in which it assumes intensity and tension and, forcing it to the limit, maintains itself vertiginously in it, allowing a glimpse into transcendence as pure imminence.

In this sense, it could be said that Kafka's is an aesthetic skepticism, according to very specific terms. Kant, great thinker of the law that he was, closed all cognitive accesses to transcendence. Consciousness of duty remained the fundament of a relationship to transcendence that could only be articulated in terms of postulates, whose certainty does not arise from any other instance than consciousness itself. Any possibility of an *experience* of the transcendent was condemned as fanaticism, superstition, and an equally ungrounded and excessive claim of "seeing beyond the limits" of experience itself. Nevertheless, the analytic of aesthetic judgment, with its opening onto the principle of the general knowability of objects by virtue of their free appearance out of the fundament of nature, opens a breach that may be called analogic or allusive, which will be fervently exploited by the Romantic heirs—through Schiller—and the idealist successors.[28] The trace that emanates from this breach outlines an entire aesthetical culture that, on the ruined foundations of metaphysics and religion as secure forms and ways of accessing transcendence, erects the premises of art, more delicate and unstable but at the same time more ductile and versatile, which give in their way, always allusively, a glimpse of the transcendent in the guise of an experience not of what exceeds the limits of experience but, rather, of exceeding itself. This exceeding, as an endurance and persistence at the limit (on "the last frontier"), along with the radical renunciation of representing what transcends it, is the stamp of Kafka's writing.

I move now to my last point, a debt I incurred almost from the beginning. Allowing my hypothesis on the Kafkan tropes (I hope to have suggested how they intertwine and communicate, modifying one another), although I am certain that it is unfeasible to provide an exhaustive and definitive catalog of them, I deem it possible to describe the general mode of their functioning. This is not an easy task either, but a brief attempt to meet its requirements would perhaps lend a semblance of verisimilitude to what I have proposed. I intend to do nothing more than evoke and comment on a pair of innuendos from accredited specialists on Kafka's work.

Kafka's skepticism has been debated abundantly, always in a manner more or less incidental—that is, without this attribution being endorsed by a *concept* of skepticism that does justice to the essential strategy of the latter and its historical varieties. The sole study that meets this requisite, as far as I know, is from Stanley Corngold, included in his brilliant book *Lambent Traces*.[29] Corngold discusses with extraordinary acuity and very persuasively many of the issues I have touched on here. In his interpretation, Kafka practices an "aesthetic of skepticism" that is pushed to the extreme, at which point it reverts, through an "immoralism of skepticism," toward an ethical stance that can no longer be called skeptic, although this very stance cannot be carried out by the finite subject, upon which it nevertheless presses heavily as conscience and anguish. "[Kafka's] claim that, as a finite individual, he is unable to realize the task—of doing the right thing—is inferior to the claim that the right thing to do is real, transparent, and an authentic burden" (*Lambent* 141). In his study, the author discerns what he sees as a central operation of Kafka's writing, with reference precisely to the complex of relations around which I have been circling:

> The formal device in Kafka's late work most apt to generate the aura of the transcendent (in both positive and negative senses) is a type of deconstructive logic that works through what might be called "chiastic recursion." In such a pattern, each new term, consisting of elements syntactically and conceptually parallel to those of a previous term, arises by means of an inversion of these elements. (121–22)[30]

Corngold exemplifies his approach with the brief narrative *The [Spinning] Top*, *The Great Wall of China* (a major narrative, and one of Kafka's most substantial pieces), and lastly the famous parable *On Parables*, each of which (like so many other stories) provokes a markedly disturbing effect, one that associates them with the form of paradox. In a previous note, I referred to Gerhard Neumann's old and outstanding study on the nature of paradox in Kafka, in which he argues that Kafka's kind of paradox is notoriously *sui generis* and different from the classic paradox, which operates mainly through the device of inversion. Validating the latter as a specific moment, he adds a second moment of "deviation," which radically estranges the former, generating a hermeneutical context (one could almost say a trap) in which the usual relations and inferences that regulate logical thinking and common sense are led astray.[31]

I have the impression that both Neumann and Corngold hit the mark, each one of them from the point of view of their specific models. In fact, I think that the same model lies at the basis of their hypotheses: the procedure of inversion is the axis in both, and what Neumann tries to conceive as Kafka's peculiar mode of inversion through the idea of deviation, which constitutes the "sliding paradox," is described by Corngold by way of the figure of the chiasm, which has the advantage of determining in logical and rhetorical terms a generative process of Kafka's writing. In both cases, it is about understanding how this sort of thought paralysis is produced, this *paranoesis*, as I called it, this suspension of every conclusive moment and of every judgment that would communicate the definitive sentence; it is about understanding how this writing manages to open, in that very suspense, the breach of a meaning that is asymptotic with respect to all the complex of significations that it mobilizes (through images, metaphors, allegorical turns, etc.). At the beginning I suggested that this is a structure of scissions (semantic and syntactic, I might say, following Corngold and Neumann), which resonate with one another and call into crisis (but do not annihilate) the possibility of meaning. This crisis that does not annul meaning but suspends it, that does not negotiate significations but counterbalances them according to their respective forces, maintaining their mutual relation in their scission, moreover, in their reciprocal exclusion, is the very form of (im)possibility. One of the aphorisms expresses this in the guise of a little fable: "A reversal. Lurking, fretful, hoping, the answer creeps around the question, peers despairingly in its averted face, follows it on its most abstruse journeys—that is, those that have least to do with the answer" (Kafka, *Zürau* 76 bis).

The reversal (*Umschwung*) is an essential recourse of Kafka's writing. Just as it is the headache of so many scholars, it puts the reader in the (im)possible situation of deciding the undecidable and, for this very reason, of experiencing error—that is, of erring across the exile of meaning, which is the same as being exposed to the unquestionable and pressing condition of keeping oneself open to meaning. It is a writing that tightens the rope just above the ground: to stumble on it is the only way to follow the path.

POST-SCRIPTUM

At the threshold of my catalog of (Kafkan skeptical) tropes, I warned of what seems to me an intractable task—namely, the construction or reconstruction of the logic of Kafka's writing. In what I think is a brilliant book, Paul North has made a sizeable step forward in this direction. Indeed, the excursus appended to the book's first part ("Kafka's Being and Time") is entitled "For a Kafkan Logic." North argues for the existence of "two logoi": the "logic of sense" and the "logic of speech." I am not going to comment on the whole argument sagaciously deployed in this epilogue; I will only refer to something he says about the second logical operation of the "logic of sense": negation. He considers the latter to be "the central logical operation of the thoughts" (alluding precisely to the Zürau "aphorisms," which constitute the essential matter of North's entire argument), corresponding to "a logic whose objective is to slow rather than to promote the movement of truth across premises" (North 155). There is no reference to skepticism in North's book, but I think that the description I have just quoted, and especially the notion of slowing down the "movement of truth" to a complete stop, insinuates the connection for which I'm arguing, and I would say, furthermore, that the crucial instance of the operation of negation that North invokes is particularly illuminating with respect to this issue. The point is to conceive a mode of negation that does not posit in turn; insofar as I negate something, I affirm its opposite, and—insofar as negation is negated—the result turns out to be an affirmation: a negative times a negative equals a positive. Necessary is a mode that would be able to preserve negativity as such and not just to serve dialectically (or mathematically) as mediation toward positivity, much less a higher one.

North cites a letter sent to Max Brod in February 1919 in which Kafka tells his friend about the "common and yet astounding phenomenon" of a young girl, "not Jewish and yet not not-Jewish, not German and yet not not-German [*Nicht Jüdin und nicht Nicht-Jüdin, nicht Deutsche, nicht Nicht-Deutsche*]" (Kafka, *Briefe* 216/*Letters* 213). The young girl is Milena Jesenská. This absolutely peculiar mode of negation, contends North, may be termed an "indefinite negation" (158), and he takes recourse (critically) to Kant's concept of an "infinite negation" in which the predicate is negated. The discussion of this concept is meticulous and lucid, and I'm not going to enter into its details here. I will only retain the Kantian principle of a "thoroughgoing determination," according to which, North writes, "infinite judgment is an epistemological measure taken in a world whose thoroughgoing determinacy is posited a priori and the description of this determinacy is: *tertium non datur*" (161). Given an "all" of possibilities as the condition for this thoroughgoing determinacy, and granted that this "all" is not just a "transcendental presupposition" or an "ideal of pure reason," as it is in Kant, but rather a progressive totalizing and realization of possibilities up to its absolute fulfillment, I think one could also speak of an un-determining negation: different from, though not opposed to, the fundamental principle of dialectics that Hegel adopted from Spinoza, according to which *omnis determinatio est negatio*, a negation the negativity of which points teleologically to a saturated positing. Yet, cardinal here, as I said before, is that "'not and not-not' is an attempt to negate without thereby also positing" (North 159)—that is, to negate without determining anything. Negation in this sense is not opposed to dialectic negativity because, at the moment it would oppose the latter, it would necessarily posit itself as something given; otherwise said, it would affirm itself as negation: it (un)limits itself to open the possibility of the third (and the fourth)—that is, the *other*.

To a certain extent, Kafka's absolutely peculiar kind of negation—impervious to any form of affirmation, positing, and givenness—reminds me of Swift's "the thing which was not," which is the way the rational horses of Gulliver's fourth voyage are able to explain the practice of lying, universally widespread in the human world, and absolutely unknown to them.[32] This "not," if taken to characterize Gulliver's place in Houyhnhmnland (for there he is "the thing that is not"), is a negation without a contrary: Gulliver has no place in this world; he *is* a no-place (*ou topos*), impossible to fit into the binary scheme of Houyhnhmns and Yahoos—a radically *other* in a world that is fully determined. In this sense, Swift's "not," which neither posits nor opposes, as I argue elsewhere, reenters itself and becomes sheer potency ("La verdad y su doble" 161), which also has something of a liberating effect. This would be the potency of Kafka's negation.

But let us leave Swift to himself. Anyway, I would like to believe that any self-respecting skeptic would value Kafka's "not and not-not" as a genuine finding. You may recall in this context some of the codified utterances of the Pyrrhonian skeptic recorded by Sextus Empiricus: "I determine nothing [*ouden horizo*]," which Sextus explains as "an expression indicative of our own mental condition [*pathous hemeterou*]" rather than an affirmation about things not manifest (Sextus 197). Or again: "All things are undetermined [*panta estin aorista*]," which is intended not as an assertion about existing things but, rather, as the announcement about how things presented by the dogmatists appear to the skeptic (198). All express the skeptic's present state of mind in view of what presently appears—that is, in view of the *phenomenon*, which Sextus calls the criterion of skepticism. In any case, if you examine Sextus's catalog of skeptical formulas, you won't find anything as cogent as Kafka's doubling of the negation, with the exception, perhaps, of the second expression: *aphasia* consists in refraining from *phasis*, assertion in its general sense as either affirmation or negation, so that aphasia does not entail that things really lead to non-assertion but, rather, indicates "that we now, at the time of uttering it, are in this condition regarding the problems [*tôn zetoumenon*] now before us" (193). The one and only difference is that Milena is nothing for which you are searching (*zeteo*); she is not a problem but, rather, something that is at the same time a "usual and ... astonishing appearance," which is precisely what *phenomena* should be for a skeptic.

Chapter Six

Borges

ESSAY AND FICTION

TWO OF THE MOST COMMONLY OBSERVED ISSUES in the analyses of and commentaries on the work of Jorge Luis Borges (1899–1986) are, on the one hand, the relaxation and even the erasure of the limits separating essay from fiction and, on the other, the skeptical disposition of his writing. The first concerns a sort of literary peculiarity that, while it is not exclusive to Borges, reaches what is perhaps its most complete and purest expression in his work. Concerning the second issue, I prefer to think that it defines a certain atmosphere and an effect, instead of a standpoint or an intellectual affiliation attributable to Borges. I'm interested here in establishing a relation between these two issues.

The essay, as we well know, has skeptical roots and frequently, if not always, breathes a skeptical air ever since its original inception by Montaigne, who in turn, in his *Apology for Raymond Sebond*, famously divulges the arguments of Sextus Empiricus, with the subsequent repercussion that these arguments would have throughout the development of modern philosophy.[1] The intimate relation between essay and fiction, which might at first be mistrusted because it has the air of confounding truth and deception (the calling of the essay, although it confesses its lack of conclusiveness and is essentially reluctant with respect to dogma, is always the truth, whereas fiction presents us with a contract according to which we tolerate being deceived in exchange for a bonus of pleasure or amusement), is arguable mainly because in both cases, in essay and in fiction, the discourse is located on the level and the horizon of the hypothesis, of the "as if." In turn, the tentative inscription of that relation in the context of skepticism supposes something particularly interesting, for there is some ground for suspecting that fiction also has a certain place therein precisely because of the incidental use that the skeptic makes of hypothetical arguments (such as "supposing that" or "let us think as if") in order to disappoint the dogmatist's pretensions to truth.

AN EXEMPLARY TEXT

"Tlön, Uqbar, Orbis Tertius" is frequently mentioned as a paradigmatic case of the fluidity between fiction and essay, such that it would be possible to extract from it the general clues for the comprehension of Borgesian writing. There are people who believe that its inclusion as the first piece of *Fictions* (and therefore as the first fiction that Borges acknowledges publicly with his signature)[2] gives something of a wink in this direction. Nevertheless, this would probably amount to falling victim to the tricks of that writing and of other winks in Borges's narrative, which the author uses to warn his readers about the hidden but decisive signification of marginal details and lost corners of the world. It is possible that the very concise prologues, not exempt from equivocal hints, should be considered with much more attention, especially—as concerns the present case—what Borges says in the prologue to the *Garden of Forking Paths*, the book in which that first "fiction" was first included; in a sort of typological sketch of the texts that form the book, three classes are distinguished: a detective story (which gives the collection its title), four "tales of fantasy," and, lastly, some "notes on imaginary books" (*Obras* 1: 457/*Collected* 67),[3] which is the category to which our present text belongs.

In fact, "Tlön, Uqbar, Orbis Tertius" is comprised of three notes that each report a different finding: an unusual encyclopedic entry in the first note, a whole volume of an alien encyclopedia in the second, and a letter in the third, which supposedly clears up the mystery promoted by the two previous notes. The three are linked by a couple of discreet and oblique clues.

Notwithstanding the fact that Borges seems to play down the significance of this narrative in his prologue, it obviously has an unequivocal importance for his entire work. It is a sort of pattern book of procedures that could be interpreted as the peculiar tropes of this writing; in turn, Borges's writing transforms those tropes into fundamental modes of the production of fiction.

The peculiarity of these tropes consists in the fact that they are not merely rhetorical forms but are codified with the help of certain objects that are also somehow their schemes.

Two of these objects, which are eminent from every point of view in Borges's work, appear at the very beginning of the narration: the mirror and the encyclopedia. A certain mirror, located at the end of the corridor of a country house where the narrator and Bioy Casares are lodging (the "I" by which the former identifies himself announces unequivocally that he should be read as the real Borges), is the occasion for Bioy to quote from memory a sententious phrase on mirrors that he had found in one of the volumes of an apocryphal encyclopedia, which, under the ostentatious title of the *Anglo-American Cyclopaedia*, was nothing other than the unauthorized reprint of the 1902 edition of the *Encyclopaedia Britannica*. The place from which Bioy picks out the quotation is an article on Uqbar, which, according to subsequent investigations, figured only in four additional pages of the copy possessed by the friend, whereas the country in question—allegedly located in Asia Minor—is not to be found in any map whatsoever.[4]

It might seem that the mirror has an incidental function; a remark on the silent and ominous glimmer of the mirror in the corridor—the narrator says that "the mirror was spying on us [*el espejo nos acechaba*]" (*Obras* 1: 461/ *Collected* 68, translation modified)—motivates the evocation of the phrase. But this very phrase makes it clear that the case of the mirror is far from being trivial: "mirrors and copulation are abominable, for they multiply the number of mankind" (461/68),[5] recalls Bioy. This censurable virtue—the blame betrays a kernel of misanthropy—is an oblique insinuation of the story's central issue, and, of course, as everybody knows, it is an obsessive theme in Borges's work. The mention of the mirror refers in turn to the encyclopedia, which is another fundamental scheme in this work: John Irwin recalls that medieval scholars called those treatises that pretended to expound the sum (*summa*) of human knowledge *speculum*, suggesting that this sum (a predecessor of the modern encyclopedia) is the place in which all things are reflected (286). At a point, then, which, if you wish, can be conceived as asymptotic, at the end of the mirror or at the beginning of the encyclopedia, encyclopedia and mirror are the same.

This amounts to saying that what Borges calls at the very beginning of his story, using a word that one might suppose to be carefully calculated, a "conjunction" ("I owe the discovery of Uqbar to the conjunction of a mirror and an encyclopedia" [*Obras* 1: 461/*Collected* 68]) describes both the incident—the coincidence—that gives occasion to the story, let us say to its content, and at the same time the form and the character of the story. Unlike the narratives that are supported by the development of their respective anecdotes (no matter the derivations that may follow), this one very quickly shows its strategy and its consciousness of its strategy. As Paul de Man says in "A Modern Master," this narrative is more a philosophical tale (a *conte philosophique*), which was so assiduous in the eighteenth century (de Man, *Critical* 125); playing a little with this theme and with the aforesaid conjunction, we could perhaps speak of a "speculative tale."

But there is a clear difference between this story and the philosophical tale of the eighteenth century; the master of the genre was, of course, Voltaire (with those wonderful books *Candide*, *Zadig*, and *Micromégas*), without omitting some outstanding pieces by Sade. The philosophical tale serves a critical intention with respect to the established social conditions and relations concerning power, beliefs, and customs, while the Borgesian model seems to be perfectly innocuous in this range of issues, at least if one thinks of explicit and direct discursive functions. Whereas the former, due precisely to the critical efficacy that is its essential aim, appeals to satirical resources in order to chastise misconceptions and prejudices and hides a nucleus of philosophical contents with primarily moral implications beneath a narrative form, Borges's "tale" *seems*—please note my emphasis here—to dispense with every allusion to an external context and incorporates into its economy, as internal elements, all the referential data to which it resorts. If the *conte philosophique*, much like satire, is a mirror that sends back the distorted image of a determinate reality in order to accentuate its censurable traits in a way similar to caricature, Borges's tale is a mirror that turns back upon itself, producing an effect of derealization entirely in accordance with the apparent abstention on which I am commenting, and it has irony—self-irony, it should be said—as its essential resource. At least in principle, because, from the point of view of the hyper-complex treatment of the relations between fiction (representation) and reality that Borges develops, this narrative should be considered infinitely more treacherous and captious in view of those same contexts to which I am alluding.

I'm talking about an effect of derealization. To say that this is a process that occurs in the narrative might sound like an oddity or pleonasm, because in the end it is a story gathered, together with the rest of its kind, under the title of "fiction," and this makes it clear for the reader that what is from now on offered to his or her attention is a collection of "pieces," of "eight pieces" as Borges himself calls them (*Obras* 1:457/*Collected* 67, translation modified),[6] whose limits of consistency are, if I may put it so, "para-real." However, this narrative initially predetermines the world from which it is told as the real world, particularly in its first chapter, under the auspices of the names of actual people—although the majority of the circumstances in which they appear and some of the works attributed to them are fictitious—and the relations of those people to the "self" of the narrator seem to identify the latter as Borges himself. This determination therefore becomes a necessity for a narrative whose denouement is the contamination, the invasion, of the real world by the imaginary and purely speculative world of Tlön.

Furthermore, the whole first chapter has the aspect of a report on the bibliographic—and in a certain way detective—inquiry undertaken by "Borges" and his friend in order to clear up the enigma of the anomalous edition of the illicit *Anglo-American Cyclopaedia*. It is true that this aspect mirrors at the same time the pure research of knowledge for knowledge's sake and police investigation. It is also true that the air of invention that surrounds the report disturbs the referentiality that should guarantee the mention of real people with their real inclinations and intellectual traits.[7]

The second part is, as I said, a new note. Unlike the specifications of the incidents in the first chapter, this one starts under the misty effect of the invocation of the late Herbert Ashe, of whom it is said that his "limited and waning memory ... still lingers ... in the illusory depths of the mirrors" of a certain hotel in Adrogué, and that, "in life, [he] was afflicted with unreality, as so many Englishmen are; in death, he is not even the ghost he was in life" (*Obras* 1: 463/*Collected* 70).[8] This aura of phantasmal unreality is, so to speak, the portico through which a major finding is to be made: as the only legacy of the dead man, the narrator finds months later, in the hotel's bar, the eleventh volume of "*A First Encyclopaedia of Tlön*" (464/71; the English comes from the original as well), which is the visible sign of an entire planet. (The report adds insidiously that this eleventh volume has 1,001 pages, obviously alluding to the *Arabian Nights* that Borges admired so much, frequently evoking the central night in which Scheherazade begins the entire narration anew, with the abyssal effect or suggestion that her story will reach the night in which she began to tell the whole story.) From this point forward, after detailing the conjectures that such a finding motivated throughout the learned world—Néstor Ibarra, Martínez Estrada, Drieu La Rochelle, and Alfonso Reyes are all fallaciously mentioned—and determining that "the fundamental problem" (465/72, translation modified) consists in identifying the inventors of

Tlön (and briefly alluding to what will constitute the clue to the enigma in the third note), Borges's narration centers on a description of the peculiarities of this unsuspected planet, which vividly brings to mind the specious reports of books on utopias.

But these peculiarities are neither wonders nor anecdotic aberrations but—and the narrator asks for a few minutes of attention—the "conception of the universe" (*Obras* 1: 465/*Collected* 72) that prevails on Tlön. So, the dossier concerning the "congenital idealism" (465/72) of its inhabitants is discussed, with clearly Berkeleyan characteristics: the Bishop is mentioned at the threshold, and the ironical objection that David Hume made to his philosophy is recalled.[9]

PLANETARY IDEALISM

The interest that the narrator declares in communicating the Tlönian "conception of the universe" has a special meaning for Borges's strategy. The *idea* of a world the inhabitants of which are congenital idealists—spontaneous adherents to the principle *esse est percipi*—is stated in the antipodes of the beliefs with which we organize our lives, what for us amounts to saying in the antipodes of belief as such, granted that we can admit that the very nature of belief consists in the spontaneous adhesion to the existence of an outside world and of independent things filling it up. So, this idea defines in a parodic and paradoxical way a planet on which beliefs are the contrary of belief as such. The matrix of all those beliefs is the conviction that the world "is not a concourse of objects in space" but "a heterogeneous series of independent acts" (*Obras* 1: 465/*Collected* 72–73, translation modified) in time (and it's understood that these acts are mental acts and are independent from each other).

The narrator's interest may be expeditiously attributed to Borges. The brilliant exposition of the peculiar beliefs that prevail on Tlön serves diverse purposes, but they all revolve around a concept, a program, and a practice of writing that is the inalienable characteristic of his work. I will summarize the stages or episodes of this exposition.

The first concern is language, as the means by which and in which human beings administer their relations to reality. There are two hemispheres of Tlön: in the southern hemisphere verbs prevail, and in the boreal hemisphere, monosyllabic adjectives; in both, nouns have been abolished or simply do not exist, which coheres with the aforesaid conviction. If there is nothing but mental acts, if there are no things, only perceptions, there cannot be nouns, which are the indispensable recourse of *our* belief in the existence of an external world and of things in it. It is not necessary to insist on the consequences that Borges extracts from this double assumption: whatever they might be, verbs or adjectives, the ways of speaking of events take on a poetic appearance, although this effect is ironically toned down because in the southern hemisphere you can only notice it in translation—due to the very uncomfortable cacophony of the original—and in the northern you have to postulate the effect, benevolently admitting that only one word, made up of unending combinations and compositions, can truly enjoy such a poetic quality. Some people might have the impression that the hint toward the entity of the poetic is unequivocal, that what is implied here is that the poetic shares the disbelief in nouns, that it plays them down, surrounding them with swarms of events until finally dissolving them. Be that as it may, the volatilization of reference that lies at the core of the omission of nouns, of *names*, the merely expressive character of the verbal constructions, their irrepressible creativity, results in a most abundant spreading of nouns, which is especially evident in those "*poetic object[s]*" (*Obras* 1: 466/*Collected* 73)[10] of the boreal inhabitants of Tlön.

The second stage or episode is a direct corollary of the primordial Tlönian conviction: the only discipline that it knows or admits is psychology, taking into account that there are only mental processes and nothing subsistent. Setting aside the incongruities contained in the exposition of this principle (incongruities scattered throughout the text), its consequences entail a philosophical joke: since everything that exists is mental and therefore temporal, relations between independent states or acts are not conceivable if not as associations of ideas. The preponderance in Tlön of George Berkeley's grand fiction converges on the challenge to causality that his critic Hume promotes. So, the truth of Berkeley's idealism as supported by Tlönians is Hume's idealism.[11]

The joke is the preamble to that which could be considered the core of the provocation that this text and all of Borges's work addresses to philosophy and in general to the pretensions and institutions of knowledge. I mean *provocation* in a double sense, for it is at once harassment and irresistible incitement; where this writing hurts the expectations of the cognitive dominion over reality, there it awakens them at the same time, though not to urge them to reestablish themselves with the same purpose but to search and find, following writing's equivocal traces, the subtext of their own liberating critique: it functions, in the skeptical mode, as a purgative. This bifid provocation (for it has much of a serpent's seduction), promoted by devious as well as flagrant incongruities, has its inception in the sequel of what the text calls "total monism or idealism" (*Obras* 1: 466/*Collected* 74, translation modified): the invalidation of science and even of mere reasoning. The invalidation follows—and by now this should not surprise us—Hume's destructive *innuendo*: a subject's state not being inherently linked with another, the abusive attribution of causal connections to the supposed things of the supposedly external world has repercussions on the perceptions that lead—in us—to such presumption, so that the explanation is void. But this uselessness, remarks the narrator, by now speaking as a thorough connoisseur of Tlön's peculiarities, is a motive not for the inexistence of the sciences but for their uncontainable multiplication:

> the fact that every philosophy is by definition a dialectical game, a *Philosophie des Als Ob*, has allowed them to proliferate. There are systems upon systems that are incredible but possessed of a pleasing architecture or a certain agreeable sensationalism. The metaphysicians of Tlön seek not truth, or even plausibility—they seek to amaze, astound. In their view, metaphysics is a branch of the literature of fantasy. They know that a system is naught but the subordination of all the aspects of the universe to one of those aspects. (467/74)

This is such a thoroughbred Borgesian statement that commentators agree in omitting its mediations (a radically foreign and apocryphal encyclopedia unwillingly bequeathed by an ashen Englishman and a reader of that encyclopedia who is probably a fallacious or imprudent narrator and who looks too much like the assumed author, an assumed author, of course, because he is captiously invested in the narrator and the whole as the supplies for a fraudulent story) and straightforwardly attribute it to Borges himself, knowing well that Borges spent most of his life disavowing the opinion that there could be something like Borges *himself*, immune to the *other*, that there could be "selfness" exempt from total "otherness."

As should be clear by now, the provocation that this statement proposes is biting and fulminating, and it perhaps reveals the clue for all that is said about Tlön and its oddities. In a certain way it could be like the vision that Kant had of the wide and multifarious tradition of philosophy that reached him as an undertow once he was alerted by Hume's corrosive critique. But the statement is due above all to the idea that philosophy—and all undertakings of knowledge—is a disconsolate exercise of pure fiction; the reference to Hans Vaihinger's "as if" points in this direction. It is possible that truth was the primeval glimpse of some perplexed people who didn't give up in assigning privileged importance to their own discomfiture; it is possible that, harassed by their perplexity and some happy findings that seemed on target only to fall very soon into discredit, they had aspired at least to the probability of accessing truth or to a promissory but uncertain auspice but in the end could not yield it as fruit, condemned to be satisfied with a dim reflection of the astonishment that originally incited them to the search of truth. "In their view, metaphysics is a branch of the literature of fantasy." The phrase, half sober, half categorical, makes the philosophical flow return to its original source. Aristotle maintained that human beings have two main affections: the love of stories, which is the love of wonder, and the love of knowing. The first is universal, and the second pertains only to a few, but the whole of humanity, including the few, coincides in astonishment: lovers of myths and philosophers have the same origin and the same calling. "Borges" turns them back to that origin, and he willingly confounds them there: fantastic literature is the truth of philosophy.

From a certain point of view, this assertion is banal. When Kant refers to the history of philosophy leading up to his era as an arena, a battlefield in which the architects and champions of various, not only discrepant but also contradictory doctrines, he draws a picture that supposes or implies *this* truth: each time a new thinker makes an appearance, wholly persuaded that he is the bearer of *the* truth, he tells us a new tale. The problem is that he doesn't know the literary virtue of his discourse, and, instead of gaily consenting to entertaining himself and his fellows or, at least, his peers, he erects an unassailable and gloomy fortress of dogmatism.

The smiling paradox that the text highlights—the proliferation of systems occasioned by the general disbelief in something like *the* truth—is, then, a consequence of the skepticism in which the idealism of the Tlönians ends up, something of an inverse consequence at which one curiously arrives by a straight path. And precisely this fateful inference is no longer as trivial as the previous steps might have been, or seemed to be, because the reduction of philosophy (of metaphysics as its speculative coronation and as the effort of giving an account of the whole universe) to the status of fiction provokes the beginnings of a trembling that will spread to the entire compass of discourse, to all of reason's aspirations. Something happens to *the* truth with *this* truth, which paradoxically and parodically includes it as a subordinate member. (A particular truth might not be part of *the* truth; its particularity might stand in a tense relation with the latter's universality.) So, the acknowledged arbitrariness of the systems stipulates a different rule for what we call truth. It is not improbable that this rule is very closely, or perhaps essentially, related to the nature of the essay, and it is not improbable that it lies in the nearest neighborhood of skepticism or that it is a skepticism sui generis. I will return to this in the final section of this chapter.

Another step: the showcase of systems advocated by the Tlönian schools demonstrates an imaginative fertility that promptly penetrates deep into the jungle of absurdity. There's the tricky indication that among all those systems the one that has been most outrageous is materialism, which, if we overlook its enunciation and its name, is, one would say, for us the spontaneous certainty of common sense. The discussions aroused by this doctrine, particularly the "sophism of the nine copper coins" (*Obras* 1: 467/*Collected* 75) conceived by a heresiarch from the eleventh century (this number haunts the text) who wants to prove the identity and continuity of the nine coins even when nobody perceives them, turn out to be new avatars, which follow and substitute the initial idealism (or mentalism) and radical skepticism, consisting in an idealist pantheism, proposed by an opponent of the heresiarch one century later (we have been warned that in Tlön—as in England, we might add—the duodecimal system prevails). The pantheism in question refers all mental acts (being could be predicated on nothing else) to a unique, indivisible, and eternal subject that is refracted, let us say a bit phantasmagorically, in the plurality of beings of the universe. The final triumph of this new creed, which is somehow the caricature of Spinoza, who is mentioned earlier in the text, and for which forceful arguments are made, has considerable effects on mathematics and literature: in the former, it is established that the obtainment of the same numeric results by diverse persons is due to the association of ideas or to good memory; in the latter, every idea of originality, and therefore also of plagiarism, is omitted, and all works are attributed to a unique, anonymous, and timeless author. This last detail, which implies the abolition of the concept of authorship, is, we know, a cherished theme for Borges.

The report on the "conception of the universe" to which the Tlönians adhere or according to which they live—which turns out to be not only one but many conceptions, many contained in one master conception, granted that the stubborn idealism is the matrix of all the variations, including those that deny it—is in the end, despite all its sophisms and idle pursuits, or merely because of them, too familiar: *de tua res agitur*. It doesn't take any work to recognize the history of human urges—of those urges of those human beings driven by the metaphysical *élan*—in search of an explanation of the universe, fatally unsuccessful but not lacking interest.[12] The "conjunction of a mirror and an encyclopedia" of which the initial sentence of the story speaks comes to be fulfilled in a very unexpected way. The eleventh volume of an improbable encyclopedia, which casually contains the exposition of the Tlönian philosophy and science and permits its reader not only to report it as public information but also to incur conjectures that might intervene, correct, and extrapolate, is, in what amounts to all this, the mirror in which the terrestrial history of thought is reflected. And, so, the narrator's report, which reflects the Tlönian mirror, remains involved in the same game too. There is only one difference between that planet and ours: like every lucid mirror, the Tlönian one knows about its condition, unlike the blind mirror of human knowledge. Hence the phrase that is the center of the exposé and that actually is in the middle of it: "In their view, metaphysics is a branch of the literature of fantasy." This feeling has the air of a smiling abdication of all the pretensions that constitute the fundamental unease of human beings searching to decipher the secret of the universe.[13]

The last step of the second note is something of a marginal comment and at the same time a conclusion or, if you like, a definitive statement about the things that are at stake in all of this. It concerns the *hrönir*, "secondary objects" that are, "though awkwardly so, somewhat longer" than those that they emulate (*Obras* 1: 470/*Collected* 77). In their initial condition, they are duplicates of lost objects, caused by the eagerness of a second seeker. Their methodical production, says the narrator, is recent, and it "has been of invaluable aid to archaeologists, making it possible not only to interrogate but even to modify the past, which is now no less plastic, no less malleable than the future" (470/77–78). This docility permits the fabrication of a past that is—if I may give it a Borgesian title—the size of their hope. For it is possible that hope is the breath of memory, that it is directed more to the past than to the future, granted that the most to which a mortal can aspire is that the past from which he comes is ordered and made to measure. In the text it is said that the *ur* is, at times, stranger and purer than any *hrön*: "the object brought forth by hope" is "stranger and purer than any *hrön*" (470/78). And it is called by a name that should be intimately evocative for us, an *ur*: "ur" is "original" in German, etymologically that "from which," and it also refers to the ancient great reign of Sumeria, etymologically just "the city," which in the eleventh edition of the *Britannica* occupies the place that the story (fallaciously) attributes to Uqbar in the corresponding volume of the *American Cyclopedia*. I set aside the gradations and degradations that the *hrönir* admit, which, even as they might betray their derivation from a model, also have a proclivity to take the place of their models in the fashion of the Platonic *eidola* (the *hrön* of the eleventh degree—it couldn't be anything other than the eleventh—surpasses the original in definition and purity), because all of them depend on the fact of duplication and on the "fact" that such duplication is due to rushes of the mind, to mental processes. What in the calculated progression of the story satisfies this marginal comment is the indication that the Tlönian "conception of the universe" is not innocuous with respect to that which could stubbornly continue to be reality and that the latter does not remain unhurt by the power of representation. Therefore, the comment is also a conclusion. A conclusion that allows for the poetical rapture of the narration:

> Things duplicate themselves on Tlön; they also tend to grow vague or "sketchy," and to lose detail when they begin to be forgotten. The classic example is the doorway that continued to exist so long as a certain beggar frequented it, but which was lost to sight when he died. Sometimes a few birds, a horse, have saved the ruins of an amphitheater. (471/78)

A DOUBLE REALITY

Duality, duplication, duplicity, splitting: it is not only about the weirdness of the congenital predisposition of the inhabitants of Tlön to grant a "reality" that exists only according to the rhythms and changes of thinking. It is also about the strategy and the paratextual structure of the story,[14] which folds systematically on itself, in itself, and betrays in its own writing, form, and procedure the same motifs that it exploits as narrative material. Splitting is a trope that gives an account of what is at stake in what I named earlier the allied schemes of mirror and encyclopedia, which, by the way, makes the story at the same time a story, a fiction, an essay on that fiction, and an essay on fiction as such. Philosophical tale, encyclopedic tale, speculative tale.

Splitting appears, then, as an essential resource, which one is tempted to attribute to the entire Borgesian work in (at least) three directions: in the first place, and precisely here, it is the splitting of everything (materiality/ideality) and the uncertainty of perception as soon as one attempts to identify that which is perceived (*esse est percipi* is also posed as a question); in the second place, this uncertainty has to do with the deferral of perception, always shaded by memory and expectation—that is, by its unavoidable unpunctuality; in the third place, it is the splitting of the narrator (the narrating "self"), which points to the contract between writer and reader (the writer as reader, and the reader as writer; I will return to the issue of the self). This last aspect, this contract, occurs outside legality or, rather, generates a legality of its own, for it has the character of complicity.

In his early essay on Borges, de Man lets his reading key be dictated by the *Universal History of Infamy* or, more exactly, by the notion of infamy and by the criminal nature of certain actions that constitute the motif or the center of the stories.[15] In all of these cases, in one way or another, it is a crime of impersonation, which suggests that splitting is never innocent. De Man's hypothesis is sharp, and, seeming to fit naturally with the Borgesian recreation of the detective story, it can be extended to the rest of Borges's narrative production, an extension that de Man actually undertakes. However, I think that the equation of infamy with mere crime runs the risk of simplification. Obviously, this is not de Man's approach. But he does not point to an issue that I deem of primary importance—namely, that infamy, having a moral and legal signification, is not limited to crime. It suffices to think that the *Universal History of Infamy* is not only a museum of human iniquities (superbly told) but also a lesson on history, which is to say on reality and narration. A lesson that has its reason in precisely infamy, not as a moral concept but in its primary etymological meaning, in-famy, from "fame," itself from *fari*, "to speak": the in-famous is the unsaid and that which resists being said—that is, that which resists entering into the space of universality.[16] Transgression and crime are privileged forms of the exacerbation of such resistance, just as they are violent irruptions of contingency. The Borgesian title's oxymoron not only notoriously points to this rebellious singularity but also suggests that writing, this kind of writing that makes the inscription of the deed (the wicked action) and the teleological ideality of the narration swing against each other impetuously, brings about the possibility of doing justice to such singularity.

Certainly, "Tlön, Uqbar, Orbis Tertius" complies with many of the characteristics of the detective story: there is an enigma to decipher; the narrator and Bioy act as detectives in the first note, and, as the enigma spreads and attention is increasingly attracted, a cohort of new investigators is added to the original two;[17] there are hints and traces that are casually revealed or discovered; there are exhumations and seals; there are deaths, surely not by another's hand, although not exempt of a certain dose of violence, deaths that obviously contribute to the whole issue; there is a persistence of the enigma at the end of the first two notes, which the narrator says he published in 1940 in the journal *Sur* and in the *Antología de la literatura fantástica* (which was actually published that year by Borges, Bioy, and Silvina Ocampo and included the complete tale); there is a (presumed) solution in the postscript that perhaps does not clear things up to the extent desired; there is a supplementary mystery that is marginally annotated ("there is still, of course, the problem of the *material* from which some objects are made" [*Obras* 1: 473n1/ *Collected* 81n6]); and, finally, there is an abyssal process—the usurpation of the real world by the fantastic universe, right now in course—which ends up making the story border the genre of science fiction.

All this you can find there. But the Borgesian rewriting of the detective story does not simply propose a particular mystery; it is not restricted to offering a more or less exciting or disturbing sequence of events and a more or less surprising denouement; in fact, this can be easily verified in such paradigmatic narratives as "The Garden of Forking Paths" or "Ibn-Hakam al-Bokhari, Murdered in His Labyrinth." In each of them, rewriting does not consist in the proposal of a new procedure or a new form for structuring the events but presents itself thematically, explicitly on its own terms; it is true that this rewriting is inextricably overlapped with the events narrated, but it is also clearly discernible as such. This assigns to such rewriting an essentially epistemological feature, which in turn is in accordance with the original and cardinal calling of the genre, and you know that the fundamental instigator and model of this genre, with exactly the same traits and scope, is Edgar Allan Poe.[18] The epistemological feature is manifest in a most extraordinary fashion in the reflexive, self-inclusive, and auto-ironic character of the Borgesian story; it has in the aforesaid splitting its principle and makes the statute of fiction—and of course its relations to the supposedly "real" (which cannot continue to be thought of as referential or merely representative)— the nuclear problem of literature, of language. The deployment of all these attributes and all these qualities is what makes "Tlön, Uqbar, Orbis Tertius" a foundational text.[19]

The point is that the story reflects itself. The "polemic" that keeps Borges and Bioy entertained in the after-dinner talk deals with "composing a first-person novel whose narrator would omit or distort things and engage in all sorts of contradictions, so that a few of the book's readers—a very few—might divine an atrocious or banal reality" (*Obras* 1:461/*Collected* 68, translation modified). And it turns out that the story about Tlön corresponds to that kind of narrative economy, with the exception that it is not a novel but, according to a preference for the less laborious that Borges declares in his prologue, a "note" or a sequence of three notes; all the rest is there: the narration in the first person, the omission or disfiguring of facts, the various contradictions, the glimpses reserved for a very scarce number of readers, and you could also name the idle practice of reading as a divination exercise, which is a Borgesian paradigm. At least, the final revelation—that which allows itself to be divined by the few selected readers—is probably the very essence of the story; the invasion of the real world by the phantasmagoria of the planet Tlön has exactly this character, an invasion that the narrator reports as an inexorable fact that reaches the condition of a universal evidence and leaves the inhabitants of that first world nothing but the sad certainty of a total expropriation of the real by the fictitious, which is a sort of tide, as it were: the progressive intromission of fantastic elements into the real world has as its counterpart an undertow that bleeds this world dry of all its own components, which vanish, absorbed by the imaginary order. In the end, the "atrocious or banal" quality—which one is tempted to rephrase as "atrocious and banal," both at once—is perhaps the definitive predicate that Borges reserves for what we know or believe we know as "reality" and is—if not always, most of the time—the half defeated, half mordacious lesson of his texts. That reality—what we represent to ourselves as reality and to which we are condemned—is expropriated from the beginning. This is (perhaps, and let us say it marginally) the *Orbis Tertius*.

SOMETHING THAT HAPPENS
(THAT HAPPENED) TO THE SUBJECT

Something happens to or with the "self," to the first person, when she or he takes into account the evidence I was just mentioning. (And I employ the word *evidence* not necessarily in the logical or epistemological sense but, rather, in the legal and policing sense; between the two series there is a link but also a difference, because in the latter sense what we call "evidence," as dazzling as it might be, is due to a hypothesis.) Something happens to the first person (the "I") when you use it as a deictic of the place (language and affection) from which, if not the evidence, at least the (partial, fragmentary) set of traces that lead to it is enounced.

"Tlön, Uqbar, Orbis Tertius" is written in the first person. As I already said, this person (you will recall that the etymological meaning of that word is "mask") is Borges and "Borges," and perhaps many other names in the story; for the same reason, she is Nobody, like Odysseus. It is important, then, to find out what happens to that first person, that "I."

The use of the first person is typical of the essay and also of the report in which one gives account of the facts or events one has witnessed. It is true that these two cases are distinct, for in the essay the "I" manifests its permanent disposition to be involved in the issue he approaches not only by way of opinion but also affectively, even existentially; in the report the first person who informs about the facts or events she has witnessed must instead remain aloof, not committing to the meaning that those facts or events might eventually have for her person. However, between both cases there is a discreet connecting thread: both carry out the labor of the witness. And, for the essayist, if she is not a present and bodily witness of the matter, as the reporter has to be, that condition of presence is accomplished precisely by the declaration of the effect that the matter produces in her; she is, let us say, an eyewitness of this effect.

The use of the "I" is a *signed* use. In one case, the signature (the name) is like a deictic: it is the indication not necessarily of a personal identity but rather of a position—the incidental position in which the first person has found herself at the moment of dealing with a given matter—and, therefore, it's the mark of a point of view. In the other case, it is like a credential: a certificate of authenticity that risks the veracity of the one who signs.

"Tlön, Uqbar, Orbis Tertius" has a signature, and it lacks a signature at the same time. Its inclusion initially in *The Garden of Forking Paths* and definitively in *Fictions* obviously refers it to the authorship of Jorge Luis Borges. But the "I" who narrates, who reports, who utters his opinions and expresses his perplexities is and is not Borges, or, rather, is "Borges," a character in his own story who collects or betrays traits that are peculiar to Borges, the (real) person. It is the *same* Borges and the *other*, who seem to converge only at one point—precisely the final point, the end of the tale—although asymptotically. "That makes very little difference to me; through my quiet days in this hotel in Adrogué, I go on revising (though I never intend to publish) an indecisive translation in the style of Quevedo of Sir Thomas Browne's *Urne Buriall*" (*Obras* 1: 474/*Collected* 81).[20]

I spoke earlier of a supplementary mystery (the mystery concerning certain Tlönian objects infiltrating our world). It has been frequently observed that there is in this last declaration something that could also be considered a last enigma, which winks at the plot of the whole story. Why the mention of the baroque writer Thomas Browne? Why does his brilliant work (*Hydriotaphia: Urne Buriall, or, A Brief Discourse of the Sepulchrall Urnes Lately Found in Norfolk*), originally published in 1658, have something to do with the imaginary planet and its aberrant traits? What could occasion the translation of this old work with its ominous title? What, if not laziness completely given up to its own caprice? Why a Quevedian translation? Why uncertain? Why a translation at all? Those are surely too many questions, and any attempt to answer them would take me beyond my present possibilities, without taking into account my ignorance of the many issues that would be indispensable to that task.[21] I would just underscore the posthumous air that the declaration breathes, which is also the posthumous air of the subject who proffers it. This subject finds in Browne, if not an intimate companion, at least a mentor and a model for the art of writing as an art of memory. The recent finding of some urns buried in the neighborhood with a number of bones, ornaments, and accessories prompts Browne's meditation, which concerns memory, forgetfulness, and mortality, in a tenor not distinct from that of Quevedo, the third fellow upon whom "Borges" calls to help manage the translation;[22] the pondering on depredation finds refuge only in the faith and devotion of the Englishman. In the posthumous air of *his* meditation, the stench of mortality and the consoling breeze of redemption are intermingled, though the hope for redemption does not remove from the heart the deep melancholy, for the permanence to which the living once aspired is vain and dissipates with the ashes of the dead, and memory is fragile and fraudulent. Without the least consolation, being sure of the eradication of his world, which is ours, the narrator (who, as I said, is and is not, at the same time, Borges "himself") seeks refuge in the mindful exercise of his translation. Mindful and posthumous. The postscript that is closed with such a declaration is a postscript in an absolute sense. Its date to come feigned, even extending a hundred years hence to the time when the hundred volumes of the *Second Encyclopedia of Tlön* will have been found, it seals the inexorable temporality of death and seals death as the meaning of temporality.

And time is certainly an essential index of what is at stake in the story. It is not only about time being the stuff of which things are made for the inhabitants of Tlön: a heterogeneous series (a sequence) of acts (mental acts) that are connected to each other only by associative games. Besides this, the narrator is particularly meticulous with the indication of dates. The two notes and the postscript mark three chronological milestones: 1935, the year of the first finding; 1940, the year to which the writing of the two first notes is dated; 1947, the year of the postscript. But there are many other dates mentioned in those sections, and, just as with the description of events and situations and with the catalog and survey of ideas and arguments, it doesn't seem possible to fix a definite order provided with strict coherence. The *Anglo-American Cyclopaedia* dates from 1917 and reproduces an edition of the *Encyclopedia Britannica* from 1902; the troubling entry on Uqbar alleges a concise bibliography that refers to a book by Silas Haslam published in 1874 and to another by Andreä from 1641; Ashe dies in 1937; in the postscript the year 1941 figures as the decisive year in which the letter elucidating the mystery of Tlön is found, referring its origins to the beginnings of the seventeenth century and to the conspiracy of a secret society, which, conceiving the invention of an entire country, wastes some years shaping the idea; the fraternity, having suffered persecution, reappears in 1824 (in Memphis, Tennessee, a city with a convenient Egyptian name) when the extravagant, despotic, and awful millionaire Ezra Buckley, informed by a sectarian, judges that what really makes sense is the invention of a whole planet, and the project reaches its final and enormous scope; we are told that four years later Buckley is poisoned and dies; in 1914 the *First Encyclopedia of Tlön* is sent to the hidden collaborators; 1942 is the year in which "the plot thickened" (*Obras* 1: 472/*Collected* 79), with the unexpected intromission of objects that are not from this world; in 1944 the forty volumes of the *First Encyclopedia* are exhumed from a library in Memphis. As far as these facts are considered, everything seems to be in order, an order that looks extremely well constructed. But there are other pieces of information provided by the narrator: the article on Uqbar mentions the "impostor-wizard Smerdis" (462/69) who gets hold of the Persian Empire after Cyrus's death;[23] it also mentions that during the thirteenth century there are religious persecutions against the Uqbarian, orthodox faithful; the eleventh volume of the *First Encyclopedia* indicates the eleventh century (which, calculated according to the duodecimal system, opportunely suggested by a footnote, should be reckoned as extending from 1440 until 1584, on condition that the Tlönian calendar coincides with ours) as the epoch in which a brilliant heresiarch invents the sophism of materialism, and one century later another man of genius, orthodox, thinks up its refutation. In the end,[24] as I said, there's no need to search for contradictions between the various dates detailed in the text; it is clear that its management does not obey an instructive purpose and is not motivated by a zeal for accuracy but, rather, seems to be much more of a distracting maneuver and deliberate gibberish.

One is tempted to think of Borges's multiple preoccupations with the problem of time, which always appears to him as a problem of identity and difference (both things simultaneously), as the anxiety regarding what is to come and the certitude that everything has happened already, as fate and determination, as the condition and definitive nullity of that thing that we call "I." One thinks of the colophon of the remarkable essay "A New Refutation of Time":

> *And yet, and yet . . .*[25] To deny temporal succession, to deny the ego, to deny the astronomical universe, are apparent desperations and secret assuagements. Our destiny (unlike the hell of Swedenborg and the hell of Tibetan mythology) is not horrible because of its unreality; it is horrible because it is irreversible and ironbound. Time is the substance I am made of. Time is a river that carries me away, but I am the river; it is a tiger that mangles me, but I am the tiger; it is a fire that consumes me, but I am the fire. The world, alas, is real; I, alas, am Borges. (*Obras* 2: 157–58/ *Other* 186–87, translation modified)

The other great Borgesian scheme, the labyrinth, appears in this story only in a footnote and under the auspices of the aforementioned Haslam,[26] the apocryphal author of *A General History of Labyrinths*. But the entangled game of dates, which points to a remote past and penetrates into a distant future, proposes that time is a lineal labyrinth, each moment of which is at the same time a bifurcation and an inescapable destiny.[27] The self, the "I," the subject is, *at the same time*, Theseus and the Minotaur.

One could ask if this is the lesson, the moral, of this fable, if in the end it is the question of the subject and its temporality (its melancholic and fateful temporality) that circulates between the lines of the narrative only to come to the surface at the last moment, in the manner of a testimony. I believe there's something (or much) to this. But there's more. The story doesn't leave its reader unhurt. The dated milestones in the notes and the postscript form, according to the sequence of the narrative, a progression that follows the rhythm of the gradual entrance of the thoroughly imaginary world of Tlön into the real world that "we" share, up to the final seizure of the latter by the former: "The world will be Tlön" (*Obras* 1: 474/*Collected* 81). But the time of this gradualism gives account of an entrance that, if it is certainly fragmentary in its occurrence, nonetheless has at its basis a previously constituted complex, a "cosmos" of which "the innermost laws which govern it have been formulated, however provisionally so" (465/72). I've spoken before of complicity as a characteristic of the contract established between writer and reader. This complicity is undoubtedly grounded in the motifs of the text; it is nourished by interest and expectation, by incredulity and by the amazement that overcomes that incredulity, as happens with every good story. But it is founded deeper on the grounds of language and its rhetorical devices, which do not activate without the assistance of the reader but evidently precede it. The same time of progression is the time of reading in such a way that, in a specular manner, the fragmentary and gradual entrance of the imaginary world allegorizes the process of the production of the story itself and teaches the difference between an order previously constituted (language), its deployment, and its always incomplete appropriation by the subject. There is no subject without time. And if there is no subject without language, if there is no subject outside of language, the story gives an account of that difference and evidences the final impossibility of the subject, which can only coincide with itself at the moment of its disappearance or, rather, has its consistency only in memory, in a *postmortem* condition, in a postscript condition. The subject dwells in the difference between time and language, and it is this difference that determines its mortality.

The "I"—that *punctum*—is the point in which the same and the other vertiginously coincide and at the same time, at the same moment, separate, irretrievably split from each other. It is the point of inscription, of writing. If *esse est percipi* is the golden rule of Tlön, *esse est scripsi* is that of "Tlön, Uqbar, Orbis Tertius." And if to write is to alter, to become another, unavoidably to address another, then writing is also a posthumous act. Thence its melancholy. With its evocations of Quevedo and Browne, the last sentence marks the instance of death, which determines and makes possible (and impossible) the subject.

The reader remains trapped in this entanglement. The last sentence is an intimation addressed to her or to him, whispering that the subject is nothing other than a web of readings.

ESSAY AND FICTION

In 1944 Borges gathers the narratives that comprise *The Garden of Forking Paths* (published separately in 1941) and *Artifices* under the common title of *Fictions*. It is not improbable that the generic title under which Borges joins his two collections not only refers the "pieces" to the vast and diffuse category of inventive narrative but also names an entirely peculiar kind of writing, which administers what I earlier called the flow between essay and fiction. I say a *flow*, for it obviously is not an illustrative exercise, as if the aim were to offer symbolic equivalents for an idea or a thesis. The inclusion of the philosophical motifs of idealism in the narrative makes them elements and resources of fiction and, at the same time, makes evident the imaginative performance that gives rise to them, skeptically rendering meaningless their truth pretension. They are played down, and the more or less concealed passages that put them into communication with their denials and contestations aggravate their blurred aspect, though they never come to mockery. It's a use, a literary and rhetorical use, that maximizes the power of fiction. "I'm neither a philosopher nor a metaphysician; what I have done is exploit, or explore—a nobler word—the literary possibilities of philosophy.... I do not have any theory of the world," says Borges in a dialogue with María Esther Vázquez. "In general, as I have used the various metaphysical and theological systems for literary ends, my readers have believed that I professed those systems, whilst the only thing I have done is to take advantage of them for those ends, nothing more" (Vázquez 107). You will also recall the epilogue of his book of essays, *Other Inquisitions*, dated 1952; there he confesses "to evaluate religious or philosophical ideas on the basis of their aesthetical worth and even for what is singular and marvelous about them. Perhaps this is," he says, "an indication of a basic skepticism" (*Obras* 2: 163/*Other* 189).

One way to allude to this flow, to the peculiarity of this writing, having "Tlön, Uqbar, Orbis Tertius" in view, is to say that its clue is the *conjunction*. Let us recall the calculated formula that the narrator employs to open his story: "I owe the discovery of Uqbar to the conjunction of a mirror and an encyclopedia." It is arguable that Borges's choice of the term has in view its diverse meanings. A conjunction is an accident, an astral event, as well as copulation, condemned, as Bioy recalls, by a heresiarch from Uqbar with a categorical sentence; a conjunction is always something of a synthesis, but it is always also a synthesis that happens by chance (or by a hidden law, which is more or less the same). The nature of the conjunction is unfailingly contingence. And it is precisely this contingence that could be an important sign concerning what I call the peculiarity of Borgesian writing, which is also its economy. I venture that this economy consists—according to the terms I've just sketched—in a conjunction of essay and fiction, which has as its rule of synthesis the continual *friction* between such orders.

With Borges the boundary between essay and narrative becomes imprecise, loses stability, and expands as a vast and unexplored zone, which writing can now trace with unforeseen consequences. But, to tell the truth, the boundary between essay and narrative has never been a firmly defined line. Smuggling between both provinces, in fact, has been the rule. The reason is structural. The essay is interested, no less than narrative, in the vindication of the singular and the factual. Each does so in different ways. The essay seeks to make an experience of the singular, an experience that appeals to concepts to get its credit, but interrupts at every moment the course of the chains of reasoning and of inference in order to indicate the difference that constitutes the singularity of the singular, the facticity of the factual, and the contingency of the contingent. Narrative, instead, wishes to attend the pristine emergence, the first spring (the *Ur-sprung*), as it were, of the singular, the birth of this Venus that has only the breath of language as its instigating force. This agreement of interests explains why the essay calls upon the resources of narrative for help.

Yet, with Borges something else happens. The progression of which I spoke in the previous section, concerning which I argued that it is not only a narrative resource shut up within the limits of the story but also a request that the reader take on her own temporal condition, is also a progression of the essay toward fiction,[28] and, at the same time that the former essentially modifies the latter, fiction recurrently acts on the essay. The consequence of the Borgesian transformation of the boundary into a free-trade zone is of an all-encompassing magnitude, like a long tremor that shakes all the orders of discourse and its relations (referential, representative) to the supposedly real and true.

Is it possible to think that this tremor is the catastrophe of truth as the aim and original determination of discourse, that meaning is hanging by a thread (the thread of narration and the thread of the "I" who relates and who reads, always feeble and controvertible), that fiction is in the end the truth of the truth and of the real? That the nature of the Borgesian exercise is nihilist in the end? I wouldn't say so. In the sequel of the dialogue with Vázquez quoted earlier, Borges says, "Besides, if I were to define myself, I would say that I am an agnostic, that is, a person who doesn't believe that knowledge is possible" (Vázquez 107). It is easy to presume that this agnosticism (the use of the term here is faithful to etymology, not to the religious context in which it is usually understood) is the confession of a fundamental defeat and that literature and aesthetics remain as the only problematic shelter and as a meager consolation. I abstain from concluding this. The agnosticism in question is a skepticism of a rare quality, which, although it might show a dissuasive and even destructive face, also has another face that is efficient and secretly positive.

I mentioned at the beginning that the essay has a primary intention of truth. It is either a conjecture about an aspect or circumstance of the world, the persistent sounding of oneself, or even—as usually happens—both at once, given that the essayist doesn't have much more than his own experience (and a baggage of readings, of course) as an instrument of investigation. In the case of Borges, the essay does not abandon its calling for truth, but truth suffers a decisive transformation by virtue of its unlimited exchange with the space of fiction. Borges's writing permits truth to become entirely aestheticized but in a very precise sense. Truth isn't different here from what Borges himself calls "the aesthetic fact"—that is, nothing other than the "imminence of a revelation, which does not happen," says the famous conclusion of "The Wall and the Books," the first essay of *Other Inquisitions* (*Obras* 2: 15/*Other* 5, translation modified). This conclusion is preceded by the mention of diverse things ("music, states of happiness, mythology, faces molded by time, certain twilights and certain places"), which all coincide in that they want to tell us something or that they have told us "something we should not have missed" (15/5). It is probable that this "something" is not some other thing that those events, states, or circumstances could reveal but their mere and pure presence, which is announced but constitutively escapes, flickers only to fade away. But precisely this revelation, forever and ever imminent, speaks of the truth that lies in the aesthetic dimension and certainly of that which is indelibly temporal in truth: truth is nothing other than the fugacious trace of an event. Borges's conjecture ("this imminence of a revelation, which does not happen, is, *perhaps*, the aesthetic fact" [15/5, translation modified; my italics]) marks the Borgesian agnosticism, his skepticism, which disbelieves not only the pretensions of human knowledge but also their aesthetic compensation, as if in this experience (and Borges takes care to underscore its elusive and never present character) the truth that is forbidden for knowledge could shine. It would follow that Borgesian skepticism, however sui generis, is also a first-rate contribution to skepticism as such. What Borges contributes to skepticism—which, I would say, he approves from a skeptical and ironical distance—is probably an aesthetic skepticism.

What is its effect? It's a reminder, an intimation. The attribution of time to truth whispers the memento of the subject's temporality, addressed to the "I" that vests it. It presses the "I" to recognize and to assume its temporality and to ponder the fact that the latter inexorably affects its relation to truth. In the end, truth escapes every human projection, every desire of possession. The great project of Tlön shows here its desperate face. As a plan to supplant a reality—atrocious and banal—the order and legality of which remain unknown for us, it satisfies the excessive desire of a "reality" made to the subject's measure, obedient to its design. "Tlön may well be a labyrinth, but it is a labyrinth forged by men, a labyrinth destined to be deciphered by men" (*Obras* 1: 474/*Collected* 81). It is the corrected and augmented version of the "symmetr[ies] ... with an appearance of order" (473/81) that fascinate human beings, driving them to the worst form of ruin. With a wink to history and conjuncture, dialectical materialism, antisemitism, and Nazism are mentioned. You see that the seeming absence of referentiality to which I alluded at the beginning is suddenly suspended in the most unexpected way, discovering under the smiling face of the apparent divertimento the grimaces of a broken reality;[29] through the interstice of a passing remark, at the moment when the fictitious condition of the text we are reading reaches its utmost peak, the force of history, of an unmentionable, infamous reality, fills with its echoes all the corridors of the labyrinth. Truth necessarily escapes the text, escapes this text that radically questions any pretension of truth, including its own, but this escape is the truth of the text, and one can only fleetingly allude to it in a passing remark, which incalculably opens the text to something that is irretrievably other to the text itself.

One is tempted to ask what impression this text might have produced on its coetaneous reader, who had the war as his background, and what that kind of deceiving apocalypse that is the scandalous end of the whole (hi)story could have said to him. Perhaps, besides the divertimento, it addresses to him a reminder that everything, reality, the things that fill reality, he himself, and all those of his kind, are made of pure contingence. That should be the reminder of the remainders of a universal urn burial.

I think that this is the calling of the essay, that it is also the calling of narrative, that it is not different but, rather, inseparable from the vindication of singularity that both advocate, and, lastly, that the two are secretly paired in the recognition of contingence, of the truth of contingence, and the contingence of truth.

"There is still, of course, the problem of the *material* from which some objects are made," perfidiously states the last footnote of the story regarding a little cone of unsuspected weight and unknown metal found among the pitiable stuff of a rustic who died after a night of hard drinking. In a most paradoxical manner, matter is the faithful symptom of the invasion of the real world by a fantastic universe inhabited by fervent idealists who radically disbelieve the tangible. But it might also be—at the same time—the other way around. Perhaps this contradictory mention of matter is something like a wink discreetly calling attention to what I've termed contingence.

A Few Words of Conclusion

> There is still, of course, the problem of the *material* from
> which some objects are made.
> —BORGES, "Tlön, Uqbar, Orbis Tertius"

IN THE PRECEDING CHAPTERS, I've tried to interrogate the strange kind of material of which some objects, which may seem absolutely familiar to us, are made. The usually unnoticed strangeness of these objects consists in that they are all products of imagination. Their familiarity is due to the fact that we live on imagination. But the fact that we live on imaginary creatures, when we become aware of it, gives these objects their disturbing strangeness.

Yes, the texts that I have chosen to peruse are such products of imagination, by which I mean fictions, but in such a way that all of them imply—at times expressly, at times tacitly—a sort of subtext or, perhaps better, a paratext that critically accompanies the narrative performance, ironizes it, reflects upon it, at times feigns to disbelieve it or overtly belies it, and in the end doubtfully takes distance from itself, surrendering all rights to a final truth at the very moment it comes to the surface.

Nevertheless, it could be doubted that I've paid tribute to imagination's rich ingenuity, or else it may be esteemed that this alleged tribute, if it is one, is rather questionable.

I do not need to call attention to the fact that, in my attempt to lend some credibility to the idea of a skeptical condition of literature, I have made recourse mainly to essays and aphorisms or else to borderline texts that tend to avoid attributions of a discursive or literary identity. One could easily object that such a procedure eases the task of demonstration. Essays and aphorisms—those are products of thinking, not of invention; they are eminently discursive, if not straightforwardly argumentative, and for that reason they tend to suppress or drastically reduce all narrative performance together with the drive that imagination lends it. Moreover, they have to do in some way or another with truth, be it problematically or in a sentious tone.

However, one central point of that idea is that literature—let me restrict the terms here to modern literature, that is, to literature "in hard times," as Hölderlin would have it—necessarily involves a reflective interrogation about its own nature, its necessity, its sheer (im)possibility. (Modern) literature cannot project a place for itself, which is always an impermanent, precarious place, without thinking about this (im)possibility. Its proximity to a kind of philosophical inquiry tends to be transgressive. It is something quite different from the glorious and joyful impudence in the *alethe diegemata*, "true stories," of Lucian of Samosata, whom I would be inclined to celebrate as the first modern writer. Nevertheless, his magnificent challenge to the reader, his scandalous use of poetic license (*mythologein eleutherias*), his boastful honesty in proudly confessing that he lies, although he lies in a "far more honest" way than his predecessors, "for though I tell the truth in nothing else, I shall at least be truthful in saying that I am a liar [*aletheuo legon hoti pseudomai*]" (Lucian 253): all of this lies far away from modern tempers, which—whether ironical, melancholic, angry, or merely ludicrous—always betray a structural duplicity. In Lucian's case, since he is "writing about things ... which, in fact, do not exist at all and, in the nature of things, cannot exist [*mete holos onton mete ten archen genesthai dynamenon*]," he tells his reader that they "should on no account believe [*medamos pisteuein*] in them" (253). Wherever you may find similar intimations in modern literature, they are not straight warnings: they are traps.

Yet, the understanding—the faculty of concepts and truth—does not control and subordinate the imagination here. At stake between the two is a kind of peculiar interaction (I would be tempted to say an intercourse) that, far from a "free play," is rather a cannibalistic struggle whose outcome, if the antagonists survive, is fiction. Yes, it is about fiction. It is about the truth of fiction. Let me take a first instance.

In *Kant's Dog*, a relatively recent book, David Johnson undertakes—quite successfully, I would say—the difficult task of giving a comprehensive reading of Borges's work that intends to show how it systematically complicates philosophy and literature. Not that he points out the many philosophical references and allusions you may find in the Argentinian writer's oeuvre, which has been done many times; he intends to show, rather, how Borges's writing—in narratives, essays, and notes—inscribes and stresses fundamental issues of philosophical thought: temporality, memory, imagination, language and meaning, identity, otherness, God. The complication to which I'm alluding presupposes an essential relation and at the same time an essential difference between literature and philosophy: "each inscribed at the limit of the other" (Johnson 23). This limit, in turn, prevails in a common expression that inextricably knots both uses of language: "as if." This linguistic tool at the service of analogy is the instrument that Johnson employs in order to bring to light that complication—I would say, more accurately, that *complicity*. Stated in the simplest way, the "as" in the "as if" stands for philosophy: understanding, truth, presence; the "if" stands for literature, art: imagination, error (or fiction), future (or past, which would in any case be an immemorial past, not a historical one). In this sense, the "as" functions as a widget that signals identity or resemblance, scanning beings in reference to their specific being: it opens the order of the categories. According to the conditionality that it expresses, by contrast, the "if" produces a sort of blurring, a certain unreality and virtualization affecting the state or the action to which it is prefixed. The point is that the "if" in the "as if" has already modified the rule of the "as" insofar as it disturbs the movement by which, on the assumption that the resemblance is categorically controllable, a thing is referred to itself or to something that resembles it. While the meaning of the "as" is to guarantee the sameness of something, whatever it may be,[1] the "if" persistently *others* the something, leading it astray in its movement. And you do not have to think of the "if" as if it were exclusively the effect of thinking or speaking or writing in the "as if" mode: wherever "as" (*hôs*, *qua*, *als*) is meant, an "if" silently accompanies it, as a disquieting shadow.

So, this is the first instance.

Allow me now to make recourse to another mode of connoting the complex fabric of fiction; this mode is particularly notorious. At the beginning of chapter 14 in his *Biographia Literaria*, published in 1817, Samuel Taylor Coleridge speaks about the poetic program outlined in the company of his neighbor and friend William Wordsworth: "the sympathy of the reader" was at the center of their conversations, whether motivated by "a faithful adherence to the truth of nature" or by the novelties due to "the power ... of imagination" (145). This was the occasion of the *Lyrical Ballads*, Coleridge's fantastic, supernatural kind of endeavor that, combining both sources of interest, consisted in transferring "from our inward nature a human interest and a semblance of truth sufficient to procure for [the] shadows of imagination that willing suspension of disbelief for the moment, which constitutes poetic faith" (145). Coleridge's felicitous wording—"willing suspension of disbelief"—has the scope of a principle expressing the condition under which the reception of a product of fiction is accomplished. The willingness of which the formula speaks indicates the active participation of the viewer, hearer, or reader in order to bring about the proper effect of the work. A sort of temporal complicity ("for the moment"), or if you will—and I think it's more accurate—a contractual arrangement between author and recipient, sanctions the admissibility of fiction.

Anyway, I would like to linger a bit on the phrase, pondering the somewhat strange formula: "suspension of disbelief." Obviously, "disbelief" refers to an essential, original tendency of our disposition to believe, which becomes engaged only by that which bears the signs of usual reality and familiarity. Disbelief awakens where these signs are absent or debilitated. This is the reason why an act of will is necessary to overcome such a primary refusal to believe in extraordinary things—a refusal that at least leads to casting doubt on them. The willingness needs to be facilitated in the exposition of such things, however, by the presence of marks of its non-deceptive character—that is, marks of its fictional character. "Poetic faith," which is the result or the product of this act of will, thus implies both: the acceptance of the "shadows of imagination" that, in this case, the writer offers his or her reader, as well as the compliance with the condition of a certain sincerity, that is, of giving evidence of the unreality of what is told. Of course, this "faith" is something absolutely new over against the belief of our natural, everyday attitude; it is another, heterogeneous kind of "belief" due to the aforementioned "suspension."

I would like to think of this suspension not just as a change in the receiver's frame of mind due to his or her decision. Ultimately, the latter is much less a decision than surrendering to a seduction; a willing surrender, yes, but one that pays tribute to a seduction that is grounded on the specific operations and on the specific rules that govern fiction, operations and rules that have as a whole, I would say, the structure of a suspension. In this sense, this suspension is not a subjective feature but rather a property, or better, a potency of language as the material of which fictional objects are made. Language, as such, has this peculiar power—which may be considered also, or rather, as an impotence—of deferring everything that might be signaled, announced, alluded to, revealed by language itself: reference, the function that we use to assign as the regular task of language, is inevitably difference and deferral. This opens a space—and a time, of course, one should say a space-time—where (and when) language folds up over itself in order to make itself capable of signaling, announcing, alluding, referring, and revealing. Suspension is the opening of this space-time that is the space-time in which fiction takes place, the space-time of fiction in both directions of the genitive *and* in an extended sense of fiction, which involves not only the variegated fabric of imagination but also the entirety of our capacity to think: concepts, too, are fictions we need and produce in order to come to terms with what we experience.

Insofar as I am speaking of a kind of suspension that would be essential to the constitution of the literary phenomenon—inasmuch as it would open the space of fiction—and insofar as I am implicitly surmising that this suspension has something to do with the skeptical *epoche*, it should be imperative to lend some credibility to this kinship, to which I have referred intermittently—and I fear a bit annoyingly—throughout the preceding essays. Of course, the skeptical *epoche* has, in principle, nothing to do with the appeal, virtues, and deceptions of the literary: it is an epistemic attitude. As Sextus explains, *epecho* (I suspend judgment) means, "I am unable to say which of the objects presented I ought to believe and which I ought to disbelieve" (Sextus 196). This is due to the equipollence (*isosthenia*) of the conflicting propositions that might be formulated about a certain fact or statement.

What should be taken into account here is the fact that skeptical suspension is linguistically performed or, better said, the modes that lead to suspension (the skeptical tropes) are accompanied by "certain expressions [*phonas tinas*] indicative of [the] skeptical attitude and tone of mind [*hemas pathous*]" (Sextus 187). And Sextus goes on to explain the specific scope of various utterances, such as "not more," "perhaps," "possibly," "I suspend judgment," "I determine nothing," etc. It is possible to discern three different types of relation to language, which are three modes of expression skeptically modulated. There is the use of language that is loose, indifferent, and functional (191), which is on the one hand the merely everyday use, words, and expressions embedded in common life and commerce. On the other hand, however, this first use responds to the dogmatist's dispute about the meaning of words and statements, something of which he is irresistibly fond. Another use belongs entirely to the confrontation with the dogmatist: aphasia, summarily said, is the renunciation of affirming or negating anything insofar as the issue remains undecided. This, as a matter of fact, is the trope of all skeptical tropes, since it is the skeptic's self-imposed prohibition against dogmatically stating anything about things manifest. But there is a third use, which in the order of things is in fact the first. It might be called the "expression of what happens to me," not a statement but, rather, the expression of an affection (pathos): the affection produced by the presence of the phenomenon. In this sense, what the skeptic calls phenomenon bears an essential correspondence to *pathos*, to the point that the word *phantasia* equivalently means for him/her the appearance—the presence—that forces involuntary assent (cf. Sextus 19), as well as the perception of this appearance. A second feature of the phenomenon—and this one especially interests me—is that it bears in each case an indelible index of temporality (*nun*, now), so that it might be properly conceived of as an *event*. In this sense, Sextus says that the skeptic "relates what he/she feels [*ho paschei diegoumenos*]" (197, translation modified). This relating is a *diegesis*, then, a narrative performance—an atomic or minimal narrative yield—quite consistent with the first characterization of the skeptic that Sextus offers: "we simply record each fact [*peri hekastou*], like a chronicler [*historikôs apangellomen*]" (4). Like a chronicler, furthermore, the "I" who tells what happens to him- or herself is also one and the same with the event, a phenomenon amid phenomena. Let's simply think of the possibility of expanding the present of this encounter, of lingering on this kind of testimonial account, of persisting in suspense and telling what happens—what *is* happening—under the condition of this suspense: such a stance might be the opening of a time, a space of time—an *epoche*, if I may—for other uses of *diegesis*, perhaps for a plethora of *phantasiai*. It would be the epoch of suspense.

In the previous chapters, my intention has been to suggest what seems to me to be diverse uses of *diegesis* that may take place in the temporal dilation of suspension. Allow me to go over some instances of these uses that—I hope—should have emerged from what has been discussed in those chapters or to which I have at least alluded in this conclusion.

To begin, there is a particular feature of Lichtenberg's writing that I have mentioned in passing (see chapter 3, note 7): his frequent—I would be tempted to say *systematic*, according to the sense in which Lichtenberg speaks of his *Gedankensystem*—use of the subjunctive mood (cf. Schöne 1993). Notoriously, this feature combines the physics professor's experimental practice with his irresistible penchant for writing and, in writing, for inventing all sorts of situations, processes, and outcomes that stretch well beyond the domain of the ordinary, predictable, or arguably possible: they go far into the field of the (im)possible, if I may insist on this rather artificial way of putting it, or—maybe better—far into the subjunctive field of the virtual. The gist of this multifarious procedure (for its applications are various and numerous) is that all of its intentions aim toward truth, but its very versatility makes truth burst into many flashing little truths ("penny-truths," as Lichtenberg calls them [*Sudelbücher* F 1219]) that are all versions of the (im)possible. At every step, it transgresses the boundary between scientific research—the formulation of hypotheses, the assumption of certain conditions (what if?), and the alternative outcomes that, given such conditions, might result (Lichtenberg frequently leaves the reader wondering what these outcomes could be)—philosophical doubt, literary invention, and the probing of the astounding and at times definitively treacherous versatility of language.

In a certain sense, it could be said that Lichtenberg's subjunctive, triggered by the simple question "what if?" that in itself suspends the given state of affairs to which it is applied, creates a bridge that connects its many divergent directions with Borges's dizzying blending of fiction and reality, the vertigo of which is hypercritical. This blending is, from the reader's point of view, at least twofold. On the one hand, it entraps the reader in an interchange with the author that tends to spectralize both, if I may say so. This critical side concerns the subject. On the other hand, it is a warning under the guise of a reflection back onto the act of narrating. Without renouncing itself, narrating returns to itself critically, pondering its own performance, in a sort of meta-discourse (which has an essayistic, speculative guise) that suggests that something exceeds this performance, not necessarily as its origin or as its motif but, in any case, something sufficiently stubborn not to enter into the game. You could call it reality if reality were not, from the first moment, involved in the game. (Reality—that is, your sense of reality—for this sense, which cannot but be articulated as an opinion and as belief, is what literature challenges and disrupts in the first place.)

On a different but not structurally distant strand, Kleist's mastery consists in his ability to suggest insidiously that our sense of reality—inevitably cast in opinion, as I said—is a compound of diverse forms of discourse that intersect one another and, though offering occasionally (in fact, rarely) reciprocal confirmation, most of the time undermine or even bely one another, casting shadows—or shades, in any case—over the purported appropriateness of the specific form in view of the intention it should serve as a vehicle. Narration, essay, drama, scientific and technical descriptions, fairytale, aesthetic appreciations, theological or philosophical speculation, chronicle and journalistic notes—all come together to suggest that the blurring of the boundaries between reality and fiction is due to the inevitable interface connecting the various discursive forms in which we try to coin truth, facts, events, experiences, our notion of reality, or merely our fleeting impressions.

This contamination of discourses places in parentheses Aristotelian *metabasis eis allo genos*, which is, at the same time, the foundation of Western epistemic building *and* of the Western permission for poetic rendering. Indeed, poetic license presupposes the limit within which a circumvention of the non-*metabasis* principle is possible and acceptable, under the condition of analogy—that is, under the condition of the "as if," provided that it is governed by the "as." In this sense, the limit presupposes the strict separation of reality and fiction, of truth and fantasy; insofar as the "if" essentially disrupts the rule of the "as," the latter becomes open to the whirlwind of (im)possibilities. In the end, that limit is grounded in the principle of the excluded third. If you make recourse to analogy, you know that the terms of the analogy aren't identical, but they share some common feature that defines the analogy's resemblance no matter how distant its terms are in our common world. Matching the ostensibly different terms doesn't make way for their identity, of course, or for their absolute difference. Something in between remains suppressed, something different from identity and difference or, better, indifferent to identity and difference, something fundamentally *other*. Perhaps no one knew this better than Kafka. Take, for instance, his abysmal parable "On Parables." The wise speak in parables that are of no use in daily life, which merely implies that the incomprehensible is incomprehensible. An argument begins: one says that, if one would follow the parables, one would become a parable, relieved from daily cares. The other bets that this is also a parable. "The first said: You have won. / The second said: But unfortunately only in parable. / The first said: No, in reality: in parable you have lost" (Kafka, *Complete Stories* 457). This is Kafka's "not and not-not," neither an abolition or falsification of truth nor its relativization. It's an instantaneous outburst of truth magnetized by events, which is the same as the stillness at the center of the whirlwind.

If I may recall something that I tried to argue when addressing the famous Swiftian dichotomy of fools and knaves, at this center stands Swift's implied fourth, the prudent advocate of a common sense that is not given but has to be produced in the first place, one who does not yield to believing, that is, to credulity. This advocate, I suggested, results from the exclusion of the unhappy third—the madman—from the unfortunate alternative of fool or knave. The advocate, I would like to think, has a kind of freedom to deal with the ranting of the other three.

When confronting the blurring of the borderline between reality and fiction—that is, when trespassing the "and" but still lingering on it (not being a fool, a knave, or a madman)—you have various options to give an account of this curious "and," of this "between." These options include the "as if," the "willing suspension of disbelief" (which consists not in belief but, rather, in an absolutely different kind of "faith"), the Kafkan "not and not-not," Swift's "the thing that is not," and yes, of course, the subjunctive mood that is, so to speak, the lieutenant of the "between." This is the point: to stand and to stay in between. To hold on there, precisely there, would be happiness—or serenity, in the Pyrrhonian mood—due to "the rarest of gifts, a perfectly balanced mind" (Carroll 754), as Lewis Carroll (another name that should be considered here) would have it. And this is not far from the figure of a scale, Montaigne's skeptical emblem, which so resembles the shrugging of one's shoulders.

I am certainly not advocating for a Babelic blending of all kinds of languages or for an immersion of truth intentions into something that someone would call the swamp of imagination. *Amicus veritatis*, I just wanted to say some words about the truth of fiction. In short, I am merely suggesting that freely handling diverse types of discourse, without lodging them in closed compartments that do not communicate with one another (even if these compartments are meant to secure truth against fiction's ambushes or, in turn, fiction against truth's severe demands and pretensions), might bring about nonnegligible fruits. In the end, it is the freedom for which Montaigne vehemently longs: "I so hunger after freedom [*Je suis si affady après la liberté*] that if anyone were to forbid me access to some corner of the Indies I would to some extent live less at ease" (*Essais* 1119/*Essays* 1216). I don't know why I'm led to think of this corner—this *coin*—as a forested one, as the jungle that the Indies—that is, America—would have seemed to be for any European at the time. All that the sieur de Montaigne claims for himself against the rigidly constraining imposition of the law is "ma liberté d'aller et venir" ("my freedom to come and go"; 1119/1216), to which no place in the world, no matter how remote, should be forbidden. I would say that this is a fair claim when it comes to texts too. At stake, in the end, is our ability to simply wander freely through the forest of discourses.

Notes

INTRODUCTION

1. The paragraphs of the present exposition refer in brief to the sections that follow.

2. Consistent with this, obviously, is the key that would also allow for a theoretical explanation of the overcoming of the paradox: the repetition of experience takes place not on the same level of the original experience but in the order of fiction.

3. All dual references will cite the original language first and, wherever available, the English translation second.

4. Cf. the notes by the editors in Benjamin, *Schriften* 2, pt. 3: 1276–88.

5. Perhaps I should elaborate on what I mean by "truth content": It is not just about a determined content that common experience puts at the disposal of its bearers as a basis of communication among them, but about experience as a condition of appropriation of any contents whatsoever, under the sole condition that they are, in one way or another, truly communicable. It is precisely in this sense that Benjamin connects the loss of the capacity to share experiences— a capacity that the art of storytelling cultivates and develops—with the crisis of experience itself.

6. To this extent it seems to me valid to say that Benjamin does not restrict his remark to the communicability of experience, as if it were a process external to it; on the contrary, I assume that the remark presupposes that communicability is inherent to experience, and that a breaking of the former amounts to a breaking of the latter.

7. Certainly, this synonymy reduces the efficacy of return to which Derrida refers and that implies in its spectral condition a crisis of the distinction between reality and fiction. Nevertheless, it seems to me interesting to continue to work with the concept of fiction—that is, to remain within the metaphysical frame of the literary—not just because it allows, as I think it does, the critical elaboration of the relation between literature and skepticism, but also because a more radicalized version of the fictitious itself presupposes a fundamental analysis of what we could call the "logic of erasure" or of "negation" that would be at work in the literary operation. One could venture that, insofar as it is possible to conceive this logic from the standpoint of a temporal vector—and, more precisely, from the vector of deferral—one might also go further toward the problem of "return" (of *revenance*) to which Derrida refers.

8. Let us remark here, as a complement to what was said in the preceding note, that this "space of fiction" arises from a double "erasure" or "negation": on the one hand the erasure of narration in favor of the narrated event—that is to say, in view of the singularity and punctuality of its becoming—and on the other hand the erasure of the event in favor of its narration—that is, in view of its memorable preservation. This duplicity would mark the structure of repetition of repetition that we attributed to narration, and it would only be necessary to conceive each of these "erasures" together with their mutual relation in a temporal key in order to understand that the fabric of the "space of fiction" is woven by deferral.

9. This "virtualization" presupposes the relative suppression of the ontological difference between reality and fiction on the basis of their common reference to the sphere of the possible, as the latter depends on what I term a "general faculty of format" and is administered by it: and this would be the properly technical way of overcoming that difference. It is, then, a reluctance to grant fully the absolute efficacy of this technical way that drives me to insist on the concept of fiction.

10. Certainly, although the word *fiction* is alien to Aristotle, it is not only possible to maintain that the term *poiesis* is to some extent an equivalent of it, but also to argue that Aristotle, in discussing *poiesis*, establishes the fundamental criteria for the determination of "fiction" (*plasma, argumentum, fictio*): the presentation of events that are articulated by a causal and not merely a temporal sequence (as is the case of historical narration), the exposition of the universals that are implicated in such a sequence (in the sense of what a certain character would do in a given situation and context), the imbrications of truth and falsity under the general principle of verisimilitude (conceived of as real probability rather than as psychological credibility, although the latter is not excluded as a persuasive resource of the poet). In the most ample terms, the whole of these criteria may be reduced to a fundamental purpose of intelligibility of experience, which literary creation would serve on the basis of its specific logic.

11. So it is with narration in its inherited character: the primary suspension of judgment would widen the range of possibilities in order to bring about in it the configuration of a "story." We might be asked if a literature that would present suspension itself should be possible.

12. Of course, one might argue that this equivalence lacks the necessary symmetry, for the notion of aura does not involve communicative factors, at least not explicitly. However, it would also be meaningful to think that this difference strengthens the equivalence, not in an analogical sense, but complementarily: what Benjamin conceives of as auratic experience—"the unique apparition of a distance, however near it may be [*einmalige Erscheinung einer Ferne, so nah sie sein mag*]" (*Schriften* I: 479/*Writings* 3: 104–05)—defines the case of an experience that is in itself fullness of sense, without requiring any narrative mediation in the process of its happening. The mysticism of experience that involves the phenomenon of aura cuts, on the one hand, intersubjective participation, but on the other it simultaneously makes possible an indirect communication of such an experience in terms of aesthetic communication.

13. The exception I am making here has, I presume, some bearing: it is certainly of no consequence to speak about a "subject" of the experiences that are shared among a community of narration, precisely to the extent that what we call a "subject" presupposes a break with such a community—that is, with the context of meaning within which the member of that community lives, as it were, spontaneously. This means that the "subject" presupposes the dissolution of this context and that it becomes a subject as it resolves by itself and for itself the problem that—as experience of uncertainty or perplexity, as the sole undeniable experience that remains—such dissolution poses. In this sense, it could be said that the "individual" is a structural moment in the genesis of the "subject."

14. The first edition of the *Essays* dates from 1580, followed by a second eight years later, which includes a third book; Descartes publishes his *Meditations* in 1641.

15. Of course, my charging Montaigne with lacking any method is hyperbolic. There is indeed a method in his procedure, or, put differently, there is in everything what Montaigne calls a fundamental power at work, one that has the capacity to adapt itself to the peculiarity of every issue. This power is *judgment*.

16. Montaigne as well as Bacon dates the origins of the essay to antiquity: the former to Plato and Xenophon, the latter to Seneca.

17. Cf. Bacon in the *New Organon*:
Now just as the end and goal of the sciences is poorly defined among men, so also even if it had been well defined, yet the road which men have chosen for themselves is totally erroneous and impassable. It would strike the mind dumb with amazement, if one thought about it properly, that it has been no one's care or concern that a regular, well-built road should be opened and constructed for the human understanding from sense and experience; but everything has

been left to the darkness of traditions, or to the eddy and whirl of arguments, or to the waves and windings of chance and casual, unregulated experience. Let anyone think soberly and carefully about the kind of path men have commonly used in the investigation and discovery of anything. And first he will surely note the simple, nonscientific method of discovery which is most familiar to men. This is simply that in preparing and equipping himself to find something out, anyone first researches and reads what others have written on the subject; then adds his own thoughts, and with much mental agitation interrogates his own spirit and calls upon it to open its oracles to him. This procedure has absolutely no foundation and simply spins around on opinions.

Another person, to aid discovery, might call logic in, which belongs to the subject under discussion only as far as its name is concerned. For a discovery of logic is not a discovery of the leading principles and axioms in which the arts consist, but only of those which seem to be in agreement with them. For the more inquisitive and insistent questioners, those who take the trouble to accost her with demands for proofs and discoveries of principles or of the first axioms, are met by logic with a very well-known response which throws them back on faith and the oath of allegiance (so to speak) which anyone must give to any art.

There remains mere experience: which is chance, if it comes by itself; experiment, if sought. This kind of experience is like a brush without a head (as they say), mere groping, such as men use in the dark, trying everything in case they may be lucky enough to stumble into the right path. It would be much better and more sensible to wait for day or light a lamp, and then to start the journey. The true order of experience, on the other hand, first lights the lamp, then shows the way by its light, beginning with experience digested and ordered, not backwards or random, and from that it infers axioms, and then new experiments on the basis of the axioms so formed; since even the divine word did not operate on the mass of things without order.

Therefore let men cease to wonder that the sciences have not finished the course, since they have wholly lost their way; they have altogether deserted and abandoned experience, or trapped themselves in it (as in a maze) and gone round in circles; since a properly organised order takes one through the woods of experience by a steady path to the open country of axioms. (66–68)

CHAPTER ONE

1. Quotations and paraphrases, with the indication of the corresponding page number(s), refer first to the French edition and second to the English translation.

2. The question *Que sais-je?* is engraved under the image of a pair of scales on a medallion that Montaigne had made at the beginning of 1576. The motto was added to the frontispiece of the 1635 edition of the *Essays*, which was prepared by Mademoiselle De Gournay.

3. I will refer to this below, in the section entitled "The Written Self."

4. Reason, I argued before, is a faculty of law and interpretation, and the overlapping of both functions is indiscernible. In this sense, Montaigne's attack against civil laws combines perfectly with his disparagement of the obsessive urge to know. As forensic interpretations are to civil laws, philosophical interpretations are to the law of nature: "[Scientific investigations and inquiries] have nothing to do with knowledge so sublime: the philosophers are very right to refer us to the laws of Nature, but they pervert them and present Nature's face too sophistically, painted in colours which are far too exalted, from which arise so many diverse portraits of so uniform a subject" (1120/1218).

5. "What an ingenious medley is Nature's [*Ingénieux mélange de nature*]" (1116/1213), proclaims the passage—quoted above—in which Montaigne underlines this duality. Nature's adequacy to human needs presupposes that, in spite of its infinite variety, it offers—by virtue of the principle of similarity—everything that is wanted, not for its knowledge, but in order to follow its rule.

6. The general characteristics of humankind, Montaigne claims them multiplied about himself. Compare this with the ironical beginning of the ninth essay, "On Liars": "There is nobody less suited than I am to start talking about memory. I can hardly find a trace of it in myself; I doubt if there is any other memory in the world as grotesquely faulty as mine is! All my other endowments are mean and ordinary: but I think that, where memory is concerned, I am most singular and rare, worthy of both name and reputation!" (55/32).

7. Certainly, writing may be considered a persistent act of stalking and capturing the self in the various moments of its exposure to the world's constant variability, which is one and the same with what Montaigne calls "experience," but it is also a complex and ambiguous act. Allow me to return to the chapter's penultimate quotation in which, upon recounting the almost deadly accident he suffered, Montaigne says, "I must not overlook the following: the last thing I could recover was my memory of the accident itself [*Je ne veux pas oublier cecy, que la derniere chose en quoy je me peuz remettre, ce fut la souvenance de cet accident*]." An alternative translation could be the following: "I don't want to forget that the last thing I could recall was my memory of that accident." The "I" that expresses here its intention, its desire, is a written "I," not a psychological subject. This sort of "will to remember" indicates three different operations of writing that take the place of memory (*je ne veux pas oublier—la derniere chose en quoy je me peuz remettre—la souvenance de cet accident*), which in its turn is an ersatz recollection of the irretrievable present of the accident—the unexperienceable present of one's own death. In a chapter focused on the essay upon which I am commenting, Lawrence Kritzman speaks of a "simulation of death" (87–103). And, yes, Montaigne affirms, "it does seem that we have some means of breaking ourselves in for death and to some extent of making an assay of it" (*Essais* 389/*Essays* 417). The assay is the accident, turned into something of an experiment, though not in Bacon's manner, of course, but rather as a

simulation—and not just a "simulation of death," but rather the simulation of a simulation of dying, being dead, and returning from death, as if it were a kind of syncopated, disrupted *cogito*. And this simulation of simulation is writing.

8. The last line of this citation (*Les plus mortes morts sont les plus saines*) has been entirely omitted in the English translation.

9. "Nothing is so beautiful, so right, as acting as a man should: nor is any learning so arduous as knowing how to live this life naturally [*nouvellement*] and well" (1160/1261).

CHAPTER TWO

1. December 1697 is the date inscribed in *The Epistle Dedicatory, to His Royal Highness Prince Posterity*, one of the many prolegomena included in the work. It is also the year indicated in the preambular "The Bookseller to the Reader" in *The Battel of the Books* as the date of this text together with the *Tale*. The *Apology* that Swift adds in the fifth edition (1710) maintains that the book was almost finished in 1696.

2. The *Apology* is a text that is not entirely trustworthy from many points of view due to its intention to confront the commotion brought about by the *Tale*, which covered literary, scholarly, religious, and politic aspects, and also to protect the hidden author from the prejudicial consequences in which the whole thing could result¾obsessively insists on this point, concluding the defense in these terms: "*and I believe there is not a Person in* England *who can understand that Book, that ever imagined it to have been any thing else, but to expose the Abuses and Corruptions in Learning and Religion*" (Swift, *Tale* 10). The defense is perfectly valid, for the *Tale* actually handles those issues, but the tone in which it is formulated and the scope attributed to it make it so patently a disclaimer that it seems to be a covert confession of the implications of the book, which go much further than a mere vindication of the institutions in question. In addition, the putative author protests that he has done nothing other than make use of the many corruptions he criticizes as material for a satire (cf. *Tale* 5), that "*there generally runs an Irony through the Thread of the whole Book, which the Men of Tast will observe and distinguish*" (8), and lastly, "*that, as wit is the noblest and most useful gift of humane nature, so humour is the most agreeable; and where this two enter far into the composition of any work, they will render it always acceptable to the world*" (9), nothing of which is objectionable except, again, the tone and the scope. The entire *Apology* seems to serve the purpose of restricting the *Tale*'s effect, and in a certain way it ends up being another of the misleading maneuvers that are proper to its strategy, not to mention that the "author" who produces here the defense of the anonymous work is a definitively equivocal figure. I will return to these issues from other angles.

3. In *Jonathan Swift and the Millennium of Madness* (2006), a book of copious erudition, Kenneth Craven has identified the web of intellectual relations

exploited by the *Tale* and in which it intervenes parodically. In what follows I will profit from some of the results and motives of his rich investigation.

4. The point is of the utmost importance: Swift's epoch is extraordinarily rich in intellectual experiments and provocations, devoid to a considerable extent of the jurisdictional provinces to which the very outcome of its process has led and which modern posterity takes for granted. Inasmuch as there is no accurate outline of the jurisdictional boundaries between the emerging natural sciences and the esoteric disciplines (alchemy and astrology, for instance), the beginnings of human sciences stimulated by the rapid rise of the former (in attempts as dissimilar as Descartes's, Hobbes's, and Spinoza's), the progress of medicine, and the most varied range of disciplines, some from remote antiquity and some more recent, all unavoidably testify to the absence of homogeneous or comparable criteria of epistemic assessment. In this mixed context operates Swiftian satire, and it is indeed a privileged watchtower from which to observe the whole scenario. In this sense, *A Tale of a Tub* is a most important piece, although not the only one. The satire of astrology in *The Bickerstaff Papers*, of economy in *A Modest Proposal*, and, in an all-embracing way, the acid criticism of *Gulliver's Travels* should not be left unmentioned.

5. In a well-documented paper, Marcus Walsh has discussed the use of marginalia, footnotes, lists, and catalogs in *A Tale of a Tub*, highlighting "how conscious Swift was in the *Tale* of the manifold conventions of the book, more especially of the learned book, and how alive he was to the rich possibilities they offered to a satiric pen" ("Swift's *Tale*" 115).

6. On these aspects, see, among others, Mueller 208–11.

7. The first page reference is to the German edition, the second to the English translation. The numbering system here is a bit complex. *Die Metaphysik der Sitten* is a book contained in vol. VIII of the Suhrkamp edition of Kant's work; in this volume is also included the book *Die Religion innerhalb der Grenzen der blossen Vernunft*, of which 128 corresponds to the original editions (1797 and 1788), identified as A and B, so it is AB 128, but in the Suhrkampo edition, it is page 405. The scholarly standard citation of Kant's works refers to "AB" or to the Akademie Ausgabe "AA," (volume number AA and page; in this case: AA 6: 290).

8. The case of anonymity and many others: mercenary writing, for instance, which is a particularly relevant case for Swift's work.

9. The paper was originally published in 1969 and is now included in *The World, the Text, and the Critic* (2006).

10. Perhaps the essential characteristic of the "author" whom we call "Swift" is the annulment of what Derrida, in *La voix et le phénomène*, calls the "vouloir-dire" (meaning to say) through a process of exacerbation of his parodic writing, which makes him an ironically asymptotic "author," a vanishing point of multiple discourses, at the same time present and absent in all of them, not even as signature, but as intensity. Phiddian aims at this issue by making use

of the "Derridean notion of erasure" (and of the spur) in order to account for the "process of parody, particularly of parody as fugitive and indeterminate as Swift's" (13–19).

11. Kenneth Craven's aforementioned study provides abundant background on this matter.

12. The motif of surprise is closely related to Leavis's thesis on the radically negative nature of Swiftian satire: "Swift's is essentially a matter of surprise and negation; its function is to defeat habit, to intimidate, and to demoralize" (75).

13. Leavis himself acknowledges that "a method of surprise does not admit of description in any easy formula" (76).

14. I would like to think that this circulation is already epitomized in the formula that records what I have called the hermeneutical accident: "but how to analyse the Tub," as index of a reversibility that makes the word *tub* at the same time as *but* an exception that mobilizes the constant rotation of meanings and that in its repercussion unfailingly engages the "butt," the mockery's target, the laughing stock of satire.

15. If we consider the previous remarks on the author, on his obsessive nature and his anxiety, the eminently evasive character of his condition, his essential inconsistency, we should say that the neutrality vis-à-vis meaning to which I'm pointing here becomes the counterpart of what I called earlier the hypothesis of the author.

16. The *sack-posset* is a creamy Elizabethan dessert made out of eggs and flavored with sack (Madeira wine).

17. Compare with Marcus Walsh's introduction to the Cambridge edition of the *Tale*. See also Walsh, "Text," 82–84.

18. Section 10.

19. *The Scripture's Genuine Interpreter Asserted* (1678), in Walsh, "Text," 88–89.

20. The name *high church* alludes to the observance, theologically grounded, of the liturgical formality of the cult under strict sacerdotal guidance, with an emphasis on rite and ceremony. Its expression in Anglicanism approaches the cultic forms of Catholicism. The *low church*, instead, does not follow ceremonial ordinances or established ritual patterns, dispenses with special garbs and symbols, and favors spontaneity in preaching and prayer.

21. To this effect, it may be said that the *Tale*, dragging everything along, including the putative author himself, becomes complicit with this abolition. So, then, the people who judged that the book was the most corrupted and calamitous way of advocating for the interests of the ecclesiastical institution and for the principles of established religion had some reason on their side. Of them, William Wotton was the reader of the most prompt and acute perspicacity.

22. This is the happy English translation of the German original ("wenn die Sprache feiert"—when language feasts). See Wittgenstein 23.

23. I say not very promising, because it is assigned to the learned reader to dedicate his or her whole life to the speculations that this "miraculous Treatise" provokes at every turn.

24. This defense is scandalous: apart from the fact that the author promises the prompt publication of *A Panegyrical Essay upon the Number* THREE in the list of his "discourses" (4), triads abound in the text, starting with the oratorical machines (section 1), and continuing with the three brothers and their three respective creeds (section 2 on), the three kinds of critics (section 3), the three great types of revolutions (conquer, system, and vision, specifically referring to empire, philosophy, and religion, section 4), and concluding with the three readers (section 10).

25. It can only be a negative hint, because the fourth sense, common sense, as I will underline in what follows, is not given in any way. I come back to the apologist's alibi of number four, which nevertheless betrays a discreet wink toward something that I deem to be a central axis of the *Tale* as a whole. This axis runs from start to finish and ideally relates a fourth party (the dead father), whose definitive absence leaves his sons free to undertake their adventurous wanderings, equipped with a plain testament that they will not take long to pervert, with another fourth party that the text may request as its truthful reader, or else as the reader of the "testament."

26. An inhabitant of Bedlam (formerly Bethlehem), the London asylum for lunatics, a society of which the narrator is proud to have been a member, and to which he will undoubtedly return with honor.

27. I share Denis Donoghue's view, contrasting with F. R. Leavis's opinion, in support of the thesis of the trap. Donoghue thinks that the passage refers to Swift's patron, Sir William Temple, and that it commends secluded life in the Epicurean garden: "To be a fool among knaves is consciously and conscientiously to seek the life in the garden, rejecting the life of the world which, in this Epicurean setting, is the work of knaves. It is Temple's choice, one kind of folly rather than another, Moor Park rather than the Court. So the sentence is not a trap. But it drives the reader from one idiom to another without warning; the energy at work is critical, skeptical, and subversive" (56–57).

28. I presume that—in formal terms—the various groups of three elements (I think especially of the three sons, which are so related to these figures: Peter the knave, Jack the madman, and Martin the fool) result in the *Tale* from the subtraction (by absence, death, original lack) of the fourth. In the arithmetic I was imagining, three is the product of the lack of a fourth element, and two—always in bitter opposition—the product of the (self-)exclusion of the third.

29. In any case, this "casuistry" is not a mere accumulation of arguments. Sextus Empiricus observes that there is a hierarchical organization that subordinates the remaining nine tropes to the trope of relativity and distinguishes them between those that correspond to the one who judges, to the judged thing, and to both the judge and the judged together (38). So, the sequence of arguments

makes clear that the ten tropes build a single great argument—or a general argumentative strategy—in which each of its moments complements and strengthens refutation, provided that the refutation does not concede and that a new premise is produced in order to oppose it. One may marginally comment that the development of the ten tropes is not devoid of sarcastic winks that may perfectly be counted as a satire *in nuce* of dogmatism: as a supplement of the contestation of the alleged superiority of human sense impressions as against the "so-called 'non-rational' animals," Sextus indicates that, besides the arguments of this contestation, skeptics "do not consider it unseemly to poke a little fun [*katapaízein*] at those conceited braggarts [*tetyphómenoi kaì periautológountoí*], the Dogmatists" (62, translation modified). In another passage concluding the exposition of the second trope, he lays the blame on them as narcissistic (*philautoí*), because when judging things they prefer themselves to other people and because, when the dispute concerns one single person, they speak of a visionary "Sage [*oneiropoloúmenos sophós*]" (91). Skeptical challenges to the Dogmatists are not unlike those that may be found in satiric invectives; the latter figures insistently in Swift.

30. It is interesting to pay attention to the various pieces of information provided by Kenneth Craven regarding the conflict between Galen's and Paracelsus's medical paradigm, Swift's support of the former and his rejection of the latter, and, finally, the satirical use of both, particularly in the *Tale* (cf. Craven 159–78).

CHAPTER THREE

1. Let's recall two of Pascal's *Pensées*: (1) "Cleopatra's nose: had it been shorter, the whole aspect of the world would have been altered" (162). And (2) "Cromwell was about to ravage all Christendom; the royal family was undone, and his own for ever established, save for a little grain of sand which formed in his ureter. Rome herself was trembling under him; but this small piece of gravel having formed there, he is dead, his family cast down, all is peaceful, and the king is restored" (176).

2. Wherever possible, citations of Lichtenberg are taken from either Steven Tester's translations in *Philosophical Writings* or from R. J. Hollingdale's anthology in *The Waste Books*. Neither, however, contains all the entries of Lichtenberg's *Sudelbücher*; at times, they contain only partial translations of a single entry. I retain the standardized method of referring to the *Südelbucher* (the letter refers to the individual notebook, the number to the corresponding entry), and any entry not to be found in *Philosophical Writings* or *The Waste Books* is my own translation.

3. The abbreviation *KA* refers to the book Κέρας Αμαλθέας (Amalthea's horn, the cornucopia). Let me quote an early note that strengthens the idea,

emphasizing the examination of causal chains whose links used to go unnoticed: "The greatest things in the world are brought about by others, to which we pay no attention, insignificant causes that we overlook but that eventually accumulate" (A 19).

4. Gerhard Gamm values this last sentence—"to find difficult the easy things"—as the genuine maxim of philosophy (64).

5. This is the first mention of the "waste book" in the *Waste Books*. The reference it contains alludes to another note: "In the waste book [*Sudel-Buch*], the witty ideas [*Einfälle*] that one has can be set out with all the involvedness into which one usually falls while the thing is still new to him or her. After one becomes familiar with the thing, one sees the unnecessary and seizes it more succinctly. This happened to me when I wrote my Timorus. I [have] often shaded an expression with what was an essay in the waste book" (E 150).

6. I say "thought figures," but I clearly do not mean it in the rhetorical sense of "figure" or of "figures of thought." Therefore, I say "something like logical figures," although this does not properly reflect what I have (or think I have) in mind either: these "thought figures" could also be named—if you'll permit the apparent counter-sense—"figures of nonthinking," for they are (or would be) that unpredictable and ephemeral foliage that is formed when thinking and its course—its discourse—are, as it were, electrified and interrupted by something else, something other that assaults it and resists being organically incorporated into that course. And this resistance is not simply extrinsic: it is the resistance that thinking itself opposes to its merely lineal configuration, to the simple inertia of its continuity. And that's because thinking couldn't be "electrified" by something external to it if it were not in itself open to exteriority and otherness. We have a standard instance of this in digression, which is perhaps the principle of the never fully accomplished relation of thinking and language, which happily sparkles in the *ocurrencia*, in the event and its fortunate coincidence with thinking. I'll soon refer to this. (Maybe one could say "occurrence" in immediate connection with the "event." The point is that we have in Spanish this term to signify an "idea," a "bright idea.")

7. By way of complementing what I said in the previous note, this is an opportune time to recall that one of the major forms for treating the constellation of entries in the *Sudelbücher* consists in paying attention to Lichtenberg's assiduous use of the subjunctive mood. The relevance of this approach concerns its kinship with Professor Lichtenberg's mastery in physical experiments, to which his teaching in Göttingen largely attests. Subjunctive is the mood of thought experiments: "If this were not there now [*Wenn dieses gar nun nicht da wäre*], what would then become [*was würde alsdann werden*]?" (KA 340). I guess that the combination of this approach with the one I'm trying here would yield some interesting results. For an elaborate analysis of Lichtenberg's subjunctives, see Albrecht Schöne's *Aufklärung aus dem Geist der Experimentalphysik*.

8. "Acumen is a magnifying glass [*Vergrößerungs-Glas*], wit a lens of reduction [*Verkleinerungs-Glas*]. The latter, however, leads to the universal [*Allgemeine*]" (F 700).

9. Another note rephrases this in a more serious tone, so as to refute Leibniz's theory of the best of all possible worlds (K 69).

10. For a discussion of Lichtenberg's and Wittgenstein's respective approaches to language and the subject, see Rolf Wintermeyer, *Lichtenberg, Wittgenstein et la question du sujet*.

11. Lichtenberg includes this self-annihilating implement as the first item in an auction list in "Verzeichnis einer Sammlung von Gerätschaften, welche in dem Hause des Sir H. S. künftige Woche öffentlich verauktioniert werden soll," a fake translation from English in Swift's manner (*Schriften, Dritter Band* 452). The first instance of this witticism is found in a letter to Christian Gottlob Heyne from July 23, 1793: "Regarding the *camera obscura* [in a list of instruments partially defective of a physics device], for which it is necessary to make anew a box [or a case] and a convex lens, the idea came to me of a knife without a blade, from which the handle is missing." You can *see*, one could say, how various threads of Lichtenberg's operations and figures become interwoven here: the unusual glance, the device, the impossible object (a purely verbal creature), and something like the nirvana of comprehension.

12. "UB" (*Undatierbare Bemerkungen*) is the abbreviation used for the notes of unknown date.

13. It is true that we have also a confession from Lichtenberg that, like everything else that he says, certainly cannot be taken at face value: "One is never happier than when set upon by the sharp feeling of living *only* in *this* world. My misfortune is to exist not in *this* world but, rather, in the numerous possible chains of relations that, supported by my consciousness, my imagination [*Phantasie*] creates; thus passes a part of my time, and no reason is capable of overcoming it" (J 948).

14. Heidegger's text is "Die Kunst und der Raum" (1969). It is worth stressing that, if both the automatism *and* autonomy of language produce mirages that condition the way in which the subject envisages reality and herself and that need to be rectified for this reason, they at the same time favor the subject's capacity to think for herself, if she sufficiently pays attention to the "wisdom recorded in language."

15. In turn, as Loescher says referring to Lichtenberg's literary and scientific productions, "writing is an automatism that generates ideas. The stubborn repetition of some figures of thought and formulations should be understood as a strategy the aim of which is to bridge 'gaps' in the process of writerly ideation by way of motoric writing in the sense of recurrent 'mantras'" (233).

16. "If someone gathered close together all of the witty ideas [*Einfälle*] of his or her life, it would result in a good work. Everyone is a genius at least once in life. The geniuses properly so-called only have the witty ideas gathered more

closely together. One thus sees how much hinges upon writing everything down" (G 228).

17. I have examined this most notorious annotation, confronting it mainly with Kant's "I think," in "External Things, the Subject, and Language."

CHAPTER FOUR

1. In citations of Freud, the first reference is to the original German (*Studienausgabe*, volume 3), and the second is to Alix Strachey's translation.

2. I have touched on this point in my essay, "La cuestión de lo siniestro en Freud."

3. Freud speaks of a "faint touch of satire" with which the author treats Nathaniel's "idealization of his mistress" (251/227).

4. Citations of Kleist will refer, first, to the original German in volume 3 of Kleist's *Sämtliche Werke und Briefe* and, second, to Peter Wortsman's translation.

5. See de Man, "Aesthetic Formalization: Kleist's *Über das Marionettentheater*," in *The Rhetoric of Romanticism*, 263–90. As will become evident, I will allude on more than one occasion to this lucid essay.

6. This passage has the additional interest of being the first that registers the name *Grazie* (the adjective *graziös* was already used at the beginning, as I was just mentioning), while the term in the preceding passages has been *Anmut*. It is something like a dividing line in the text that separates the use of these names. They will continue to alternate in the narrator's account, so as to prove the knowledge he declares here, and afterwards he will be talking about *Grazie* until the end.

7. But I don't think that this should be emphasized too much, as if you were adding theses upon theses when reading a text to which it is impossible to attribute a doctrinal intention. In the change on which I was commenting in my previous note (the change from *Anmut* to *Grazie*), you may observe a certain permissiveness transmitted to the terms used. *Grazie* is not, properly speaking, a religious word (*um Gottes Gnaden* is the expression that is used to say "by the grace of God"), and it clearly evokes mythological themes (think of the three Graces). Just as Kleist plays with the ambiguity of a "fall" that is understood at times in a physical register, at times in a metaphysical sense, so, too, the dogma of the Fall is used less as a dogma and more as a myth, as a tale of which the only thing that differentiates it from the others that we read here is that it is merely alluded to but not told.

8. Cf. José M. Cuesta Abad's remarks in *La palabra tardía*, where you may find a passage on Kleist's text (starting at 32).

9. In *The Rhetoric of Romanticism*, De Man rightly refers to another little miscellaneous piece by Kleist, which is entitled "Über die allmähliche Verfertigung der Gedanken beim Reden"/"On the Gradual Formulation of Thoughts While

Speaking" (Kleist, *Sämtliche* 3: 221–26/*Selected Prose* 255–63). The narrator recommends, when you don't get the fruit of knowledge through reflection and meditation, to talk about the issue with the first person you meet and to expect that the chat will bring you the idea you are searching for. It is, of course, a peculiar kind of spontaneity, the logic, if I may say so, of a spirit and a wit that, delivered to the automatisms of language and unconcerned by the demands and rigors of sense and meaning, suddenly realizes what it seeks. There is no one who has not experienced it and some of us have made it a method that it actually cannot be. This is also the way in which de Man understands the lesson of the marionette text: the supreme achievements of discourse are obtained at the price of a loss of control and by delivering oneself to the extreme formalization of grammatical cases (*Rhetoric* 290).

10. The voyage of knowledge to infinity: the dialectics that this dialogue abbreviates to the point of parody.

11. The French call it *Le tireur d'épine*. The piece at the Louvre is one of many copies of this famous sculpture from the first century BCE, of which the original is in the Palazzo dei Conservatori, in Rome.

12. One must not overlook the fact that this very condition is reflected by the speaker's narration, which also needs the assistance of a witness, no longer for the assurance of grace, but for the veracity of the story with which he wants to certify his awareness about the harm of consciousness and in which, for the same reason, he sees himself reflected.

13. The whole issue of believing, crediting, and attesting refers to Kleist's central concern with the inaccessibility of truth, which he reads in the Kantian subtraction of the thing in itself. As Kleist writes to Wilhelmine von Zenge in a letter from March 22, 1801: "we cannot decide whether what we call truth is really truth [*wahrhaft Wahrheit ist*] or whether it merely appear so [*nur so scheint*] to us" (*Sämtliche* 4: 205). This concern, known as the "Kant crisis," forces the young Kleist to abandon his epistemic vocation, and it receives an especially pointed formulation in his later work. It is the theme coined in the phrase "probability is not always on the side of truth [*wie denn die Wahrscheinlichkeit nicht immer auf Seiten der Wahrheit ist*]," which stands in the final segment of the novella *Michael Kohlhaas* as a preamble to a most unlikely incident, about which the narrator declares to be "duty-bound to permit any reader so inclined to doubt" (*Sämtliche* 3: 134/*Selected Prose* 246). Three stories told by an old officer to a bewildered audience in "Improbable Veracities" ("Unwahrscheinliche Wahrhaftigkeiten," *Sämtliche* 3: 376–79) constitute in some sense the formalization of the theme. On this point, see, for instance, Adams 208.

14. This "likewise" is an insidious extenuation: analogically to what occurs with the intersection of lines in geometrical space and with the image in physical space, consciousness and knowledge would have to cross *an* infinity, but which one?

15. By contrast, *"the spirit can't go wrong if there's no spirit to begin with,"* as the narrator says to himself (216/269).

16. How not to acknowledge that here the *uncanny* announces itself in an unrestrained manner? An additional allusion may be permitted. Freud considered Hoffmann the author of the uncanny par excellence. In Hoffmann's story "Elementargeist," the narrator describes the major's body in such a way that none of his limbs are related to the others, while a nonhuman characteristic is attributed to each of them (Cf. Kayser 197n12.) The theme of the amputated limb that has or takes on autonomous life is mentioned by Freud among the many motifs that complicate his catalog of the uncanny ("Das Unheimlihe"/"The Uncanny" 266/244). Then again, however, amputated limbs may be disarticulated words, as Tim Mehigan argues following de Man, "words ... severed from their rightful context at every step of the way" (98) and culminating in a single word, *zerstreut*, that "disrupts the creation of the mythicized world ... and strews its carefully arranged component parts in all directions" (101).

CHAPTER FIVE

1. "Scepticism is an ability, or mental attitude [*dynamis*], which opposes appearances to judgements [*pahinomenon te kai noumenon*] in any way whatsoever" (Sextus 8).

2. Quotations are taken from the English edition of the *Zürau Aphorisms*. The numerals in these references refer to the corresponding aphorism. Slashes (e.g., "70/71") denote a single aphorism; when the number is followed by "bis," this indicates that the aphorism in question was written by Kafka in substitution of the aphorism that was originally identified by that number.

3. Kafka says that the suicidal individual "is the prisoner who sees a gallows being erected in the prison yard, mistakenly thinks it is the one intended for him, breaks out of his cell in the night, and goes down and hangs himself" (*Schriften* 76).

4. The "belief in a personal god," notes Kafka, is a form of "concealment" of the essential faith in the indestructible (*Zürau* 50).

5. This means—and I deem it important for the comprehension of a central knot in Kafka's thinking—that the law is never something previously given, an imperative of fulfillment emanating from its consistency and content, an obligation of acting: law is given in and with the exigency itself, and it does not exist for us in any other form than that of exigency. In this sense, I have stamped the latter with the attributes of "pure" and "absolute."

6. A note from Notebook G reads, "The fact that our task is exactly commensurate with our life gives it the appearance of being infinite" (*Schriften* 71/*Blue* 36).

7. I speak of aphorisms, although the name is somewhat misleading. In a certain sense, I would agree with Paul North in that these texts of varying

lengths are more akin to Pascal's *Pensées* than to the copious tradition of aphoristic writing (North 4, 12). In fact, North calls the Zürau texts "thoughts" (a "treatise of thoughts"). Nevertheless, I will continue to speak of aphorisms for the sake of custom.

8. Obviously, the names I will apply are my personal choices, and I will not deny that they may sound a little arbitrary; what interests me is the logical suggestion that they carry.

9. Even more radically, knowledge of this difference is knowledge of difference as such; if it neither takes place nor announces itself, if the difference is clouded or obscured, there is only evil: not to distinguish between evil and good is evil; therefore, to make the difference is necessarily to do the right thing.

10. This point, together with the previous observations, finds a clear expression in following terms: "For us there exist two kinds of truth, as they are represented by the Tree of Knowledge and the Tree of Life. The truth of the active principle and the truth of the static principle. In the first, Good separates itself off from Evil; the second is nothing but Good itself, knowing neither of Good nor of Evil. The first truth is given to us really, the second only intuitively [*ahnungsweise*]. That is what it is so sad to see. The cheerful thing is that the first truth pertains to the fleeting moment, the second to eternity; and that, too, is why the first truth fades out in the light of the second" (Kafka, *Schriften* 83–84/*Blue* 43).

11. This aphorism was crossed out by Kafka.

12. See Kafka, *Schriften* 32/*Blue* 15.

13. My translation. Michael Hoffmann has the following: "It seems more like a tripwire than a tightrope."

14. "This world is our going astray, but as such it is itself something indestructible, or, rather, something that can be destroyed only by means of being carried to its logical conclusion [*durch seine Zu-ende-führung*], and not by renunciation" (*Schriften* 83/*Blue* 43).

15. In this sense I spoke about an "error of error," for there is also a truth of error, which would be what I am trying to suggest. I think that no one has better conceived this point than Blanchot: "The impatience at the heart of error is the essential fault, because it misconstrues the very trueness of error which, like a law, requires that one never believe the goal is close or that one is coming nearer to it. One must never have done with the indefinite; one must never grasp—as if it were the immediate, the already present—the profundity of inexhaustible absence" (79).

16. This, which seems to be the best prospect of guile, lacks in the end every solid expectation: "Everything is deception: the question is whether to seek the least amount of deception, or the mean, or to seek out the highest. In the first instance, you will cheat goodness by making it too easy to acquire, and Evil by imposing too unfavorable conditions on it. In the second instance, you cheat goodness by failing to strive for it in this earthly life. In the third instance, you cheat goodness by removing yourself from it as far as you can, and Evil by

maximizing it in a bid to reduce its impact. Accordingly, the second option is the one to go for, because you always cheat goodness, but—in this case at least, or so it would seem—not Evil" (Kafka, *Zürau* 55).

17. Different, of course, is the human situation: "We were created to live in Paradise, and Paradise was designed to serve us. Our designation has been changed; we are not told whether this has happened to Paradise as well" (Kafka, *Zürau* 84).

18. In his study "Umkehrung und Ablenkung: Franz Kafkas 'Gleitendes Paradox,'" Gerhard Neumann says that Kafka's "'inversion' is not ... that of classical paradox; rather, it appears constantly associated with a 'deviation' from the conventional paths of thinking, and it thereby achieves two decisive effects: on the one hand, two poles ... enter into a relationship as determinate as strange, and it seems that Kafka's issue is precisely this relation; on the other hand, this relation does not allow itself to be reduced to any of the usual connections of thinking" (464, my translation).

19. The parable *The Shield of the City* also deals with the topic of the tower, and it names the undertaking with a remarkable wordplay: *Himmelsturmbau*, which—as George Steiner notes—allows two readings at a time: the "construction of the tower (of/toward) heaven" (*Himmels/turmbau*), and the "construction of the assault on heaven" (*Himmel/sturmbau*) (Kafka, *Schriften* 318–19 and 323; Steiner 1998, 69–70). The parable's title, as in many other cases, was added by Brod.

20. This phrase is found in the "Forschungen-Heft [Notebook of research]," dating around 1922.

21. Compare this point with the following aphorism: "It is conceivable that Alexander the Great—for all the military successes of his youth, for all the excellence of the army he trained, for all the desire he felt in himself to change the world—might have stopped at the Hellespont, and never crossed it, and not out of fear, not out of indecisiveness, not out of weakness of will, but from heavy legs" (*Zürau* 39).

22. It could be objected that I put too much emphasis on this quotation with its final equation of "believing" and "being" and that it would be necessary to contrast this quotation with another, which plays with the ambiguity between a verb and a possessive pronoun: "The German word *sein* signifies both 'to be there' and 'to belong to Him'" (Kafka *Zürau*, 46). Yet, the key lies in the concept of the indestructible, which I address immediately hereafter.

23. Bloom declares his agreement with Ritchie Robertson about the centrality of this concept for Kafka's work. Indeed, Robertson remits to Schopenhauer and his meditation on death in *The World as Will and Representation* and, further, calls the indestructible "Kafka's impersonal divinity" (Robertson 123; see also 121–22).

24. A crisis that seems to have a faithful expression in this aphorism: "Belief in progress doesn't mean belief in progress that has already occurred. That

would not require belief" (Kafka, *Zürau* 48). If I am not grossly mistaken, progress is addressed here as a form of secularized transcendence that has its temporal dimension in the future, and Kafka exploits the semantics of the verb *to believe* according to its strictest meaning: obviously, I can believe in something that has already happened on the basis of reports and accounts, but this goes no further than helping me to form an opinion that may be erroneous due to the imprecision or falsity of the reports. But believing in progress means having faith in its (not already given) reality, faith in the fact that the future remains open, and this is more a bet and a hope than an opinion or a forecast, for which reason it is undermined by a doubt and an anxiety that tend to suppress the very possibility of "believing."

25. *Asthenia*, regarding belief, manifests itself as what could be called the alibi of happiness: "Theoretically, there is one consummate possibility of felicity: to believe in the indestructible in oneself, and then not to go looking for it" (Kafka, *Zürau* 69).

26. If this condition and destiny were clear for Kafka at an early date, then it was the famous night of September 22–23, 1912, during which, over the span of eight hours of uninterrupted writing, he produced *The Judgment* (*Das Urteil*). This night provides Kafka the truth of his calling and the shape of its fulfillment: "Only *in this way* can writing be done, only with such coherence, with such a complete opening out of the body and the soul" (Kafka, *Tagebücher* 461/ *Diaries* 213).

27. This determines also the security of art, its very possibility as well as the insistence in difference. An annotation of Notebook G, resounding with this quotation, says, "Art flies around truth, but with the definite intention of not getting burnt. Its capacity lies in finding in the dark void a place where the beam of light can be intensely caught, without this having been perceptible before" (Kafka *Schriften* 75–76/*Blue* 39).

28. A dissonant echo in Kafka, who is faithful to the transience of the glimpse: "Language can be used only very obliquely of things outside the physical world, not even metaphorically, since all it knows to do—according to the nature of the physical world—is to treat of ownership and its relations" (Kafka, *Zürau* 57).

29. I am referring to chapter 7, "'A Faith Like a Guillotine': Kafka on Skepticism" (126–41).

30. See also Corngold, "Kafka's Later Stories and Aphorisms," 104.

31. Neumann distinguishes three maneuvers "by which Kafka leads the reader to a domain where all rigid conceptuality slips ... [:] the *semantic displacement*, ... the *placement of quotations*, ... [and] the *strange metaphor*" (486–87).

32. Swift writes, "having Occasion to talk of *Lying*, and *false Representation*, it was with much Difficulty that he comprehended what I meant ... For he argued thus; That the Use of Speech was to make us understand one another, and

to receive Information of Facts; now if any one *said the Thing which was not*, these Ends were defeated." (*Gulliver's Travels* 354).

CHAPTER SIX

1. See chapter 1 of the present volume, "Montaigne: Writing and Skepticism."

2. This doesn't mean that the inaugural meaning of this text is absolute. The fact that Borges included the first "note" that concludes the *History of Eternity* (1936), "The Approach to Al-Mu'tasim," in the first edition of *Fictions* (1944) is already a sign of this. And indeed one cannot omit the *Universal History of Infamy* (1935), which contains Borges's first narrative exercises. For all these facts, see Nicolás Helft's *Jorge Luis Borges: Bibliografía completa*.

3. Hurley's translation has "imaginary" italicized, which is not to be found in the Spanish original.

4. Patient inquirers of Borges's work established that the referred publication actually exists, with a slightly different title: *Encyclopaedia*, instead of *Cyclopaedia*: it is effectively a reimpression of the *Britannica*, although not of the tenth edition, but of the ninth. The volume that mentions Bioy and that contains the mysterious addendum on Uqbar is—really, too—volume 46, which goes from *TOT* (and not *TOR*, as said in the narration) to *UPS*, with an article on Upsala at the end of it; the following volume begins with *URA* and its first article deals indeed with the Uro-Altaic languages. Moreover, Alan White, a particularly successful researcher, discovered (in accordance with a finding by Nicolás Helft) that the eleventh edition of the *Britannica* (which was Borges's favorite, as he adds) includes, after Upsala, exactly in the place where the insidious entry on Uqbar would figure in Bioy's unique issue, an article on Ur, the ancient Babylonian city. The conjecture on the geographical location of Uqbar in Asia Minor favors the connection. White indicates in addition that Ur, in another of its meanings that he considers especially important, is the name of a Gnostic sub-deity, represented as a serpent or a louse. See Alan White, "An Appalling or Banal Reality."

5. Once again, Hurley adds italics where there are none in the original Spanish.

6. There are seven in the first edition from 1941 (*The Garden of Forking Paths*), to which an eighth piece is further added (in *Fictions*, from 1944), which, as already mentioned, literally reproduces the first of the notes that close the *History of Eternity* ("The Approach to Al-Mu'tasim").

7. It will be recalled that both friends amused themselves with table talk about "composing a first-person novel whose narrator would omit or distort things and engage in all sorts of contradictions, so that a few of the book's readers—a very few—might divine an atrocious or banal reality" (*Obras* 1: 461/ *Collected* 68, translation modified)

8. There is also the conjecture that Ashe could be a figure that recalls Borges's father, and, certainly, the date of Ashe's decease (1938) is relatively close to the date of Jorge Guillermo Borges's death (1937). However, Félix Della Paolera, in *Borges: Revelaciones*, maintains that he is one Mr. William Foy, who perfectly matches Ashe's portrait, with the exception that the narrative makes him die prematurely. I cannot help hearing "ashen" in the name, with all its deathly resonances.

9. "Hume declared for all time that while Berkeley's arguments admit not the slightest refutation, they inspire not the slightest conviction" (*Obras* 1: 465/*Collected* 72). Hume's categorical judgment is to be found in a note of his *Enquiry Concerning Human Understanding* and refers to Berkeley's claim to have made a case with his work against all skeptics, atheists, and freethinkers: "But that all his arguments, though otherwise intended, are, in reality, merely sceptical, appears from this, *that they admit of no answer and produce no conviction. Their only effect is to cause that momentary amazement and irresolution and confusion, which is the result of scepticism*" (Hume 155n1).

10. Hurley replaces Borges's italics with quotation marks in the English.

11. Despite their opposition, Borges labels both "apologists of idealism" in his "New Refutation of Time" (*Obras* 2: 147/*Other* 175).

12. I agree with White that "the apparently fantastic doctrines the narrator finds in *A First Encyclopedia* are no more fantastic than those espoused by various terrestrial metaphysicians, and that at least many have direct terrestrial counterparts" (84).

13. I would like to add something that may be summarized in a few fables and a lot of philosophies. The protagonist of "The Gospel According to Mark," a young medicine student named Baltasar Espinosa trying to understand the passionate interest shown by his precarious audience when he reads the gospel out loud, says to himself that, "throughout history, humankind has told two stories: the story of a lost ship sailing the Mediterranean seas in quest of a beloved island, and the story of a god who allows himself to be crucified on Golgotha" (*Obras* 2: 477–78/*Collected* 400). Taking for granted that Borges omits a third story, which in a certain way concerns him, the story of a pilgrim who, without knowing, murders his father, kills a monster, wins as a retribution his victim's kingdom and wife, and blinds himself as he discovers the atrocity of his deeds, with philosophy it is exactly the opposite: it is interminably plural, and men advocate countless explanations of a reality that remains unscathed and indifferent to them.

14. Cf. Claire de Obaldia's *L'esprit de l'essai* 390–91.

15. Cf. de Man, *Critical* 216.

16. To be more precise: the Indo-European root is *bhā* (to speak), which in Greek gives *phemí* and in Latin *fari* (to speak, to say), as well as *fama* (rumor, reputation, renown), from which comes the adjective *infamis* (discredited, dishonored).

My attention to this theme was called by Kate Jenckes's beautiful book *Reading Borges after Benjamin: Allegory, Afterlife, and the Writing of History*; in 2002, at the Universidad de Chile, I was lucky enough to have the opportunity to comment upon the doctoral thesis upon which this book is based.

17. All of them are in their entirety erudite bibliographical inquirers, but this doesn't say anything against the detective appearance of the issue; in the end, inquirers and detectives (and archeologists, historians, paleologists, paleontologists, etc.) share what could be called the *science of vestiges*.

18. Irwin's aforementioned book offers a remarkable exposition of the relations between Borgesian narrative and Poe's great series of detective stories. Let us incidentally say that the proverbial Dupin is first of all an epistemological hero and undoubtedly a skeptic who knows that truth is only discoverable on condition that one doesn't believe in it.

19. The use of this term (*foundational*) might be nonsense, I know, granted that Borges's arguments go always in the opposite direction. I keep it just in order to call attention to the fact that this "foundation"—which may be plainly conceived in this way from the standpoint of the Argentinean writer's literary evolution—is a sort of foundering and that the latter has to do radically with the statute of fiction.

20. It may be observed that this last phrase, apart from the allusion upon which I will soon comment, has an aftertaste of irony and paradox: not long before, at the moment in which the narrator intends to report the recent events that "have changed the face of the earth," he declares: "Here I end the personal portion of my narration" (*Obras* 1: 473–74/*Collected* 80–81).

21. I refer, among other studies, to Irwin's *The Mystery to a Solution* (129–37) and to Mercedes Blanco's "Arqueologías de Tlön, Borges y el *Urn Burial* de Browne" (19–46).

22. Borges indeed, together with Bioy, publishes in the journal *Sur* in 1944 a version of the fifth chapter of *Urn Burial*. Years before, in 1925, he dedicated to Browne one of the essays of his juvenile *Inquisitions*.

23. The mention of Smerdis is a malicious interpolation and a warning about the theme of usurpations and impersonations that stubbornly resist being unraveled. Smerdis was the younger son of Cyrus II and brother of Cambyses II. Before dying, Cyrus would have appointed him governor of the Oriental provinces of the Persian Empire. However, as Herodotus tells us, Cambyses II ordered Smerdis's murder, fearing that his brother could organize an intestine rebellion while he was conducting a campaign in Egypt. An impostor, one Gaumata, a priest of the magi of Media, proclaimed himself king of Persia by impersonating Smerdis, whose death was to be kept secret. Other sources suggest that Gaumata is the name of the impostor's brother and that he was the one who forged all the intrigue. The usurper initially enjoyed general favor, but he lost it because of certain measures that affected the religious cult and the locations of many inhabitants of the kingdom. Darius headed a successful rebellion

and ordered these events to be recorded in what is known as the Behistun Inscription. Some historians have suspected that Gaumata was the real Smerdis, that those facts were forged by Darius in order to justify his rebellion, and that he himself was the actual usurper. So, the warning I'm talking about also concerns the processes of remaking the past that the Tlönians, already experienced in the production of *hrönir*, are accustomed to carrying out willingly and artfully.

24. I set aside the insertion of multiple figures in the narration that contribute to the confusion of the dates by mere juxtaposition. For an analysis of the theme, see Cristina Parodi, "El intrincado cronotopo de 'Tlön.'"

25. In English in the original.

26. A fictional character, named according to what in English-speaking countries would be Borges's middle name.

27. This, of course, is the model worked out by "The Garden of Forking Paths."

28. Cf. Obaldia 375.

29. A first, ominous announcement of this reality has already appeared under the guise of the "reclusive millionaire" Ezra Buckley, owner of portentous wealth accrued thanks to his goldmines, the whores from his brothels, and his many Black slaves. It has been assiduously observed (recently, for instance, by Daniel Attala) that this awful man's last name is the last alias of the "cruel redeemer" Lazarus Morell, an ingenious and despicable slave trader who died in a Natchez hospital of pulmonary congestion: he passed away as Silas Buckley. Morell's final moniker adorns another nebulous character of the present story, Silas Haslam, author of *History of the Land called Uqbar*, allegedly published in 1874; it merits mention that Haslam was the last name of Frances Anne, Jorge Luis Borges's paternal grandmother.

CONCLUSION

1. Heidegger does not rely on this sort of assurance, but he certainly affirms that the "as" is inscribed in Dasein's very being as the original relation to Being. Existential comprehension fulfills itself in interpretation, which brings to light what is already present in the most primary comprehension: everyday dealing with what surrounds us is already articulated as a seeing and comprehending "something as something" (*Etwas als Etwas*).

Works Cited

Adams, Dale. "Nicht immer auf Seiten der Wahrheit: Wahrscheinlichkeit und (Un)Wissen in Kleists Unwahrscheinliche Wahrhaftigkeiten." *Wissensfiguren im Werk Heinrich von Kleists*, edited by Yixu Lü et al., Rombach, 2012, pp. 207–22.
Arciniegas, Germán. *América ladina*. Edited by Juan Gustavo Cobo Borda, FCE, 1993.
Aristotle. *Poetics*. Translated and with an introduction and notes by Anthony Kenny. Oxford UP, 2013.
Attala, Daniel. "'Tlön, Uqbar, Orbis Tertius' o la idolatría: Una lectura en clave atlántico-bíblica." *Cuadernos Lírico*, no. 19, 2018, pp. 1–32.
Bacon, Francis. *The New Organon*. Edited by Lisa Jardine and Michael Silverthorne, Cambridge UP, 2003.
Benjamin, Walter. *Gesammelte Schriften*, vol. 1, part 1. Edited by Rolf Tiedemann and Hermann Schweppenhäuser, Suhrkamp, 1972.
———. *Gesammelte Schriften*, vol. 2, parts 1–3. Edited by Rolf Tiedemann and Hermann Schweppenhäuser, Suhrkamp, 1977.
———. *Selected Writings 2: 1931–1934*, part 2. Edited by Howard Eiland et al., translated by Rodney Livingstone et al., Harvard UP, 2005.
———. *Selected Writings 3: 1935–1938*. Edited by Howard Eiland and Michael W. Jennings, translated by Edmund Jephcott et al., Harvard UP, 2002.
Blanchot, Maurice. *The Space of Literature*. Translated by Ann Smock. Lincoln, U of Nebraska P, 1989.
Blanco, Mercedes. "Arqueologías de Tlön, Borges y el *Urn Burial* de Browne." *Variaciones Borges*, no. 15, 2003, pp. 19–46.

Bloom, Harold. *The Western Canon: The Books and School of the Ages*. Harcourt, 1994.
Borges, Jorge Luis. *Collected Fictions*. Translated by Andrew Hurley, Penguin, 1998.
——. *Obras completas 1*. Emecé, 2010.
——. *Obras completas 2*. Emecé, 2010.
——. *Other Inquisitions: 1937–1954*. Translated by Ruth L. C. Simms, U of Texas P, 1995.
Carroll, Lewis. *Complete Works*. Introduced by Alexander Woollcott, illustrated by John Tenniel, Vintage, 1976.
Coleridge, Samuel Taylor. *Biographia Literaria, or Biographical Sketches from my Literary Life and Opinions and Two Lay Sermons*. George Bell and Sons, 1905.
Connery, Brian A. "The Persona as Pretender and the Reader as Constitutional Subject in Swift's *Tale*." *Cutting Edges: Postmodern Critical Essays on Eighteenth-Century Satire*, edited by James E. Gill, U of Tennessee P, 1995, pp. 159–80.
Corngold, Stanley. "Kafka's Later Stories and Aphorisms." *The Cambridge Companion to Franz Kafka*, edited by Julian Preece, Cambridge UP, 2003, pp. 95–110.
——. *Lambent Traces: Franz Kafka*. Princeton UP, 2004.
Craven, Kenneth. *Jonathan Swift and the Millennium of Madness: The Information Age in Swift's "A Tale of a Tub."* iUniverse, 2006.
Cuesta Abad, José M. *La palabra tardía. Hacia Paul Celan*. Trotta, 2001.
de Man, Paul. *Critical Writings, 1953–1978*. Edited by Lindsay Waters, U of Minnesota P, 1989.
——. *The Rhetoric of Romanticism*. Columbia UP, 1984.
Derrida, Jacques. *Schibboleth pour Paul Celan*. Galilée, 1986.
——. *La voix et le phénomène: Introduction au problème du signe dans la phénoménologie de Husserl*. Presses universitaires de France, 2009.
——. *Sovereignties in Question: The Poetics of Paul Celan*. Edited by Thomas Dutoit and Outi Pasanen, Fordham UP, 2005.
Donoghue, Denis. *Jonathan Swift: A Critical Introduction*. Cambridge UP, 1971.
Dyson, A. E. *The Crazy Fabric: Essays in Irony*. Macmillan, 1973.
Fox, Christopher, editor. *The Cambridge Companion to Jonathan Swift*. Cambridge UP, 2003.
Freud, Sigmund. "Das Unheimliche." *Studienausgabe*, vol. 3, S. Fischer Verlag, 1970, pp. 241–74.
——. "The 'Uncanny.'" Translated by Alix Strachey. *The Standard Edition of the Complete Psychological Works of Sigmund Freud, Volume XVII (1917–1919)*. Edited by James Strachey, Hogarth Press, 1955, pp. 217–52.
Gamm, Gerhard. "Ich denke, es denkt." *Nicht nichts. Studien zu einer Semantik des Unbestimmten*, Suhrkamp, 2000, pp. 58–81.

Heidegger, Martin. "Die Kunst und der Raum." *Gesamtausgabe Band 13: Aus der Erfahrung des Denkens*, Vittorio Klostermann, 1983, pp. 203–10.

Helft, Nicolás. *Jorge Luis Borges: Bibliografía completa*. FCE, 1997.

Hegel, Georg Wilhelm Friedrich. *Introductory Lectures on Aesthetics*. Edited by Michael Inwood, translated by Bernard Bosanquet, Penguin, 1993.

———. *Werke 13: Vorlesungen über die Ästhetik*. Suhrkamp, 1970.

Hume, David. *Enquiry Concerning the Human Understanding*. Edited by L. A. Selby-Bigge, Clarendon Press, 1992.

Irwin, John T. *The Mystery to a Solution: Poe, Borges, and the Analytic Detective Story*. Johns Hopkins UP, 1996.

Jenckes, Kate. *Reading Borges after Benjamin: Allegory, Afterlife, and the Writing of History*. State U of New York P, 2007.

Johnson, David. *Kant's Dog. On Borges, Philosophy, and the Time of Translation*. State U of New York P, 2012.

Kafka, Franz. *The Blue Octavo Notebooks*. Edited by Max Brod, translated by Ernst Kaiser and Eithne Wilkins, Exact Change, 1991.

———. *Die Briefe*. Zweitausendeins, 2005.

———. *The Complete Stories*. Edited by Nahum N. Glatzer, various translators, Schocken, 1971.

———. *The Diaries od Franz Kafka, 1910–1923*. Edited by Max Brod, translated by Joseph Kresch and Martin Greenberg, Schocken, 1976.

———. *Letters to Friends, Family, and Editors*. Translated by Richard and Clara Winston, Schocken, 1977.

———. *Nachgelassene Schriften und Fragmente*, vol. 2. Edited by Jost Schillemeit, Fischer, 2002.

———. *Tagebücher*. Edited by Hans-Gerd Koch et al., Fischer, 2002.

———. *The Zürau Aphorisms*. Translated by Michael Hoffmann, Schocken, 2006.

Kant, Immanuel. *The Metaphysics of Morals*. Translated by Mary Gregor, Cambridge UP, 1996.

———. *Die Metaphysik der Sitten. Werkausgabe Band VIII: Schriften zur Ethik und Religionsphilosophie*, Suhrkamp 1968.

Kayser, Wolfgang. *The Grotesque in Art and Literature*. Translated by Ulrich Weisstein, Indiana UP, 1963.

Kleist, Heinrich von. *Sämtliche Werke und Briefe*, vol. 3. Edited by Klaus Müller-Salget, Deutscher Klassiker Verlag, 1990.

———. *Sämtliche Werke und Briefe*, vol. 4. Edited by Klaus Müller-Salget and Stefan Ormanns, Deutscher Klassiker Verlag, 1997.

———. *Selected Prose of Heinrich von Kleist*. Translated by Peter Wortsman, Archipelago Books, 2010.

Kritzman, Lawrence. *The Fabulous Imagination: On Montaigne's Essays*. Columbia UP, 2009.

La Rochefoucauld, François de. *Collected Maxims and Other Reflections*. Translated by E. H. Blackmore et al., Oxford UP, 2007.

Leavis, F. R. *The Common Pursuit*. New York UP, 1952.
Lichtenberg, Georg Christoph. *Philosophical Writings*. Edited and translated by Steven Tester, State U of New York P, 2012.
———. *Schriften und Briefe. Dritter Band*. Edited by Wolfgang Promies, Carl Hanser Verlag, 1972.
———. *Schriften und Briefe. Vierter Band. Briefe*. Edited by Wolfgang Promies, Carl Hanser Verlag, 1967.
———. *Sudelbücher*. Edited by Wolfgang Promies, Deutscher Taschenbuch Verlag, 1968, 1971, 1992. 3 Vols.
———. *The Waste Books*. Translated by R. J. Hollingdale, New York Review Books, 2000.
Loescher, Jens. *Schreiben. Literarische und wissenschaftliche Innovation bei Lichtenberg, Jean Paul, Goethe*. Walter de Gruyter, 2014.
Lucian. "A True Story." *Lucian*, vol. 1. Translated by A. M. Harmon, Macmillan, 1913, pp. 247–357. Loeb Classical Library.
Marx, Karl. *Foundations of the Critique of Political Economy*. Translated by Martin Nicolaus, Random House, 1973.
———. "Ökonomische Manuskripte 1857/58." *Marx-Engels Gesamtausgabe (MEGA)*, vol. 2, part 1.1. Dietz Verlag, 1976, pp. 21–48.
Mehigan, Tim. *Heinrich von Kleist: Writing after Kant*. Camden House, 2011.
Montaigne, Michel de. *The Complete Essays*. Edited and translated by M. A. Screech, Penguin, 1993.
———. *Les Essais*. Edited by Jean Balsamo et al., Gallimard, 2007. Bibliothèque de la Pléiade.
Mueller, Judith C. "*A Tale of a Tub* and Early Prose." *The Cambridge Companion to Jonathan Swift*, edited by Christopher Fox, Cambridge UP, 2003, pp. 202–15.
Neumann, Gerhard. "Umkehrung und Ablenkung. Franz Kafkas 'Gleitendes Paradox.'" *Franz Kafka*, edited by Heinz Politzer, Wissenschaftliche Buchgesellschaft, 1968, pp. 459–515.
North, Paul. *The Yield: Kafka's Atheological Reformation*. Stanford UP, 2015.
Obaldia, Claire de. *L'esprit de l'essai*. Seuil, 1995.
Oyarzun, Pablo. "La Cosa Que era Swift." *La letra volada*, Ediciones de la Universidad Diego Portales, 2009, pp. 70–97.
———. "La cuestión de lo siniestro en Freud." *Revista de Teoría del Arte*, no. 8, 2003, pp. 53–94.
———. "External Things, the Subject, and Language." *CR: The New Centennial Review*, vol. 17, no. 2, 2017, pp. 43–62.
———. "La verdad y su doble. Misantropología y sátira en Jonathan Swift." *Una especie de espejo. Swift: Cuatro ensayos y una nota*, Editorial Universitaria, 2014, pp. 137–89.
Paolera, Félix della. *Borges: Revelaciones*. Fundación E. Constantini, 1999.
Parodi, Cristina. "El intrincado cronotopo de 'Tlön.'" *Variaciones Borges*, no. 18, 2004, pp. 81–113.

Pascal, Blaise. *Pascal's Pensées*. Translated by W. F. Trotter, with an introduction by T. S. Eliot, E. P. Dutton, 1958.
Phiddian, Robert. *Swift's Parody*. Cambridge UP, 1995.
Plato. "Parmenides." Translated by B. Jowett. *The Dialogues of Plato: Volume IV*, Oxford UP, 1877, pp. 1–106.
———. "Sophist." Translated by B. Jowett. *The Dialogues of Plato: Volume IV*, Oxford UP, 1877, pp. 281–408.
Robertson, Ritchie. *Kafka. A Very Short Introduction*. Cambridge UP, 2004.
Rosenzweig, Franz. "Die Schrift und Luther." *Der Mensch und sein Werk. Gesammelte Schriften*, vol. 3, *Stromland. Kleinere Schriften zu Glauben un Denken*. Edited by Reinhold and Annemarie Mayer, Martinus Nijhoff, 1984, pp. 749–72.
———. "Scripture and Luther." *Scripture and Translation*. Indiana UP, 1994.
Said, Edward. *The World, the Text, and the Critic*. Harvard UP, 2006.
Schöne, Albrecht. *Aufklärung aus dem Geist der Experimentalphysik. Lichtenbergsche Konjunktive*. C. H. Beck, 1993.
Sextus Empiricus. *Outlines of Pyrrhonism*. Edited by Jeffrey Henderson, translated by R. G. Bury, Harvard UP, 1933.
Steiner, George. *After Babel: Aspects of Language and Translation*. Oxford UP, 1998.
Swift, Jonathan. *Gulliver's Travels*. Edited by David Womersley, Cambridge UP, 2012.
———. *A Tale of a Tub and Other Works*. Edited by Marcus Walsh, Cambridge UP, 2010.
Vázquez, María Esther. *Borges: Imágenes, memorias, diálogos*. Monte Ávila, 1977.
Walsh, Marcus. "Swift's *Tale of a Tub* and the mock book." *Jonathan Swift and the Eighteenth Century Book*, edited by Paddy Bullard and James McLaverty, Cambridge UP, 2013, pp. 101–18.
———. "Text, 'Text,' and Swift's *A Tale of a Tub*." *Jonathan Swift: A Collection of Critical Essays*, edited by Claude Rawson, Prentice Hall, 1995, pp. 82–98.
White, Alan. "An Appalling or Banal Reality." *Variaciones Borges*, no. 15, 2003, pp. 47–91.
Wintermeyer, Rolf. *Lichtenberg, Wittgenstein et la question du sujet*. Presses de l'Université Paris-Sorbonne, 2014.
Wittgenstein, Ludwig. *Philosophical Investigations*. Translated by G. E. M. Anscombe, P. S. M. Hacker, and Joachim Schulte, Wiley-Blackwell, 2009.

Index

accident, 42–44, 93, 114, 193n7; hermeneutical, 62, 63, 196n14
Adams, Dale, 202n14
Agrippa, 83
Anabaptists, 54
Anglican(s), 75, 76, 77, 78, 80; church, 54
Anglicanism, 78
Arciniegas, Germán, 24
Aristotle, 15, 30, 112, 161, 190n10; Aristotelian, 70, 186
art(s), 1, 7–8, 14, 15, 110, 120–121, 128, 146–147, 148, 181, 206n27; Hegel's thesis of the end of, 1, 7; of living, 46; and nature, 119–120; paradox of, 114; technology and, 7; work of, 7, 18, 136. See also memory; storytelling; writing
artistic, 14, 110, 135; creation, 7
as if, 187
aura, 8, 157; auratic, 18
author(s), 50, 51, 54, 55–56, 57–59, 73, 78, 80, 84, 160, 182, 185, 194n2, 195n10, 196n15; classical, 21; feigned, 71; hypothetical, putative, 54, 60, 65, 68, 72, 194n2, 196n21; super-, 120
authorial: credential, 47; endeavor, 59

authority, 32, 68, 72, 74, 75.
authorship, 57–58, 168; abolition of the concept of, 162; annihilation of, 78
automatism, 115, 120, 124; discursive, 61; grammatical, 99. See also language

Bacon, Francis, 3–4, 20, 21–22, 23, 50, 191n16, 191n17
belief(s), 49, 99, 100, 128, 132, 143–146, 158–159, 182; and knowing, 145; and opinions, 15, 83, 165; religious, 61. See also madness
Benjamin, Walter, 1, 2–3, 4–6, 7, 8, 11–12, 14, 17–19, 20, 189n5, 189n6, 191n12; Benjaminian, 8; "The Storyteller," 1, 4–6, 17
Berkeley, George, 158, 159, 208n9
Bioy Casares, Adolfo, 155, 165, 166, 173, 207n4, 209n22
Blanchot, Maurice, 135, 146, 205n19
Blanco, Mercedes, 209n21
Bloom, Harold, 205n23
book, 46, 50–53, 54–56, 58, 59. See also truth
Borges, Jorge Guillermo, 208n8

217

Borges, Jorge Luis, 4, 25, 153, 154–177, 181, 185, 207n2, 207n4, 208n8, 208n10, 208n11, 208n13, 209n19, 209n22, 210n26, 210n29; *Fictions*, 168; *Garden of Forking Paths*, 154 (prologue), 168, 172; "Garden of Forking Paths," 166; "Ibn-Hakam al-Bokahri, Murdered in His Labyrinth," 166; "A New Refutation of Time," 171; "Tlön, Uqbar, Orbis Tertius," 154–164, 165–172, 176–177; *Universal History of Infamy*, 165. *See also* skepticism; writing
Breton, André, 101
Brod, Max, 134, 151, 205n19
Browne, Thomas, 169, 172, 209n22

Calvin, John, 50, 54
Cambyses II, 209n23
Carroll, Lewis, 187
Catholic(s), 75, 77, 80; church, 54, 70, 75; worldview, 76
Catholicism, 69, 76, 196n20
Celan, Paul, 9
Christian, doctrine, 76; religion, 54, 129; tradition, 75
Cicero, Marcus Tullius, 45
Coleridge, Samuel Taylor, 181–182
common sense, 68, 75, 79, 80, 82, 83, 102, 149, 162, 187, 197n25
communication, 11, 12, 19, 55, 189n5, 190n12; technical mediation of, 3. *See also* narrative
communicability, communicable. *See* experience
consciousness, 105, 110–111, 116–118, 122, 123–124, 202n12, 202n14; of duty, 148; of guilt, 129; of mediation, 138
Corngold, Stanley, 148–149, 150, 206n30
Craven, Kenneth, 198n30
criticism, 3, 27, 195n4
Cuesta Abad, José M., 201n8
Cyrus II, 209n23

Darius, 209–210n23
de Man, Paul, 46, 112–113, 115, 120, 125, 156, 165, 201n5, 201–202n9, 203n16, 208n15
death, 42–44, 45, 114, 116, 120, 130, 169, 172, 193–194n7, 197n28. *See also* temporality
Della Paolera, Félix, 208n8
Derrida, Jacques, 9, 190n7, 195n10
Descartes, René, 20, 21, 22, 191n14, 195n4; Cartesian, 42
desire, 12, 30; to know, 30–31, 35; of possession, 176; of power, 70; of reality, 176
disbelief, 159, 161, 182, 187. *See also* suspension
discourse, 19, 59, 63, 112, 125, 174, 185–186, 187, 195n10; ideality of, 54; meta-, 185; pretension to truth, 4; uses of, 48
dogmatic: assertions, 83; attitudes, 84, certitude, 137, frame of mind, 138, judgments and prejudices, 82; pretensions, 27
dogmatism, 16, 40, 161, 198n29
dogmatist(s), 83, 128–129, 152, 154, 184, 198n29
Donoghue, Denis, 197n27
dream(s), 85; experience of, 104–105; of reason, 68
Drieu La Rochelle, Pierre, 157
Duchamp, Marcel, 109

Eleatics, 90
Epicurus, 74
equipollence, 146, 183; of reasons, 140
essay, 3–4, 20–23, 24–25, 28, 32–35, 48, 162, 168, 175, 180, 191n16; and experience, 28; and fiction, 153–154, 164, 173–174, 175; and knowing, 25; and narration (narrative), 14, 42, 44, 119, 174, 176; and study, 34, 35, 40; and truth, 3–4, 21, 153, 175, 180
event(s), 8–9, 18–19, 36, 41–42, 44, 46; certitude of, 3; coincidence with thinking, 199n6; diversity, multiplicity of, 36, 38; minimal, 92; minuteness, singularity

of, 37, 41; monstrous, 5–6; narrated, 190n8, n10; phenomenon as, 184; random, 93; truth as, 94–95, 175, 186
exigency, 128, 129, 131–132, 135, 136, 137, 140, 145, 146, 203n5
experience(s), 1–3, 4, 5–6, 7, 8, 12–13, 17, 18, 21, 23, 32, 35–36, 38, 41–42, 46, 47, 148, 190n10, 191n12, 191n13, 193n7; aesthetic, 14, 25; common, 189n5; communicability of, 11, 15, 189n6; communicable, 11, 14; crisis of, 1, 2, 11, 18, 189n5; end of, 5; of incertitude, 20; modern, 1; mysticism of, 191n12; non-actual, 15, 16; ordered, 22; paradox of, 33–34; pluralism of, 16; possibility of, 2, 6; and reason, 35, 40; repetition of, 2, 189n2; share, sharing of, 6, 18, 189n5; of the singular, 174; singularity of, 1–2; and study, 35, 40; and technology, 18; of the transcendent, 148; vague, 22; vicarious, 15. *See also* dreams; essay; self; writing
experiment(s), 18, 22, 97, 193n7; intellectual, 94, 195n4; thought, 199n7

faith, 129, 136, 144–146, 187, 203n4, 226n24; poetic, 182
fall, 44, 110, 115–116, 201n7; original, primordial, 113, 114
fiction, 3, 4, 9, 12, 16, 25, 187; and reality, 156–157, 185, 186, 187, 190n7, 190n9. *See also* essay; space-time; truth
Fontenelle, Benard Le Bovier de, 50
Foy, William, 208n8
Franklin, Benjamin, 98
freedom, 7, 29, 37, 40, 140, 142–144, 146, 187. *See also* liberty
Freud, Sigmund, 85, 107–108, 201n1, 201n3, 203n16

Galen, 198n30
Gamm, Gerhard, 199n4
Gaumata, 209–210n23
globalization, 12–13
Gournay, Marie de, 192n2

grace, 109, 110, 111, 112–114, 115–116, 117, 118, 123, 124, 202n12
gravity, 111, 112–114, 115, 116, 120; force of, 142, 143; law of, 109, 110, 115
guilt. *See* consciousness

Harrington, James, 50
Hegel, Georg Wilhelm Friedrich, 6–7, 8, 20, 30, 151. *See also* art
Heidegger, Martin, 200n14, 210n1
Helft, Nicolás, 207n2, 207n4
Herodotus, 209n23
history, 6, 15, 165, 176; of literature, 146; "of the world," 126. *See also* philosophy
Hobbes, Thomas, 50, 61, 195n4
Hoffmann, Ernst Theodor Amadeus, 108, 203n16
Hoffmann, Michael, 204n13
hope, 144, 163, 206n24; for redemption, for salvation, 136, 169
Horace, 45
Hume, David, 20, 158, 159, 160, 208n9
humor, 32, 86, 95
Hurley, Andrew, 207n3, 208n10

Ibarra, Néstor, 157
idealism, 122, 158–159, 161, 162, 173,
idealist(s), 148, 177
impossibility, 13, 43, 44, 141–142, 144, 145, 147, 180; of knowledge, 31; of literature, 2; of narrating, 2; principle of, 12; of the subject, 172; of translation, 10. *See also* repetition
imaginary: creatures, 179; order, 167; planet, 169; world, 171, 172
imagination, 179, 180, 181, 182, 183, 187; modern, 71
impatience, 138–139, 141. *See also* patience
indestructible, 131, 144–146, 203n4, 204n14, 205n22,n23, 206n25
individual, 3, 18–19, 20, 21–22, 29, 41, 47, 48, 68, 83, 91, 92, 191n13, 203n3. *See also* judgment; self; subject

information, 11–12, 13, 15, 19
insignificance, 41, 64–67, 86, 92
insignificant, 85–87, 89–91, 92, 105; the, theory of, 89, 91, 92, 94, 105. *See also* little; trifle
Irwin, John T., 155, 209n18, 209n20
iterability. *See* paradox, repetition

Jenckes, Kate, 208–209n16
Jentsch, Eduard, 107, 108
Jesenská, Milena, 151
Jewish: religion, 129
Johnson, David, 181
Johnson, Samuel, 49
judgment(s), 16, 21, 32, 33, 34, 149, 191n15; aesthetic, 148; dogmatic, 82; individual, 32. *See also* suspension

Kafka, Franz, 24, 127–152, 186, 203n2, 203n3, 203n4, 203n5, 204n10, 204n11, 205n18, 205n23, 205–206n14, 206n16, 206n18; "A Country Doctor", 143–144; "Penal Colony", 132; "Zürau Aphorisms," 34–129–132, 134, 138–151, 203n2, 203–204n7. *See also* narrative; paradox; skepticism; writing
Kant, Immanuel, 20, 55–56, 86, 92, 99, 147–148, 151, 160, 161, 195n7, 201n17; Kantian, 202n13
Kayser, Wolfgang, 203n16
Kleist, Heinrich von, 24, 109–126, 185–186, 201n4, 201n7, 201n8, 201–202n9; "On the Theater of Marionettes," 109–126
knowledge, knowing, 2, 3, 22, 27, 29, 30, 35, 38–39, 40–41, 84, 87, 92, 111, 115, 116, 129–131, 132, 135–136, 138, 139, 142, 145–146, 155, 157, 159, 161, 175, 193n4, 193n5, 202n9, 202n10, 202n14; and existence, 132, 146; of good and evil, 128, 129, 131, 135, 136–137, 140, 142, 204n9; impossibility of, 31–32; mystical, 61; non-, not-, 4, 18, 128; and/of power, 68, 70, 73; reduction of intentional, 104; trans-empirical, 33–34; tree of, 110, 113, 115, 116, 125, 129; and truth, 95. *See also* belief; perplexity; skepticism; transcendence
Rochefoucauld, François de la, 21

language, 3, 11, 31, 79, 98–100, 101–103, 104, 135, 158–159, 166, 172, 174, 181, 183, 185, 187; automatisms, inertias of, 101, 200n14, 202n9; and event, 19; impersonality of, 104; inhumanity of, 104; machine of, 98, 125. *See also* subject
law(s), 36–38, 39–40, 41, 47, 127, 131–132, 146, 147, 173, 188; of causality, 93; civil, 193n4; 203n5; of gravity, 109, 110, 115; human, 41; of language, 31; moral, 68; reason as faculty of, 37, 193n4; thinking and, 199n6. *See also* nature
Leavis, Frank Raymond, 63, 196n12, 196n13, 197n27
Leskov, Nikolai, 4–5
Leyden, John of, 54
liberty, 40. *See also* freedom
Lichtenberg, Georg Christoph, 24, 91–105, 184–185, 198n2, 199n7, 200n10, 200n11, 200n13, 200n15; figures, 96. *See also* writing
literature, 1, 3, 12, 13, 14–15, 16, 20, 24, 25, 27, 48, 73, 82, 108, 128, 146, 162, 166, 175, 180, 185; end of, 1, 8, 19; fantastic, 4, 25, 160, 161, 163; (im)possibility of, 2, 180; and knowledge, 13; modern, 180; and philosophy, 91, 181; and skepticism, 2, 4, 13, 16, 20, 24, 25, 180, 190n7
little, 85, 88–89, 90, 91–93, 96; things, 93; truths, 21, 185. *See also* insignificant, trifle
Locke, John, 50
Loescher, Jens, 200n15
logos, 16, 47, 88
Lucian of Samosata, 180
Lucretius Carus, Titus, 45
Luther, Martin, 54

madness, 68, 73; and belief, 81; modernity as an era of, 54; and nonsense, 78, 79
Mallarmé, Stéphane, 101
Martínez Estrada, Ezequiel, 157
Marx, Karl, 7
meaning(s), 39, 54–55, 59, 71, 77, 80, 81, 86; and the book, 51, 53; circulation of, 65, 66, 72–73, 196n15; entropy of, 101; fetishism of, 70; figurative, 64, 66; hidden, mystic, occult, 69, 70; institution of, 77; leaks, vanishing(s) of, 112, 113; literal, 63, 64–65; of history, 6; possibility of, 132, 150; production of, 128; proper, propriety of, 55, 62, 64, 65–66, 70; short circuits of, 102; unique, univocal, 78–79, 120; void of, 65, 66. *See also* sense, subject
Mehigan, Tim, 203n16
memory, 42, 43, 163, 165, 169, 172, 181, 193n7; art of, 169
Methodists, 54
Meyrinck, Gustav, 108
Milton, John, 50
mirror, 39, 90, 118, 119, 121, 122, 155, 156, 157, 163, 164, 173
modern(s), 50, 53, 57, 58, 61, 62, 70, 71, 75, 108; age, 2, 122; ancient(s) and, 50, 75; encyclopedia, 155; epoch, 23; era, 20, 24, 68; experience, 1; 72, 74–75; literature, 180; novel, 18; philosophy, 153; program, project, 23, 50; science, 72; systems of knowledge and power, 68; thinking, 20; times, 17, 19, 28; wits, 60–61; world, 7, 23, 24, 50, 61
modernity, 1, 2, 7, 16, 23, 54, 72, 74–75
Montaigne, Michel de, 3, 4, 20–21, 22, 23, 24, 28–48, 153, 187–188, 191n15, 191n16, 192n2, 193n4, 193n5, 193n6, 193n7; "An Apology for Raymond de Sebond," 28, 153; "On Experience," 34–41; "On Practice," 42–45; "On Repenting," 45–47; "To Philosophize Is to Learn How to Die," 45
mysticism, 29, 40

Narcissus, myth of, 118
narration, 1–2, 3, 8, 9, 12, 16, 169, 186, 190n8, 190n10, 191n11, 191n13; art of, 15; authority of, 12; crisis of, 11; and essay, 4, 24, 42, 44, 119, 174; everyday, 14; ideality of, 165; inventive, 173; oral, 19; and reality, 165; technically mediated, 19. *See also* iterability; paradox; repetition
narrating: act of, 185; impossibility of, 2. *See also* self
narrative(s), 111.112; act, 14; communication, 18, 19; and essay, 44, 119; Kafkan, 133–134, 143; voices, 57. *See also* self
narrator, 52, 59, 62, 63, 72, 84, 160, 165
nature, 29, 36, 37, 39, 41, 61, 69, 74, 80, 121, 148, 193n5; human, 128, law(s) of nature, 41, 61, 80, 193n4. *See also* art
negation, 150–152, 190n7, 190n8
Neumann, Gerhard, 149, 150, 205n18, 206n31
Newton, Isaac, 50
Nietzsche, Friedrich, 39, 95
North, Paul, 150–151, 203–204n7
novel, 1, 2–3, 4, 14, 18, 19, 20

Obaldia, Claire de, 208n14, 210n28
Ocampo, Silvina, 166

Paracelsus, 50, 198n30
paradox, 101, 135, of art, 114; of iterability, 9, 16, 189n2; in Kafka, 140–141, 149; of narration, 2, 8, 10, 13. *See also* experience
paranoesis, 135, 149
Parmenides, 90
Parodi, Cristina, 210n24
Pascal, Blaise, 91, 198n1, 204n7
Paz, Octavio, 101
patience, 140, 142. *See also* impatience
perplexity, 3, 18, 20, 23, 30, 89, 107, 161, 168, 191n13; as condition of knowing, 22
person, first, 166, 167–168

Index 221

phenomena, phenomenon, 15, 16, 23, 35, 47, 96, 104, 107, 128, 129, 151, 152, 184
Phiddian, Robert, 57, 72, 74, 195–196n10
philosopher(s), 28, 30, 42, 69, 91, 161, 193n4; skeptical, 31
philosophical: conundrums, 79; doubt, 185; ideas, 173; inquiry, 180; joke, 159; logos, 16, 47; principle, 35; self-critique, 91; skepticism, 15; speculation, 186; stance, 28, 128; thought, 181
philosophy(ies), 27, 30, 80, 87, 90, 91, 98, 99, 158, 159, 160–161, 197n24, 199n4, 208n13; "common," 101; and literature, 181; history of, 161; modern, 153
Plato, 76, 87–91, 112, 191n16; Platonic, 164; *Parmenides*, 89–90; *Republic*, 88; *Sophist*, 87–89
Poe, Edgar Allan, 166, 209n18
possibility, 3, 9, 12, 16, 31, 131, 141; of experience, 1, 6, 13, 148; of sharing experiences, 6, 13, 18; of knowing, of knowledge, 34, 35, 127; of literature, 2, 48; of meaning, 132, 150; of truth, 46; of writing, 4. *See also* repetition
Presbyterians, 54
prosthesis, 118, 123–124, 126
Pyrrho, 27
Pyrrhonian, Pyrrhonic. *See* Skeptic(s), Skepticism
Pyrrhonism, 31

Quakers, 54
Quevedo, Francisco de, 168, 172; Quevedian, 169

reading, 9, 55, 167, 172; allegorical, 120; (non)univocal, 72, 95, 109
reality, 20, 21, 22, 48, 158, 159, 164, 167, 176, 182, 185–186, 200n14; unreality, 157, 181, 182. *See also* fiction, narration
reason(ing), 32, 35–37, 40, 47–48, 50, 61, 68, 103, 160, 161, 174, 193n4; analogical, 71; and faith, 84; "ideal of pure," and instruction, 42; and mysticism,

40; natural, 68; and revelation, 29. *See also* experience
reflection, 7, 8, 111, 115, 185, 202n9; process of, 23; self-, 124
religion, 29, 49, 72, 82, 102, 148, 196n21, 197n24. *See also* Christian
religious(ness), 28, 29, 54, 59, 75, 129, 136, 146, 174–175, 194n2; beliefs, 61; cult, 209n29; and political institutions, schemes, 60, 61, 64; thinker, 129; value, 136; word, 201n7
repetition, 2, 9, 19; of the event, 9; experience of, 2, 9, 16; of experience, 2, 189n2; of repetition, 9, 16, 190n8; of the same, 10; structure of, 9, 19, 190n8; of the unrepeatable, 8, 9. *See also* iterability
Reyes, Alfonso, 157
rhetoric(al), 72–74, 80, 112, 125, 134, 149, 155, 173, 199n6; anti-, 67; codifications, 103; devices, 51, 172; meta-, 73. *See also* tropes
Robertson, Ritchie, 205n23
Romantic(ism), 116, 121, 148; fantasy, 108; promise of redemption, 122
Rosenzweig, Franz, 2, 9–11; "Scripture and Luther," 10–11

Sade, Donatien Alphonse François marquis de, 156
Said, Edward, 57
satire, 49–50, 55, 70, 82–84, 156, 194n2; Swiftian, 73, 74, 82, 195n4, 196n12, 196n14, 198n29
science, 28, 29–30, 46, 61, 80, 82, 160, 163, 195n4; human, 195n4; modern, 72; natural, 91; progress of, 22; of vestiges, 209n17
Schiller, Friedrich, 112–113, 148
Schöne, Albrecht, 199n7
Schopenhauer, Arthur, 86, 205n23
Sebond, Raymond de, 28, 29
self, 3, 20–21, 23, 31, 33, 40–42, 44–45, 46–48, 57, 58, 59, 103–104, 157, 165, 167, 171, 193n7; -consciousness, 115,

118; and experience, 28; individual, 32, 40, 47; -irony, 156; knowledge of, 41–42, 47; narrating, narrative, 58, 84, 165; -reflection, 124; truth of, 20–21, 23; selfness, 160. *See also* person, first
Seneca, 45, 191n16
Sextus Empiricus, 28, 30, 31, 84, 128–129, 152, 153, 183–184, 197–198n29
Shaftesbury, Anthony Ashley Cooper, 3rd Earl of, 50
Shelley, Mary, 108
singularity, 9, 37, 165; absolute, 8, 131; of events, 37, 190n8; of experience, 1–2; of the singular, 174; vindication of, 176
skeptic(s) 32, 83, 84, 129, 138, 140, 152, 154, 184, 198n29, 208n9, 209n18; ancient, 134; Pyrrhonian, 152; and satirists, 83
skeptical, 2, 4, 23, 25, 35, 82, 95, 104, 129, 138, 140, 144, 146, 153, 184; approach, 40; attitude, 31; canon, 32; condition of literature, 180; critique, 50; dismantling of dogmatism, 84; emblem, 187; *epoche*, 183; formulas, 152; and knowledge, 20; matrix of literature, 16; mood, 100; operation, writing as, 28; position, 32; procedure, 83; purgative, 160; self, 47; stance, 28, 149; suspension, 183; tradition, 83. *See also* tropes
skepticism, 4, 15–16, 20, 24, 25, 27–28, 30, 32, 47, 84, 98, 127–128, 132, 134, 135, 142, 146, 148, 151, 152, 154, 161, 162; aesthetic, 147, 175; Borgesian, 175; and satire, 83; and writing, 47; essay and, 22–23; Kafka's, 148–149; philosophical, 15, 27; pyrrhonic, 82, 98, 104, 127. *See also* literature
Smerdis, 209n29
Socrates, 89, 90; Socratic, 40, 88
Spinoza, Baruc, 151, 162, 195n4
spirit, 7–8, 113, 114, 124; of exploration, 70–71; of interpretation, 70
splitting, 108, 136, 164–165, 166.69

story, 19, 111, 112, 120, 125, 126, 172, 191n11; detective, 154, 164, Borgesian recreation of detective, 165–166
storytelling, 14; art of, 3, 8, 12, 14, 189n5; end (crisis) of, 1, 2, 8, 14, 15, 19
Strachey, James, 201n1
study. *see* essay, experience
subject(s), 3, 6, 11, 12, 15, 18, 19, 29, 32, 35, 41, 42, 50, 59, 83, 125, 142, 145, 160, 169, 171, 172, 176, 185, 191n13, 200n14; finite, 149; impossibility of the, 172; individual, 143; of knowledge, 100; and language, 172, 200n4, 200n10; psychological, 193n7; as the source of meaning, 57. *See also* self; temporality
subjectivity, 43, 68, 96
subterfuge(s), 131, 137–138, 139, 143, 144
suspense, 141, 150, 184
suspension, 3, 143, 149–150, 183; of judgment, 15, 16, 23, 32, 129, 140, 183, 191n11; of disbelief, willing, 181–183, 187
Swift, Jonathan, 24, 49–55, 56–63, 67–75, 77, 78, 79–84, 152, 187, 194n1, 195n4, 195n5, 195n8, 195n10, 197n27, 198n29, 198n30, 200n11, 206n32; Swiftian, 50, 74, 82, 187, 195n4, 196n12; *Gulliver's Travels*, 60, 67, 70, 71, 84, 152; *A Tale of a Tub*, 49–55, 57–80. *See also* Satire

tale, philosophical (*conte philosophique*), 156, 164; Borgesian model of, 156
technology, 5, 18, 123, 124. *See also* art
Temple, Sir William, 197n27
temporality, 181, 184; of death, 169; of deferral, 25; of the subject, 171, 176. *See also* truth
Tillotson, John, 76
Time, 169–171, 172; of fiction, space-, 183, 184; and truth, 176
Toland, John, 50
transcendence, 141, 147–148, 206n24; knowledge of, 127–128
translation, 2, 10–11, 12, 169

trifle, 86–87. *See also* insignificant, little
trope(s), 71, 112, 136, 137, 139, 140, 141, 142, 148, 150, 154–155, 164; rhetorical and logical, 134; skeptical, 136, 150, 183–184; five skeptical (Agrippa's), 83; ten skeptical, 30, 197–198n29
truth(s), 6, 7, 25, 35–36, 38, 39, 78, 93, 131, 138, 151, 154, 159, 161–162, 173, 189n5, 209n18; aesthetization of, 175; and book, 56; catastrophe of, 174; claim to, 132; and contingence, 176; divine, 29; and error, 30, 131, 204n15; and falsity, 15, 16, 99, 190n10; and fantasy, 186; and/of fiction, 153, 174, 180, 187; inaccessibility of, 202n13; and inattentiveness, 125; and lie, 120; and meaning, 128, 135, 136; of the narrated event, 9, 16, 19; penny-, 94–96, 185; search for, 15, 27, 30, 91–92; of the self, 20–21; and temporality, time affects, 46, 47, 176; of the text, 122–123, 125, 176; transcendent, 67. *See also* essay; event; knowledge
tub, 59–62, 63, 64–66, 68, 72

uncanny, 107–108, 118, 124, 203n16
utopia(s), 68, 158

Vázquez, María Ester, 173, 174
Villemesant, Hyppolite de, 11–12
Villiers de L'Isle-Adam, Auguste de, 108

Voltaire (François-Marie Arouet), 156

Walsh, Marcus, 196n17, n19
war, 5, 6, 11, 18, 176; Great, 5, 18; technical, 6; and technology, 6
White, Alan, 207n4, 208n12
Wilson, John, 78
Witness(ing), 3, 41, 42, 117–118, 135, 168, 202n12; of the self, 23, 32
Wittgenstein, Ludwig, 79, 99, 196n22, 200n10
writing, 28, 44, 46–47, 55, 57, 58–59, 66, 76, 79, 84, 128, 135, 136, 146–147, 158, 159, 164, 165, 172, 173, 174, 181, 185, 193n7, 195n8; allegorical, allegory of, 120, 133; aprioristic, 204n7; art of, 146, 169; Borges's, Borgesian, 154, 166, 173, 175, 181; and experience, 33, 47, 136; is guilty, 135; Kafka's, Kafkan, 132–133, 136, 144, 146, 147, 148, 149–150, 158, 159–160, 165, 172; Lichtenberg's, 184; and meaning, 54; parodic, 195n10; possibility of, 4; re–, 166; satirical, 59; self and, 28, 48; Swift's, 62, 63; time of, 9
Wordsworth, William, 181
Wotton, William, 53, 196n21

Xenophon, 191n16

Zenge, Wilhelmine von, 202n13

www.ingramcontent.com/pod-product-compliance
Lightning Source LLC
Chambersburg PA
CBHW020328240426
43665CB00044B/1020